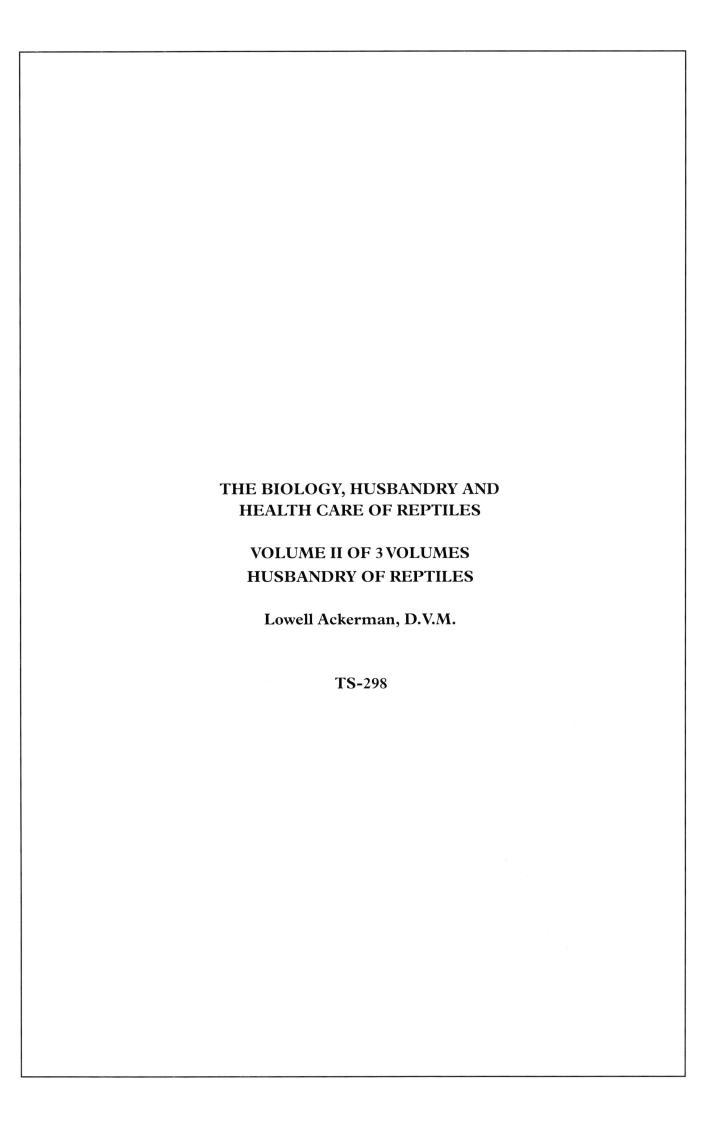

THE BIOLOGY, HUSBANDRY AND
HEALTH CARE OF REPTILES

VOLUME II OF 3 VOLUMES
HUSBANDRY OF REPTILES

Lowell Ackerman, D.V.M.

TS-298

NOTICE

The authors and editors have exerted every effort to ensure that medical information mentioned in this book is in accord with current recommendations and practice at the time of publication. However, in view of the ongoing advances in veterinary medicine, readers are urged to consult with their veterinarian regarding individual health issues.

Distributed in the UNITED STATES to the Pet Trade by T.F.H. Publications, Inc., One T.F.H. Plaza, Neptune City, NJ 07753; distributed in the UNITED STATES to the Bookstore and Library Trade by National Book Network, Inc. 4720 Boston Way, Lanham MD 20706; in CANADA to the Pet Trade by H & L Pet Supplies Inc., 27 Kingston Crescent, Kitchener, Ontario N2B 2T6; Rolf C. Hagen Inc., 3225 Sartelon St. Laurent-Montreal Quebec H4R 1E8; in CANADA to the Book Trade by Vanwell Publishing Ltd., 1 Northrup Crescent, St. Catharines, Ontario L2M 6P5; in ENGLAND by T.F.H. Publications, PO Box 15, Waterlooville PO7 6BQ; in AUSTRALIA AND THE SOUTH PACIFIC by T.F.H. (Australia), Pty. Ltd., Box 149, Brookvale 2100 N.S.W., Australia; in NEW ZEALAND by Brooklands Aquarium Ltd. 5 McGiven Drive, New Plymouth, RD1 New Zealand; in Japan by T.F.H. Publications, Japan—Jiro Tsuda, 10-12-3 Ohjidai, Sakura, Chiba 285, Japan; in SOUTH AFRICA by Lopis (Pty) Ltd., P.O. Box 39127, Booysens, 2016, Johannesburg, South Africa. Published by T.F.H. Publications, Inc.

MANUFACTURED IN THE
UNITED STATES OF AMERICA
BY T.F.H. PUBLICATIONS, INC.

THE BIOLOGY, HUSBANDRY AND HEALTH CARE OF REPTILES

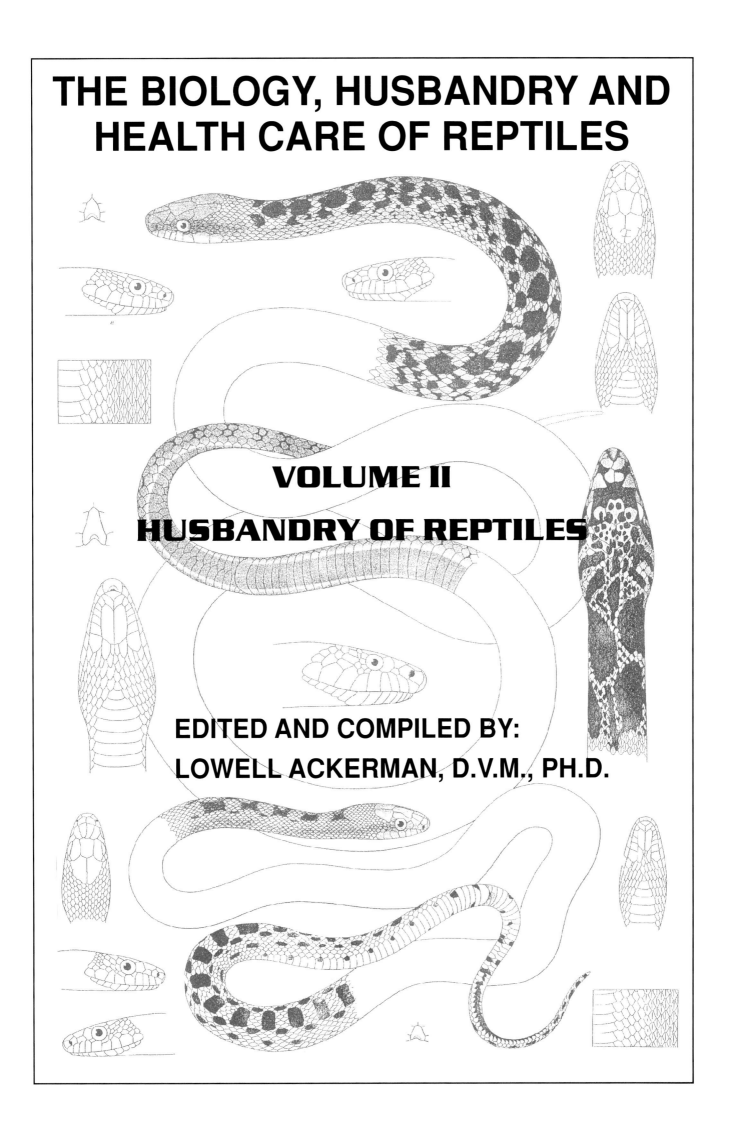

VOLUME II
HUSBANDRY OF REPTILES

EDITED AND COMPILED BY:

LOWELL ACKERMAN, D.V.M., PH.D.

In addition to being available separately as individual volumes, the three books that constitute *The Biology, Husbandry and Health Care of Reptiles* are available also as a set under that title.

Volume I, *The Biology of Reptiles*

T.F.H. Publications, Inc. style number TS-297
ISBN 0-7938-0501-5

Volume II, *The Husbandry of Reptiles*

T.F.H. Publications, Inc. style number TS-298
ISBN 0-7938-0502-3

Volume III, *The Health Care of Reptiles*

T.F.H. Publications, Inc. style number TS-299
ISBN 0-7938-0503-1

The Biology, Husbandry and Health Care of Reptiles, a three-volume set comprising all three of the above-listed books:

T.F.H. Publications, Inc. style number TS-300
ISBN 0-7938-0504-X

Please Note: The following pages include the Tables of Contents of all 3 volumes.

TABLE OF CONTENTS
VOLUME I - BIOLOGY OF REPTILES

TABLE OF CONTENTS
VOLUME II - HUSBANDRY OF REPTILES

TABLE OF CONTENTS
VOLUME III – HEALTH CARE OF REPTILES

X

TECHNICAL EDITORS
Tara K. Harper
Lowell Ackerman DVM, PhD
Herbert R. Axelrod, Ph.D., DSC

LIST OF CONTRIBUTING AUTHORS
Lowell Ackerman DVM PhD
Pet Health Initiative, Scottsdale, Arizona

Frank Austin DVM, PhD
College of Veterinary Medicine, Mississippi
    State University

Michael J. Balsai, BA
University of Pennsylvania

Sean J. Barry, MS
Section of Evolution and Ecology, University
    of California, Davis

Brad Bolon, DVM, MS, PhD, Diplomate,
    American College of Veterinary Pathologists
Pathology Associates International Corpora-
    tion, Jefferson Arkansas

Shelley Burgin, Bsc, Msc, PhD
Faculty of Science and Technology, University
    of Western Sydney-Hawkesbury, Australia

John Coborn
P.O. Box 344, Nanango, Queensland 4615,
    Australia

James C. Cokendolpher AAS, BS, MS
Department of Biology, Midwestern State
    University, Wichita Falls, Texas

Todd Driggers, DVM
Foothills Mobile Exotic DVM, Phoenix Ari-
    zona

Chantal Dupont, DVM MS
School of Veterinary Medicine, University of
    Wisconsin-Madison

Robert E. Espinoza BS, MS
University of Nevada, Reno

Luette Forrest DVM
University Laboratory Animal Resources, Uni-
    versity of California, Irvine

.
Mark F. Gerber
Boise State University

P. Gopalakrishnakone
Venom and Toxin Research Group, Faculty of
    Medicine, National University of Singapore

Michael S. Grace PhD
Department of Biology, University of Virginia,
    Charlottesville, Virginia

Ellis C. Greiner PhD
College of Veterinary Medicine, University of
    Florida, Gainesville, Florida

Steve Grenard RT
Staten Island University Hospital, New York

Janice S. Grumbles, DVM
Statesboro Animal Hospital, Statesboro, Geor-
    gia

Trudy Hagstrom, MA
Pathology Associates International Corpora-
    tion, Jefferson Arkansas

Dr. Chris J. Harvey-Clark
University Director of Animal Care, Dalhousie
    University, Halifax Nova Scotia, Canada

Craig Hassapakis BS
Amphibian and Reptile Conservation, Provo,
    Utah

Sun Huh, MD PhD
College of Medicine, Hallym University,
    Chunchon, Korea

James L. Jarchow, DVM
Sonora Animal Hospital, Tucson Arizona

Melissa Kaplan
RepEnvirEd, Rohnert Park California

Gretchen E. Kaufman, DVM
Tufts Wildlife Clinic, Tufts University School
    of Veterinary Medicine, North Grafton Mas-
    sachusetts

Michael Kiedrowski DVM
Mountain View Animal Hospital, Phoenix Ari-
    zona

David T. Kirkpatrick, PhD
Department of Biology, University of North
    Carolina-Chapel Hill

Michael Kreger, MS
AnimalWelfare Information Center, Beltsville, Maryland

Khursheed Mama, DVM, Diplomate, American College of Veterinary Anesthesia
Department of Clinical Sciences Veterinary Medicine, Colorado State University, Ft. Collins, CO

Kathy Massie
Laboratory of Reproductive Ecology, Ohio University

Mark Miller
Herpetology On-line Network; President, Philadelphia Herpetological Society

Christopher J. Murphy DVM PhD
School of Veterinary Medicine, University of Wisconsin-Madison

Willard Nelson, DVM
Exotic Pet and Bird Clinic, Kirkland Washington

Kevin A. Nunan
City University of New York- College of Staten Island

Brent D. Palmer, PhD
Laboratory of Reproductive Ecology, Ohio University

M. Jane Perkins
Laboratory of Reproductive Ecology, Ohio University

Sharon Pickavance Bsc (Hons) B Vet Med, MRCVS
Royal (Dick) School of Veterinary Studies, Edinburgh, Scotland

Adrian Renshaw, B.App.Sc.
Faculty of Science and Technology, University of Western Sydney-Hawkesbury, Australia

B. J. Richardson BSc, PhD
Faculty of Science and Technology, University of Western Sydney-Hawkesbury, Australia

David C. Rostal, PhD
Department of Biology, Georgia Southern University, Statesboro, Georgia

Juergen Schumacher, Dr. med. vet
Wildlife and Zoological Medicine Service, College of Veterinary Medicine, University of Florida, Gainesville Florida

Sue Simon
Laboratory of Reproductive Ecology, Ohio University

Craig W. Stevens PhD
Department of Pharmacology and Physiology, Oklahoma State University, College of Osteopathic Medicine

Jennifer Swofford, BS
Highland Park, Illinois

M.C.A. Uribe, PhD
Lab. Biologia de la Reproduccion, Universidad Nacional Autonoma de Mexico

Craig Smith Bsc, PhD
Centre for Hormone Research, University of Melbourne, Australia

Michael B. Thompson, PhD
School of Biological Sciences, University of Sydney, Australia

C. Richard Tracy PhD
Biological Resources Research Center, University of Nevada, Reno

Stuart K. Ware, PhD
Deparment of Clinical Sciences, University of Kentucky, Lexington Kentucky

James Watson BVSc (hons) MACVSc
Animal Health Laboratory, Depatment of Primary Industries and Fisheries, Tasmania Australia

Stan Willenbring, PhD
Department of Pharmacology and Physiology, Oklahoma State University, College of Osteopathic Medicine

Bruce Young,
Department of Biology, Lafayette College, Easton , PA.

PREFACE

Reptile biology, husbandry and health care are dynamic disciplines that involve the input of various professionals, paraprofessionals and hobbyists. Until recently, these factions have been working separately, but with a similar goal - to expand the knowledge base for reptiles and their care. This book is the first to try to assimilate, in a comprehensive fashion, the diverse information collected by biologists, herpetologists, herpetoculturists and veterinarians. I believe you'll find that this makes for very interesting reading. It also provides a single source for identifying many of the fascinating aspects of reptiles and their care that aren't available in other books.

This book provides a wealth of information on many different levels. Although it is impossible to be all things to all people, there are sections in this book to address the needs of herpetoculturists, herpetologists, veterinarians, biologists, conservationists and hobbyists. The goal was to bring together experts on reptiles, but from very different backgrounds and areas of expertise. By incorporating the work of experts from different facets of reptile care, everyone benefits from the exposure. This is not an easy task, and I would especially like to thank my senior technical editor, Tara Harper, for her diligent work on this project.

Because reptile care is far from a standardized science, you will find some differences in approaches and opinions amongst the different authors. Far from being a problem, this is a wonderful forum to express different views and explore different ideas. Controversy in science is a good thing - it stops us from being complacent and keeps us searching for the real answers. Keep this in mind while reading this book and discussing the contents with others. I hope this book keeps you asking important questions and searching for the truth.

Lowell Ackerman, DVM PhD

HUSBANDRY OF SNAKES
GENERAL INFORMATION

BY JOHN COBORN

TAXONOMY, LIFESPAN, AND HABITAT PREFERENCES

TAXONOMY AND BINOMIAL NOMENCLATURE

Taxonomy is the study of the theory, procedure and rules of classification of organisms according to the differences and similarities between them. Binomial nomenclature is the method of naming animals (and plants) invented by Linnaeus (1707-1778), a Swedish biologist.

The system is still used today, but with ever more sophisticated methods of taxonomic research, has much improved over the years. Each species is given a two-part name; the first part is the generic name and always starts with an upper case letter, the second is the trivial, or species name, and always starts with a lower case letter, even if it is derived from a proper name. Taking snakes as an example a typical binomial would be *Lampropeltis getula*, (Common Kingsnake). The generic name, *Lampropeltis* can be applied to several species in the genus (for example: *L. calligaster, L. mexicana, L. pyromelana, L. triangulum, L. zonata* and so on). Note that it is quite in order to abbreviate the generic part of the name, once it has been established in the text.

Binomials are made up of Latin words or words from other languages that have been latinized. For example, *mexicana* means "of Mexico". Latin was used because that was the international language used by scholars during Linnaeus' time and could thus break the language barrier among the international scientific community. In Europe, for example, where there are many small countries with different languages, the Common European Adder, as it is known in English, is called Kreuzotter in German; Vipere Peliade in French; Huggorm in Swedish; Marasso in Italian, and so on, but it is known to scientists as *Vipera berus*, whatever their own native language is.

When a new species of snake is discovered, it is described and named by a taxonomist, usually a qualified zoologist working in a museum or university department. Often a species may be discovered by an amateur collector, who passes it on to a taxonomist for description and naming. The original specimen described is preserved and kept as a holotype, or type specimen, usually in a museum and is used as a standard for identifying specimens of the same species. As new species have been described in the 18th, 19th and 20th centuries, some holotypes have been lost, or destroyed due to wars, natural disasters, or human blunders. In such cases, a new specimen which resembles as nearly as possible the description of the holotype is selected. This is known as the neotype.

A species is a member of a group of organisms that are essentially the same, and which can produce more of the same by reproduction. Members of different species do not normally breed together, but if they do, the offspring (known as hybrids) are usually infertile.

Taxonomists group species into genera. A genus may contain only one, or many species. A genus containing a single species is said to be monotypic. The species in a genus are all fairly similar, though not quite the same. Genera are further grouped into families, families into orders, orders into classes, and so on.

Note: some species have geographical races that may be somewhat different to the holotype, but are not considered different enough to warrant specific status. For example the Blood Python occurs in three subspecies: *Python curtus curtus* (nominate), *P. c. breitensteini*, and *P. c. brongersmai*. In captive breeding it is important to maintain individual subspecies in a pure form. Unfortunately, many snakes with several subspecies have been bred together randomly producing fertile subspecific hybrids which are no longer true to type. While hybrid breeding is an interesting part of our hobby, it is important that strict records are kept. Each snake should have a pedigree, just like that of a purebred dog, cat, or horse. Breeding stocks of original pure subspecies should also always be maintained separately from any hybrid breeding projects, otherwise we are likely to lose many natural species or subspecies forever.

LIFESPAN

It is very difficult, nigh impossible to estimate

California Kingsnake, *Lampropeltis getula californiae*. Albino specimen. Photo by W. P. Mara.

the lifespans of wild snakes. We do know that, generally, large snakes live longer than small ones and the tiniest of snake species may live only for three or four years. Another factor is the age at which snakes reach sexual maturity. Those that reach sexual maturity in one year have the shortest of lifespans; in two years they can be expected to live for six to seven years; in three years they can be expected to live for 14-15 years or more. All the records we have of snake longevity are from captive individuals, but it must be borne in mind that in the captive environment snakes are not exposed to natural predators and diseases, and are protected from extremes of climate and the related lack of food and/or water. While many captive snakes may succumb to captivity related conditions at an early age, those that have lived a relatively long period in captivity probably would not have lived so long in the wild. The following is a list of a few species that have lived in captivity for a relatively long period, with their ages, but bearing in mind that we do not necessarily know the age they were when captured:

Species	Captive Lifespan (years, months)
Boa constrictor	40, 3
Cerastes cerastes	17, 1
Crotalus horridus	28, 1
Agkistrodon contortrix	21, 6

Species	Captive Lifespan (years, months)
Drymarchon corais	25, 11
Elaphe guttata	21, 9
Epicrates angulifer	22, 7
Eunectes murinus	28
Lampropeltis getula	20, 7
Loxocemus bicolor	25
Naja melanoleuca	29, 1
Python curtus	27, 10
Python molurus	31, 1
Thamnophis proximus	15, 9
Vipera ammodytes	22

HABITAT PREFERENCES

Snakes occur in every suitable habitat on earth and are absent only from polar regions and other areas, such as mountain peaks and high latitude tundra situations where the presence of permafrost makes it impossible for them to hibernate successfully; and from a number of oceanic islands due to varying factors. In Ireland, an example of a well known snake-free country, snakes were said to have been banished by St. Patrick, but the real reason is that they were destroyed during the last Great Ice Age, and were unable to repopulate before Ireland became separated from the rest of Europe. Britain, however, separated somewhat later and now has three species of native snakes.

Blood Python, *Python curtus*. Photo by Roberta Kayne.

However, numbers of snake species increase towards the tropics and decrease towards the polar regions. A single species, the Eurasian Adder, *Vipera berus*, crosses the Arctic Circle in Europe and Asia. The most northerly American species include the Rubber Boa, *Charina bottae*; the Racer, *Coluber constrictor*; the Ringneck Snake, *Diadophis punctatus*; the Western Hognose Snake, *Heterodon nasicus*; and the Milk Snake, *Lampropeltis triangulum*, all of which range into southern Canada. Several species of garter snakes, *Thamnophis*, also occur in southern Canada, and specimens of the Common Garter Snake, *T. sirtalis*, have been found as far north as the southern part of the North West Territory at a latitude of about 60 degrees north.

In the southern hemisphere, snakes do not reach such high latitudes, but the most southerly species are *Bothrops ammodytoides*, and *Tachymenis chilensis* both of which reach a latitude of 43 degrees south in South America; and, in Australia, both the Australian Copperhead, *Austrelaps superbus*, and the Black Tiger Snake, *Notechis ater*, are found on the island of Tasmania, also 43 degrees south.

The greatest numbers of snake species occur in tropical rainforest regions. Of these regions, the tropical rainforests of Southeast Asia has the distinction of having the most species, over ninety having been recorded. In the Amazon regions of Brazil there are up to ninety species and in tropical Africa up to 75 species. However, all species are not to be found all over the same areas, the maximum number of sympatric species in a given habitat being rarely more than 30. Tropical rainforests with an average temperature of 28°C (83°F), constant high humidity, and an abundance of food throughout the year can be described as the ideal environment for species numbers. In the rainforests snakes have taken over all levels. There are burrowing species, terrestrial species, semi-aquatic species, semi-arboreal species and arboreal species.

Numbers of snake species in tropical savannah and dry tropical forest areas are somewhat less than in rainforest areas, but nevertheless still relatively substantial. Most such regions on earth can boast anything from 15-60 snake species. Such areas have marked dry and wet seasons, meaning that food is plentiful for at least half of the year. When seasons are particularly dry and food is scarce, snakes in these regions generally estivate until more favorable times arrive.

Though desert and semi desert regions are usually regarded as being "typical snake territory", there are relatively few species when compared to rainforest and savannah. However, most tropical and subtropical desert areas can boast anything from one to forty species, with lower numbers occurring in the more inhospitable areas. Most desert dwelling snakes are at least partially burrowing species, or seek out refuge from the hot sun in deep crevices.

Snake species are moderately well represented in the warmer temperate areas with a Mediterranean type climate; warm summers and cool moist winters. Snakes are active during the spring, summer and fall, but may hibernate during the colder winter months. Numbers of snake species in cooler temperate regions diminish with latitude, though some favorable areas can boast up to 20 species. Snakes in these regions generally hibernate for at least half of the year.

Most sea snakes are found in tropical oceans with the greatest concentrations occurring in the seas around the Southeast Asian Archipelago and Northern Australia, where up to 25 species may be found.

PHYSICAL CHARACTERISTICS

Everyone is familiar with the general physical appearance of the average snake. The body is elongate, flexible, and devoid of limbs, though species in a few of the more primitive families, including the Boidae, possess vestiges of a pelvic girdle, which manifests itself at the exterior of the body as a pair of short, claw-like appendages set on either side of the vent. In most species the body is more or less circular in cross section, but may vary from horizontally to vertically ovoid, or sometimes almost triangular. The belly is often slightly flattened and sometimes there is a slight ridge extending along the sides, separating the dorsal and ventral scales. The tail is variable in length and degree of taper depending on species and sometimes on sex, the tail of the male being often longer than that of the female. Species range in total length from about 10 cm (4 in) for Sundevall's Worm Snake, *Leptotyphlops sundevalli* to 10 m (33 ft) for the Reticulated Python, *Python reticulatus*

The Skin: As a relatively large area of a snake's body is in contact with the substrate or with objects among which it moves it is subject to a relatively large amount of abrasion and so must be especially tough to combat wear and tear, as well as have the more usual functions of protecting the body from injuries, desiccation and invasion of pathogens.

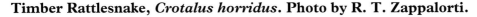

Timber Rattlesnake, *Crotalus horridus*. Photo by R. T. Zappalorti.

Arafura File Snake, *Acrochordus arafurae*. Photo by C. Banks.

The outer surface of a snake is covered with rhomboidal scales, but unlike those of a fish, whose scales are attached to the surface, those of a snake are an integral part of the skin and are formed by a series of skin folds. The actual surfaces of the scales are relatively hard and rigid, while the skin folds between them are soft and flexible. Scales may be smooth or keeled depending on species, the former often appear glossy, while the latter usually have a matt appearance. A few species have relatively small granular scales (Acrochordidae, for example). In most terrestrial and arboreal snakes, the belly scales (also known as gastrosteges) are wide, extend across the body and are arranged from the chin to the vent. Gastrosteges are used as part of the locomotory process in moving over surfaces, so are not required in seasnakes and many burrowing snakes which have fairly uniformly small scales over all the body. The scales beneath the tail, known as subcaudals, may be in a single row, or a double row; some species have a single row of subcaudals along the anterior part of the tail, changing to a double row at the posterior part. The scales on the head are enlarged in many snake families, and are sometimes referred to as shields. Numbers and arrangements of scales (pholidosis) are fairly consistant within species and are often used as a means to identification of species, and comparison with others. Identifications often revolve on dorsal scale counts at midbody; on subcaudal scale counts; on whether anal and subcaudal scales are single or divided; on arrangement of head scales, and so on.

Shedding: Also known as sloughing, casting or, more scientifically, ecdysis, regular skin shedding is an important part of a snake's metabolism. Due to growth and wear, a snake's outer skin gradually gets too small and frail, so a new skin is always being grown beneath the old one ready to replace it when the time is ripe. The outer skin layer is known as the epidermis. A complete new epidermis is formed in the layer below the existing epidermis. When the new layer is complete (most healthy snakes shed four to five times per annum; young, fast-growing snakes shed more frequently than older snakes), a lubricant fluid is exuded from glands in the inner skin and forms a filmy layer between the old and new skins. As the snake's eye-covering, spectacle or brille, is a modified scale, the fluid can actually be seen in a snake that is approaching ecdysis; the normally clear transparent spectacle becomes cloudy, or milky in appearance. Snakes cannot see clearly at this time and may be more vulnerable and thus more irritable than normal. This explains why a snake that is normally very handleable and docile may suddenly turn nasty at shedding time. As the old skin is loosened from the body, the snake becomes restless, crawling about and rubbing its chin and snout against rough surfaces. In a healthy snake, the old skin loosens around the line of the jaw and the snake pushes it back over the head by rubbing it against objects or passing through vegetation. With sinuous movements of the body muscles and with further pushing the snake gradually crawls out of its old skin, stretching it and turning it inside out in the process.

Color: Even those people who have an ineradicable abhorrence of snakes can hardly fail to marvel at the wonder of their sheens, colors and patterns, especially of those fresh after shedding. A freshly shed snake is a complete transformation of its former self. Whereas its old skin had gradually become worn, dull and lustreless, its new one has a completely different appearance. The colors and patterns are wonderfully enhanced and, under favorable light conditions, the new skin of many glossy scaled snakes, displays a remarkable sheen, often showing all the colors of the rainbow (the Rainbow Boa, *Epicrates cenchria*, and the Sunbeam Snake, *Xenopeltis unicolor* are two of the more ex-

treme examples of the effect which, however, occurs more or less in most snakes). These rainbow colors do not actually exist in the skin, but are a result of the sculptured surface of the outer skin causing white light to be split up into the colors of the spectrum.

The actual pigments which are the basis of a snake's ground color and patterns are situated below the skin surface. Although snake species show a wide range of colors, these result from combinations of only three pigments: red allophores, yellow lipophores, and dark brown melanophores. These combinations, blended with the refracted light effects described above, are responsible for all apparent colors in snakes.

The colors of most snake species are designed to camouflage themselves from predator and prey. Thus foliage living species are often predominantly green, while those living on branches are predominantly brown. The ventral surfaces of many snakes are often lighter in color than the dorsum to compensate for shadow. Desert dwelling species are often yellow to red depending on the color of the soil on which they live. Markings and patterns are intended to break up the outline of snakes and further camouflage them against the type of surfaces over which they mainly move.

Some snakes are brightly or contrastingly colored. This may be warning coloration as in the

Sunbeam Snake, *Xenopeltis unicolor*. Photo by R. D. Bartlett.

Bandy-bandy, *Vermicella annulata.* **Photo by C. Banks.**

case of North and South American coral snakes (*Micrurus* species) which are often adorned in bands of black, red, and yellow or white, or may be what is known as mimicry in which a non-venomous species tries to look like a venomous one for its own protection. The Central and South America false coral snakes of the genus *Erythrolamprus* mimic coral snakes in coloration and, as these are mildly venomous any animal living to survive a bite will avoid any snakes of such color in the future. Similar mimicry is displayed by several kingsnakes (*Lampropeltis* species). Many colorful snakes are secretive and nocturnal and their bright coloration is probably what can be described as "shock coloration". As an example the mildly venomous Australian elapid, the Bandy-Bandy, *Vermicella annulata*, when turfed out of its hiding place among leaf litter, throws its black and white banded body into loops, startling a predator during the day, or confusing it in poor light.

The Head: The snake's head may be broad with a distinct restriction of the neck, or narrow with neck and body of similar diameter. Whether the head is distinctly or indistinctly broader than the neck is a primary identification factor. It is a well known fact that snakes have no moveable eyelids. However, for protection of the delicate surface of the eye, a transparent brille or spectacle, a modified scale, covers it. In some primitive burrowing snake families, the eye has degenerated to a mere vestige hidden below a scale, and its function probably has little more ability than detecting the difference between light and darkness.

The typical snake has an amazingly large gape, and its habit of swallowing prey several times larger than its own head is well known It is not the gape alone, however, that enables the snake to do this. The mandibles are not rigidly joined at the chin, but are connected with extremely elastic tissue, which allows the mandibles to separate and stretch apart for some considerable distance. At the joint of the jaw, similar tissue allows the mandible to stretch down and away from the quadrate. The muscles and skin around the the jaws are extremely elastic and allow for expansion as prey is swallowed. The palate bones can move forward independantly of each other and the skull is totally enclosed with bone to protect the brain from the rigors of eating such large prey and providing anchorage for the complex muscle system. Numbers of teeth vary greatly from species to species. They are typically narrow, tapered, sharp pointed and curve back so that once prey is caught it can only go in one direction, down the gullet! Teeth may occur on the palatine and pterygoid bones, as well as on the upper (maxilla) and lower (mandible) jawbones where they are seated in the respective bones. As snake teeth suffer a fair degree of wear and tear they are replaced throughout life from "tooth buds" which grow just below the current teeth and move up to replace them as necessary. Most typical nonvenomous snakes have fairly uniformly sized sets of teeth though those at the front or rear of the jaws may be slightly larger. These are known as aglyphic species.

Venomous snakes have tooth specializations commonly known as fangs. Some colubrid subfamilies contain so-called rear-fanged snakes which have two or more pairs of elongated grooved teeth towards the rear of the top jaw. The groove conducts venom from modified salivery glands and is introduced into the body of the snake's victims when it bites. Such snakes are described as opisthoglyphic species.

Front fanged venomous snakes in the families Elapidae and Hydrophidae have a pair of rigidly fixed caniculate fangs at the front of the upper jaw.

Yellow-bellied Sea Snake, *Pelamus platurus*.

These conduct venom from modified salivary glands, the fangs acting as hypodermic needles as they inject toxin directly into their prey by biting, and contacting the venom glands. Such snakes are known as proteroglyphic species. In a few genera of proteroglyphic snakes (*Hemachatus* for example), the orifice near to the fang tip is directed forwards, allowing the snake to spray venom directly at aggressors by rapidly contracting its venom glands. The venom is usually aimed at the eyes and can cause severe pain and temporary blindness. Up to two or three meters (6-10 ft) the aim is reasonably accurate and it is highly recommended that persons dealing with these species wear goggles.

The most specialized fangs are possessed by the vipers and pit vipers of the families Viperidae and Crotalidae. Known as solenoglyphic species, their hypodermic like fangs are almost completely caniculate and are relatively long, those in a mature Gaboon Viper, *Bitis gabonica*, for example, being up to 2.5 cm (1 in) in length. The fangs are the only teeth on the maxilla, and when not in operation they lay back along the roof of the mouth. When the snake opens its mouth to strike at prey or an enemy, the fangs are brought rapidly forward by the rotation of the maxilla. Most viperids and crotalids have a gape so wide that the angle of

the jaw can reach almost 180 degrees during striking, and the fangs are more are less stabbed into the prey before the mandibles are closed.

The Tail: The tail of a snake is that part that extends in a posterior direction from just behind the vent. Tail lengths vary enormously from species to species. To mention two extremes, vipers of the genus *Bitis*, have a tail less than a quarter of their total length, in some cases as short as one eighth, while members of the colubrid genus *Imantodes*, may have a tail that takes up half of their total length. Most constrictors and arboreal snakes have a tail that is more or less prehensile. In most arboreal snakes the prehensile tail is powerful enough to hold the reptile's whole body as it hangs from a limb, even when it is dealing with a prey catch. In some species the tail shows special adaptabilities. In sea snakes the tail is flattened lateraly and acts as a rudder and swimming device. In many primitive burrowing snakes the tail tip ends in a sharp spine, which is thought to help anchor the snake in its burrow when dealing with prey. Natives of countries in which such snakes occur are often convinced that this spine is a dangerous sting, but of course there is no truth in this. In shieldtail snakes (Uropeltidae), the short tail ends in a flat shield, often adorned with short spines, and thought to have a similar anchoring function to the spines of burrowing snakes as described above.

The Australian death adders, *Acanthophis* species, and the Malayan Pit Viper, *Agkistrodon* (*Calloselasma*) *rhodostoma*, are examples of snakes that use their short, narrow tails as lures. Lying camouflaged among ground litter, the snakes wiggle their tails to attract small animal potential prey. Perhaps the most advanced snake tails are those possessed by rattlesnakes (*Crotalus* and *Sistrurus* species). The tip of the rattlesnake's tail is adorned with a noise producing rattle designed to warn off predators. The rattle consists of a number of loosely interconnecting horny segments. A young rattlesnake starts off with a single segment and another is added each time the snake sheds its skin. However, older segments eventually break off and a rattlesnake with more than ten segments intact is rarely encountered. The sound is produced when the rattlesnake vibrates its tail, and causes the segments to bang together, which it does when disturbed by large animals or man. The more excited the snake gets, the faster it vibrates its tail and the greater the pitch of the rattle.

SOME DIAGNOSTIC FEATURES OF SNAKE FAMILIES

While not pretending to be a formal identification guide for snake families, a few familial diagnostic features will illustrate snake diversity which, to the average novice, may not be immediately obvious. A few sample genera are included along with their geographical range. The species length range gives the shortest and longest (average adult) species length.

Family	Common Designation	Description
Typhlopidae	Blind Snakes	These are generally small burrowing snakes with small uniform, glossy scales both above and below. The eyes are small and vestigeal and are covered with enlarged scales. The tiny mouth is situated below the snout and there are typically no teeth in the lower jaw. A shovel-like rostral shield on the snout aids burrowing. The short tail typically is tipped with a sharp spine, which probably serves as an anchoring device in the burrow. A vestigeal pelvic girdle is present in some, but not all genera. They feed principally on ants and termites and most are oviparous. There are about 200 species in three genera (disputed). Genera include *Ramphotyphlops* (Australia, S.E. Asia, Africa), and *Typhlops* (Pantropical and subtropical except Australia). Due to their secretive burrowing habits they are not widely kept as terrarium animals. Species length range from 15 cm (6 in) to 80 cm (32 in)
Anomalepididae	American Blind Snakes	These are superficially similar to typhlopids but some have one or two teeth in the lower jaw. There are about 20 species in four genera including *Anomalepis* (Mexico to Peru and Ecuador) and *Liotyphlops* (Costa Rica to Paraguay). Species length range from 20 cm (8 in) to 49 cm (16 in).
Leptotyphlopidae	Worm Snakes	Sometimes called thread snakes these burrowing reptiles are even thinner than the blind snakes, several of them barely reach 3mm (1/8 in) in diameter. The rostral scale reaches far over the tiny mouth, acting as a burrowing device. There are no teeth in the upper jaw. They normally feed on ants, termites and other insects. Due to their secretive burrowing habits thay are not generally popular terrarium subjects. There are about 40 species in two genera including *Leptotyphlops* (S.E. USA, Central and South America, Africa, S.W. Asia). Species length range from 10 cm (4 in) to 40 cm (16 in).
Aniliidae	Cylinder Snakes	These burrowing to semi-burrowing snakes are round in section and the head is not distictly set off from the neck and body. The eyes are relatively small. The smooth scales are more or less uniform in size above and below the body. The tail is very short and broad. Numerous teeth are present on both the upper and lower jaws. About eleven species in three genera are normally recognised. Genera are *Anilius* (northern South America), *Anomochilus* (Southeast Asia) and *Cylindrophis* (India to Southeast Asia). Species length range from 25 cm (10 in) to 90 cm (36 in).
Acrochordidae	Wart Snakes	These almost totally aquatic snakes are found in fresh or salt water. The skin hangs somewhat loosely on the body and the scales are generally small and keeled, with a file-like texture. The tail is prehensile. The eyes are relatively small and set on the top of the head. The nostrils are valved. They feed largely on fish. There are three species in a single genus: *Acrochordus* (eastern India, through Southeast Asia and Indonesia to northern Australia). Species length range from 150 cm (5 ft) to 250 cm (8 ft).
Boidae	Boas and Pythons	Small to large, powerful constricting snakes from a variety of mainly pantropical habitats. In view of the spectacular appearance and tame docility of many species in the family, they are frequently kept as pets. The smooth scales are typically small on the dorsal surface, while those below are transversely enlarged to form a single row. The head is set distinctly from the neck. There are numerous, backwardly curved teeth set on the upper and lower jaws. The tail is relatively short and partly prehensile. Vestigeal pelvic "claws" are apparent in most species. Most species feed on vertebrates. There are about 80 species in five subfamilies and 23 genera. Genera include *Boa* (Central and South America), *Corallus* (South America), *Epicrates* (Central and South America), *Eunectes* (South America), *Morelia* (Australia, New Guinea), *Python* (Africa, India to Southeast Asia). Species length from range from 60 cm (2 ft) to 10 m (32.5 ft).
Uropeltidae	Shieldtail Snakes	A family of poorly studied burrowing snakes. The body is round in section and the smooth scales are slightly larger on the ventral surface. The snout is pointed and there are teeth on the upper and lower jaws. The tail is very short and ends in a large shield. They feed largely on invertebrates. There are about 44 species in eight genera including *Brachyophidium* (southern India), *Plectrurus* (southern India) and *Uropeltis* (southern India, Sri Lanka). Species length range from 20 cm (8 in) to 90 cm (36 in).
Xenopeltidae	Sunbeam Snake	This burrowing snake is included among the Boidae by some specialists. The head is not set distinctly from the neck and cylindrical body. The smooth, iridescent dorsal scales are small, while the ventral

369

Above: Rainbow Boa, *Epicrates cenchria*. Photo by R. D. Bartlett. Below: Racer, *Coluber constrictor*. Photo by Gerold Merker.

Yellow-faced Whipsnake, *Demansia psammophis*. Photo by John Coborn.

		scales are transversely enlarged. The eyes are relatively small. Numerous small teeth are present on the upper and lower jaws. They feed on small vertebrates. Only a single species in a single genus: *Xenopeltis* (Southern India, Southeast Asia). Length, to 100 cm (39 in).
Colubridae	Typical Snakes	The largest snake family, containing what are termed the "typical snakes". There is enormous morphological variety, and there are terrestrial, fossorial, arboreal and aquatic (freshwater) species. The head is generally distinct from the neck and tapering body. The dorsal scales may be smooth or keeled, and are generally small, diamond shaped, and overlapping. The ventral scales are transversely enlarged. The eyes are typically large. The tail is relatively long. Most species are harmless though a few are rear fanged (opisthoglyphous) and should be handled with care. There are some 2000 species in 14 subfamilies and 290 genera. Some of the more popular terrarium kept genera include *Boiga* (Africa, southern Asia, Southeast Asia to Australia), *Clelia* (Central and South America), *Coluber* (North America), *Cyclagras* (South America), *Dasypeltis* (Africa), *Drymarchon* (North, Central and South America), *Elaphe* (North America), *Hierophis*, (Eurasia), *Lampropeltis* (North and Central America), *Lycodon* (eastern and southern Asia), *Natrix* (Eurasia), *Nerodia* (North America), *Pituophis* (North America to Panama), *Ptyas* (central, eastern and South East Asia), *Spilotes* (Central and South America), *Thamnophis* (North and Central America). Species length range from 15 cm (6 in) to 3.5 m (11.5 ft).
Elapidae	Cobras, Kraits, Mambas, Coral Snakes etc.	Fixed front-fanged (proteroglyphous) venomous snakes, some of which are highly dangerous. Most species are not recommended for the home hobbyist. Superficial morphological resemblances to colubrids. The head is usually distict from the neck, but there are exceptions. The eyes are typically large and the tail is relatively long. There are some 200 species in about 50 genera. The Australian species are sometimes assigned to the Hydrophidae. Genera include *Acanthophis* (Australia), *Bungarus* (India to Southeast Asia), *Demansia* (Australia, New Guinea), *Dendroaspis* (Africa), *Hemachatus* (Southern Africa), *Hemiaspis* (Australia), *Micrurus* (Southern USA to Argentina), *Naja* (Africa, southern and Southeast Asia), *Notechis* (Australia), *Ophiophagus* (India to Southern China), *Oxyuranus* (Australia, New Guinea), *Pseudechis* (Australia, New Guinea), *Pseudonaja* (Australia, New Guinea), *Rhinoplocephalus* (Australia), *Walterinnesia* (Egypt and Middle East). Species length range from 35 cm (14 in) to 5.7 m (18 ft).
Hydrophiidae	Sea Snakes	Fixed front-fanged (proteroglyphous) venomous snakes adapted to a marine existence. Most have small uniform scales all over the body, which is typically laterally compressed. The tail is rudder-like. The eyes are relatively small, and the nostrils are valved. In view of the difficulty in providing optimum captive conditions sea snakes are rarely kept by hobbyists. There are about 56 species in two subfamilies and 16 genera including *Aipysurus* (Coastal waters from eastern India to Australia), *Laticauda* (Indian and western Pacific oceans), *Pelamis* (Indian and Pacific Oceans from eastern Africa to western American coasts). Species length range from 70 cm (28 in) to 2.75 m (9 ft).

Above: Sidewinder, *Crotalus cerastes*. Photo by Jim Merli. Below: Western Blind Snake, *Leptotyphlops humilis*. Photo by R. D. Bartlett.

Puff Adder, *Bitis arietans*. Photo by R. T. Zappalorti.

Viperidae	Typical Old World Vipers	Hinged front-fanged (solenoglyphous) venomous snakes in which the relatively large venom fangs rest along the roof of the mouth, but are brought forward by the rotation of the maxilla when the snake strikes at prey or in defense. Most species are rather heavily bodied with a relatively short tail, and many are spectacularly colored and patterned. Most are highly dangerous and are not recommended for the home hobbyist. There are about 49 species in three subfamilies and eleven genera including *Atheris* (tropical Africa), *Bitis* (Africa south of Sahara), *Cerastes* (North Africa and Arabia), *Daboia* (Southeastern Europe, and southern to Southeast Asia), *Pseudocerastes* (central southern Asia), *Vipera* (Eurasia). Species length range from 30 cm (12 in) to 2 m (6.5 ft).
Crotalidae	Pit Vipers	Hinged front-fanged (solenoglyphous) venomous snakes often regarded as a subfamily (Crotalinae) of the Viperidae. Generally similar to Viperidae, but with a heat sensitive pit between each eye and nostril. The family includes the rattlesnakes which are unique in having the segmented tail rattle. There are about 130 species in about ten genera including *Agkistrodon* (North America) *Bothrops* (Central and South America), *Crotalus* (North, Central and South America), *Sistrurus* (North America), *Trimeresurus* (Southeast Asia). Species length range from 60 cm (24 in) to 2.5 m (8 ft).

GROWTH AND DEVELOPMENT

A newborn snake is a miniature replica of an adult though its head may be somewhat proportionately larger, giving it a a typical "baby" look. Growth rate varies with climate and availability of food, which is why snakes almost always breed at times which will give neonates optimum conditions to grow and develop. Thus temperate species breed in the spring as the temperature and photoperiod increase, giving neonates the possibility to grow and develop as much as possible before experiencing their first winter. Subtropical and tropical species often time their breeding to coincide with wet seasons that will provide moisture for egg development and ensure adequate supply of food for neonates.

Newly born snakes are relatively fragile when compared to their parents, and seem less well able to cope with the environment. How much of this is due to lack of experience we cannot say, but we do know that in the first few months of life a snake is at its most vulnerable to predation. It is therefore important for young snakes to grow as quickly as possible and providing temperatures and food supplies are optimum, indeed they do. Most snakes seem to continue to grow throughout their lives though the rate of growth diminishes as each year goes by.

Rates of growth vary from season to season. A snake with abundant food and water available, and a sufficiently warm temperature will obviously grow at a much greater rate than one that is hibernating or estivating. Snakes from tropical areas, where conditions are favorable for most of the year, thus grow proportionately faster than species that must hibernate or estivate for extended periods.

Captive snakes given optimum climatic conditions probably will grow proportionately faster than their wild cousins, as they will generally receive a more reliable and regular source of food and will not have to work so hard to get it.

Small species of snakes generally reach sexual maturity at a faster rate than larger snakes. Some small species are sexually mature in one year, while larger species may not be sexually mature up to five years of age. Neonates of many species will double in length in 3-4 months given optimum conditions. Climate plays an important part in the time taken to reach sexual maturity, even among individual species. For example, the Prairie Rattlesnake, *Crotalus viridis viridis* is sexually active at two to three years of age in the southern part of its range, while in the northernmost part of its range in southern Canada it may not reach sexual maturity until seven years of age.

SEXING

While it may not be strictly necessary to know the sex of a single pet snake, breeders will find it essential to be able to distinguish between males and females. Unlike lizards, in which males often display different colors and behaviour to females, there is little immediately obvious sexual dimorphism in snakes.

In many species, the length of the tail (which starts at the rear edge of the cloacal scale(s)) is relatively longer in the male than that of the female. This is particularly evident in many viperids and boids, but not so obvious in many colubrids and elapids. In the genus *Bitis*, for example (especially the Puff Adder, *B. arietans*, and the Gaboon Viper, *B. gabonica*), the female's tail is extremely short and almost triangular, while that of the male is somewhat longer and more tapered. Having a longer tail means that the males of some species have a greater number of scales on the tail than corresponding females. Subcaudal scales are usually counted in preference to supracaudal scales as they are larger and easier to see.

Male snakes generally have a broader tail base than females. This is due to the presence of the inverted hemipenes which are housed in a pocket or sulcus which lays in a position adjacent and posterior to either side of the cloaca. In many species, adult females are larger and more robust than

Western Rattlesnake, *Crotalus viridis*. Photo by Jeff Wines.

corresponding males, though there are exceptions, and the method cannot be used for juveniles, or with inadequate comparative specimens.

Pythons and boas possess so called "claws", vestiges of hind limbs, one situated on each side of the cloaca. The claws are used by the male to stimulate the female during courtship, and may also be used to open the female cloaca to allow intromission of the engorged hemipenis. The claws of male pythons and boas are relatively large, when compared to those of the females. All of these visual methods above may be useful for cursory inspections but cannot be considered to be completely reliable.

A more reliable method of sexing snakes is the procedure known as probing, in which a narrow, blunt ended rod (appropriately lubricated with mineral oil, glycerine, or commercially available lubricant) is inserted into either side of the cloacal vent and pushed gently in the direction of the tail. In males the probe will pass inside the cavity formed by either of the invaginated hemipenes, and can be pushed for a distance corresponding to 10 or more (but usually not more than 15) subcaudal scales; in females, because of the absence of the hemipenes) the probe cannot be pushed for more than the equivalent of 2-3 subcaudal scales. After pushing in the probe, place

Blue-striped Garter Snake, *Thamnophis sirtalis similis*. **Photo by Paul Freed.**

the thumbnail of the hand you are using adjacent to the edge of the cloacal scale(s) and leave it there when you withdraw the probe. You can now measure the number of subcaudal scales that are equal to the distance in which the probe had been inserted.

Great care must be taken in selecting probes of appropriate sizes. Sets of probes are available commercially; these are smooth, ball-ended, and usually occur in sizes of 1, 2, 3, 4 and 5 mm. If you use a probe which is either too small, or too large, there is a risk of damaging the delicate linings of the cloaca and/or hemipenes, even risking a hemipenal prolapse. Use of probes is not normally recommended for snakes less than 45 cm (18 in) in total length, though some success has been demonstrated with the substitution of smooth ended intravenous catheters, or small mammal urethral catheters for the more conventional probes.

As a rough guideline you would use a 5mm probe for a 300 cm (10 ft) Anaconda or other boid

Ball Python, *Python regius*. **Photo by R. T. Zappalorti.**

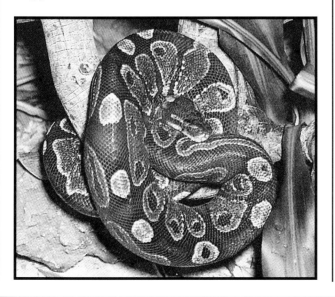

in excess of 240 cm (8 ft); a 4 mm probe for a 150 cm (5 ft) Boa Constrictor, Burmese Python or Ball Python; a 3 mm probe for a 150 cm (5 ft) Indigo Snake or Pine Snake; a 2mm probe for a 90 cm (3 ft) King Snake or Rat Snake, and a 1 mm probe for a 60 cm (2 ft) Garter Snake or Water Snake. It is highly recommended that beginners to sex determination by probing should first seek a demonstration from an advanced herpetoculturist or a veterinarian with herpetological experience.

Some herpetoculturists have been successful in determining the sexes of snakes by causing the male hemipenis to evert by applying pressure with the fingers to the area just posterior to the cloacal vent. Various veterinarians have been working on chemical stimulants which cause the hemipenis to engorge and evert, while others have taken to endoscopic examination of the reproductive organs. One method which may show promise in the future is the hormonal examination of blood, or even fecal samples. For reasons of safety it is advisable to place the dangerous end of venomous snakes inside a plastic tube when performing sex determination procedures.

SELECTION AND ACQUISITION

Careful condiderations should be given to the pros and cons of snake keeping before acquiring snakes as pets, or for a breeding project. Ask yourself the following questions first:

1. Can I afford to provide my snakes with housing and auxiliary equipment which gives them all of the necessary environmental conditions?
2. Can I ensure an adequate supply of the correct food items for the species in question?
3. Do I have the time to devote at least 30 minutes each day, plus a couple of hours every week for general husbandry?
4. Will I have an ongoing enthusiasm for my new hobby and not get bored with it after a short time?
5. Will my immediate family or apartment sharers have the same enthusiasm for this hobby as I have, or will I be able to persuade them to accept it?
6. Will I be able to afford veterinary advice if my snake becomes sick?

If you can give an honest yes answer to each of these questions then by all means go ahead and plan the accommodations for your prospective new pets. Always have the accommodations properly prepared before you acquire any specimens; never buy snakes on impulse and then have to start worrying about how you are going to house them. It is suggested that every prospective snake hobbyist should be a member of a herpetological club or society if there is one in their area. Members of such societies include novices and experienced keepers and there is always much valuable information and advice to be gained by discussion with like-minded individuals; and you will almost certainly get help with the selection of your first snake.

It is highly recommended that the beginner to snake keeping starts with one of the more common, easy to keep, and docile species (such as a Burmese Python, Rainbow Boa, Ratsnake, Garter Snake or Kingsnake for example). Maybe it is better to start with a single snake, so that you can get a good feel for its care, before getting it a mate and attempting to breed them. Involvement with common species for a period of

Rainbow Boa, *Epicrates cenchria*. Photo by R. D. Bartlett.

Blotched Kingsnake, *Lampropeltis getula goini*. Photo by R. G. Markel.

time will give you excellent experience should you decide to keep rarer, more difficult, or delicate species in the future.

While it is usually better to decide in advance what species of snake to start with, you will often be influenced in yout choice by what is available. Most hobbyists obtain their snakes from a specialist petshop or dealer, some obtain them directly from an acquaintance who has surplus stock after breeding, while a few may capture their own snakes from the wild. The latter course must be taken with great caution as many states and countries now have a total ban on unlicenced collection of snakes from the wild as they are strictly protected under wildlife laws.

The best source of snakes for the beginner is from a hobbyist who had already been successful

in captive breeding. Captive bred snakes are more accustomed to captivity than wild captured ones and will settle down better in their new quarters. In reality however, most newcomers to the hobby buy their first snake from a petshop. Fortunately the days of the dimly lit, overcrowded, dirty, untidy, smelly petshop are almost over; if you should come across one of those that are still left, give it a miss! A new breed of petshop proprietor has now come to the fore. The new age petshops and pet supermarkets are spacious, clean, clutterfree and sanitary and reptiles are displayed in an attractive manner.

The beginner should try and take a more experienced hobbyist along when going to purchase a snake so that instant advice is available. Always examine perspective purchases very carefully before making a decision to buy. Look for signs of external parasites on the reptiles or in their cages. Ask to handle a specimen that takes your fancy. If, at this stage, you are not proficient in handling,

Yellow Rat Snake, *Elaphe obsoleta quadrivittata*. 'Calico' variety. Photo by R. D. Bartlett, courtesy of Chris McQuade.

Ground Snake, *Sonora semiannulata*. Photo by John Iverson.

your experienced companion, or petshop staff will guide you. Examine the skin of the reptile carefully and choose only a specimen with clean, sleek, unblemished skin and with no shedding problems (pieces of unshed skin left on a snake are unwelcome signs of possible poor health). The reptile should be reasonably alert and show interest such as tongue flickering on being handled and should not hang limply in the hand. The body and tail should be reasonably plump, with no sunken areas either side of the vertebral column. Examine the snout for signs of injury, and the edges of the mouth for signs of inflammation or infection. Look at the vent for signs of prolapse, inflammation or diarrhea. If, after careful inspection, the snake is apparently healthy, you can go ahead and make your purchase.

TRANSPORT

Most snakes are restrained in cotton bags tied at the neck. Such bags allow the snake to breathe easily through the material, and give it a feeling of security. Each snake should be given a separate bag and the bag or bags placed in a carton, or similar for transport home. In cold weather it is recommended that cartons are lined with an insulation material such as styrofoam. Always try and get your new acquisitions home and into their cages as soon as possible. For obvious reasons, never leave snakes in a car for extended periods in excessively cold, or hot, con-

ditions. Before introducing new acquisitions to existing stock, it is highly recommended that they should first undergo a period of quarantine (see Preventive Health Care).

BEHAVIOR

Animal behavior is a science which attracts the study of many zoologists. Behavior reflects the responses to the stimuli an animal receives from its environment, together with interactions with other animals of its own and of other species. The very nature of snakes means that certain aspects of their behavior are unique and very interesting indeed. The types of behavior which are usually discussed cover reproduction (which will be discussed in detail, in the section on reproduction and breeding), locomotion, thermoregulation, defense, feeding, and social reaction.

The Senses As the senses of a snake are of prime importance to their general behaviour, these will be discussed first. Snakes have all of the essential senses that we also have but some of them operate in different ways to ours.

Sight: The first thing we notice about a snake's eyes, is that they have no moveable eyelids. However the actual eyes are protected remarkably well by the transparent spectacle or brille which is a modified scale. In other words, you can't poke a snake in the eye; it has a window before it! Some people ask: "how does a snake go to sleep if it can't close its eyes?" Although we don't really know if snakes sleep in the same way as we do, they certainly can go into long periods of immobility and torpidity. They normally do this below ground in dark cavities where the light doesn't reach and may even stick their heads between their coils for good measure. In any case, most snakes have pupils that open and close to a fair degree. In bright conditions the pupils close up, but they open up wide when it is dark. While most diurnal snakes have round pupils, many nocturnal snakes have vertically slit elliptical pupils that are even more efficient in opening and closing. Some of the nocturnal species without elliptical pupils have exceptionally large eyes; *Hapsidophrys* is a good example. There may be a few diurnal snakes with elliptical pupils, but these probably have evolved from nocturnal species.

Surprisingly, for a predator, a snake's sight is generally relatively inefficient when compared with most other predatory animals, and is nowhere as near as efficient as ours. A snake's perception of detail is apparently poor and it seems to have difficulty in focussing. There are a few exceptions: *Ahaetulla* species, for example, possess forward oriented eyes with pupils that resemble the figure 8 laying horizontally. Grooves along the snout al-low the snake to look directly forward with both eyes so that it has binocular vision, allowing it to recognise stationary prey by sight, something which most other snakes cannot do; they have to rely on the perception of movement or use a combination of other senses to recognise prey.

Hearing: Through the process of evolution all snakes have lost their external ears and middle ear cavities. However snakes can apparently "hear" in one form or another; having been proven to react to low-frequency sound waves. However, it seems unlikely that snakes are able to hear airborne sounds of higher pitch. The fact that wild snakes seem to disappear from your path before they can have seen or even scented you points to the likelihood that they have "heard" you approaching. In spite of the lack of external hearing apparatus, the inner ear of snakes is quite highly developed and seems to be extremely sensitive to ground vibrations. This is because the stapes bone, which is normally attached to the tympanum or eardrum of animals with normal hearing, is attached to the quadrate (the posterior bone of the upper jaw, which forms the point of articulation with the mandible). Vibrations thus pass from the surface over which the snake is moving, through the lower jaw, the quadrate and the stapes to the middle ear, from which a "sound" message is passed to the

African Rock Python, *Python sebae*. Photo by Paul Freed.

brain. The approach of a relatively large animal would thus seem to be make a "loud noise" to a snake. The inner ear of snakes also contains the semi-circular canals which are its organs of balance and ensure that the reptile stays the right way up, and that its head maintains a forward position when it is travelling.

Smell/Taste: The sense of smell must be regarded as the snake's most important sense. A snake can be regarded as scent oriented, using its sense of smell to detect prey, search for a mate, or avoid enemies. Though snakes have a fairly standard sense of smell operated by the olfactory epithelial cells lining the nostrils, the sense is further enhanced by the presence of an active olfactory organ in the palate, situated just below the nostrils but not directly connected to them. Known as Jacobson's organ it consists of a pair of domed cavities lined with extremely sensitive epithelium which can pass scent messages to the olfactory nerves. These vomeronasal pits correspond to the tips of the snake's forked tongue. An active snake seems to be forever flickering out its tongue through its labial notch (a device designed to avoid the bad economy of continually opening and closing the mouth). The reason it does this is to pick up scent particles on the moist surfaces of the tongue tips, from the air or from objects, and transfer them to the interior of the Jacobson's organs for analysis before the olfactory message is passed to the brain.

The sense of taste in a snake is closely related to its sense of smell. The tongue, as well as being a sensitive organ of touch and as a collector of scent particles, is endowed with a number of taste buds. This fact can be illustrated by the increasing tongue flickering and excitement of a male snake when he comes into contact with a receptive female.

Malayan Pit Viper, *Agkistrodon [Calloselasma] rhodostoma*. **Photo by W. Wuster.**

Touch: Snakes posses a fairly efficient sense of touch and it seems that the snake's skin is amply supplied with sensitive nerve endings. This can be demonstrated by touching an area of a snake's skin lightly, even with a feather (ensure the snake cannot see you). The reaction will range from a twitch of the skin at the area touched, to an expression of anger or an attempt to escape your attentions. Most snakes are happiest at rest if they can jam their bodies tightly into some form of cavity (thigmotactism); the greater the area of the snake's body touching a surface, the more secure it will feel. This shows that all parts of a snake's body are sensitive to touch and illustrates the importance of providing captive snakes with hide boxes.

Heat Sensing: Some snakes possess what could almost be called a genuine sixth sense; the ability to detect minute variations in temperature. Being able to so this is a very useful attribute for snakes that frequently take warm-blooded (endothermic) prey, which they can locate accurately even in total darkness. Heat sensing is made possible by the possession of heat sensitive organs or "pits" which occur only in two snake families: in the Boidae, all members of the subfamily Pythoninae (except *Aspidites* and *Calabaria*), and the genera *Corallus, Epicrates* and *Sanzinia* in the subfamily possess such organs along the edges of the jawline, either

John Milton (1608-1674), in his poem *Paradise Lost* described the serpent as "the subtlest beast in the field" he would undoubtedly have been thinking of the snake's remarkable ability of "going limblessly forth". It was relatively late in the 18th century before any real scientific attempts were made to describe a snake's locomotory mechanisms. Until that time serpents would have been regarded with awe and suspected of having mysterious or magical powers.

Snake locomotion, though certainly not magical, is indeed a unique and fascinating subject. Though no hard and fast evidence is available, it

Reticulated Python, *Python reticulatus*. Photo by Paul Freed.

within the labial scales (Pythoninae), or between then (Boinae). Members of the family Crotalidae get their common name of "pit vipers" from the fact that they all possess a pair of prominent heat sensing pits each one situated on the side of the head between the nostril and the eye. Heat sensory pits are lined with sensory membranes capable of detecting remarkably slight variations in temperature. Experiments have shown that pit vipers are capable of detecting a temperature variation of as little as 0.003° C with their pits, while boids are somewhat less efficient with a minimum of 0.026° C!

Locomotory Behavior: When English poet

is generally accepted that modern snakes evolved from limbed, lizard-like ancestors, and that most of their serpentine attributes arose as a result of these ancestors becoming fossorial and remaining so for millions of years. Emerging again as surface dwellers, the ancestors of most of our modern snakes again had to develop an efficient means of moving over the ground, but without the luxury of limbs.

A snake's major locomotory organ is its vertebral column and its supportive muscles. Snakes have a minimum of 130 vertebrae from the neck to the vent, and there may be as many as 300 or more. Viperids and crotalids, have the least number of vertebrae, while those with the most are the boids and the burrowing vipers (*Atractaspis*). The articulation of a snake's vertebrae is relatively complex for a vertebrate and here we will try and explain it in as simple terms as possible. Though individual vertebral joints allow lateral flexion of only about ten to twenty degrees, and dorso-ventral flexion even less, the combination of a relatively large number of vertebrae allows considerable articulation and bending power. Compare the flexion of a snake with a relatively small number of vertebrae such as a Puff Adder, *Bitis arietans*, and one with a relatively large number such as a Reticulated Python, *P. reticulatus* ! Vertebral articulation is controlled by a complex series of fibrous muscles and tendons attached to certain parts of the vertebrae and the ribs. The ribs themselves articulate with the vertebrae and, in turn, influence the movement of the broad belly scales (gastrosteges) possessed by most species.

The basic locomotory process is known as lateral undulation, in which the snake uses lateral joint flexures to "wriggle". As it does so, each bend in the body comes into contact with objects or imperfections on the surface over which it is moving and allows the reptile to push partions of its body backwards in order to pull itself forward. The importance of imperfections can be illustrated by placing a snake on a smooth surface such as a sheet of glass; it will have considerable difficulty in moving forward however quickly it undulates.

Another locomotory process is rectilineation which is practiced to a certain extent by most terrestrial snakes, but more so by large, thick bodied snakes such as boids and viperids. In this process the snake is literally "walking on its ribs". The vertebral muscles work in waves, moving the ribs like the limbs of a centipede. The ribs activate the belly scales and allow the snake to pull itself along, again using imperfections in the terrain to gain purchase. Snakes stalking prey using rectilineation often move more or less in a straight line, but if they are alarmed, they will break into lateral undulation in order to move faster.

A few snakes practice what is known as the concertina action in which the front part of the body is first stretched forward, before the rear part is brought forward to catch up with it much in the manner of but not as efficiently as an earthworm. This method is commonly used by many burrowing snakes.

Sidewinding is a specialized system of locomotion exhibited by snakes living in sandy deserts or other areas with a loose, shifting substrate. Obviously, with shifting substrate the snake would get no purchase on it when using any of the locomotory methods just described; it would just stay more or less in one spot! To surmount the problem desert snakes such as the Sidewinder, *Crotalus cerastes* of North America; the Dwarf Puff Adder, *Bitis peringueyi*, from Southwest Africa; and the Saw-scaled Viper, *Echis carinatus*, from North Africa and southwestern Asia, although not closely related, all practice sidewinding when necessary. The motion consists of throwing body loops so that the main pressure of movement is directed downwards, causing minimum movement in the loose substrate. Moving at an angle of about 45 degrees to its own body, the snake lifts it head and throws it forward while, at the same time it forms a body loop which is moved forward just before the head makes its next move. Sidewinders commonly leave a characteristic J-shaped track on the soft substrate over which they travel. Sidewinders can move in a more conventional manner in favorable conditions, while many other snake species can sidewind to a greater or lesser degree.

Most snakes can swim reasonably well, holding the head above the water and moving with undulatory movements of the head and tail. Truly aquatic species such as the sea snakes have dorso-ventrally flattened bodies and a paddle-like tail to help them skull rapidly through the water.

Arboreal snakes have further adaptations to help them move through branches and foliage. This may include a prehensile tail for stability, plus heavily keeled lateral scales and sharply angled ventrals to help them grip against bark and other surfaces. Using these adaptations many snakes can scale an almost smooth tree trunk with ease. Perhaps the most impressive means of arboreal locomotion is that exhibited by the so-called "Flying Snake" *Chrysopelea ornata*, also commonly known as the the Ornate Tree Snake. Although it cannot fly as such, this species and other members of its genus can launch themselves from tree branches and paraglide to another tree. By spreading the ribs, a concave surface is formed beneath the snake; this resists the air and allows the snake to glide for a considerable distance though it invariably lands at a lower altitude than that from which it took off.

Speed of Snakes: The subject of how fast a snake can move is one that has received much conjecture and one can find conflicting estimates even in the scientific literature. Just as the size of snakes is often highly exaggerated, so is their speed, and it is likely that only very few snake species would be able to outdistance a man walking at a fast pace. Though some snakes seem to be able to reach astonishing speeds for short periods, they are unable to keep it up for more than a few seconds at a time due to their low metabolic rate. One of the fastest North American snakes, the Coachwhip, *Masticophis flagellum,* has been reported variously to have been clocked at speeds between 3.6 m.p.h. and 14.9 m.p.h. according to various authors. The Black Mamba, *Dendroaspis polylepis*, probably holds the record for snake speed with short bursts of 19.8 m.p.h. having been reported by one authority.

Thermoregulatory Behavior Unlike the higher vertebrates, the birds and the mammals, which are endothermic and capable of maintaining an optimum body temperature by metabolic means, all reptiles are ectothermic (sometimes erroneously referred to as "cold-blooded") meaning that they must rely on external heat sources to keep their bodies at optimum operational temperatures. A snake subjected to decreasing temperatures becomes progressively less active until it reaches the critical minimum temperature, usually around 10° C (50 °F), at which it is unable to move and so must stay wherever it is until the temperature begins to rise again. Should the temperature continue to decrease, the lethal minimum temperature, usually around 4° C (39° F), will be reached and the snake will die.

As temperatures increase, the snake will become progressively more active until the optimum range of temperature is reached, usually in the region of 18-34° C (64-93°F). Within this range, snakes have a preferred optimum temperature at which its bodily functions perform at their best. The preferred optimum temperatures of snakes vary depending on species, and especially climate. Snakes from temperate regions for example, may operate perfectly at around 24° C (75° F), but snakes from tropical areas will be more efficient at say 28° C (83° F). The critical maximum temperature for many snakes is about 35° C (95 °F), at which it will start to show signs of heat stress. The lethal maximum for most snakes is between 38 and 44 °C (100 and 111 °F); any snake kept at or above lethal maximum temperature for more than a few minutes will perish.

In view of the great ranges of temperatures in the various snake habitats, and the inability of snakes to maintain optimum body temperatures by metabolic means, it follows that they must do so behaviourally. In cooler temperate regions, and also in subtropical and tropical montane regions, most snake species are primarily diurnal and habitually bask in the morning sun until they reach their preferred optimum temperature then, to avoid overheating, they return to the shade, coming into the sun again as their temperature reduces. This habit is sometimes referred to as heliothermic shuttling. At night, temperate region snakes retire into cavities and crevices below ground where the temperature is more stable than on the surface; some species, however, may remain active at night during periods of exceptionally warm weather. During the temperate winter, snakes are unable to reach optimum body temperatures so they must hibernate in semi-torpor until springtime temperatures return.

In subtropical regions where summer daytime temperatures are excessively hot, snakes have the problem of avoiding excessively high temperatures. Most desert dwelling snakes, for example, spend the hottest parts of the day below the substrate, or beneath rocks, logs and other ground litter. During excessively long, hot periods, when water and food are relatively scarce many subtropical snakes enter a period of prolonged torpor known as estivation. In areas with marked dry and wet seasons, snakes are primarily active during the latter.

In low altitude tropical regions, especially in tropical rainforests, snakes have the least problem in maintaining optimum temperatures. As the prevailing temperatures provide optimum conditions and are relatively stable, day and night, throughout the year snakes can remain active at all times. This also accounts for the greater percentage of large snakes in the tropics. A large boid, for example has no problem in maintaining an optimum body temperature in the tropics, but a similarly sized snake in temperate regions could never survive as its large body mass could not absorb sufficient heat from the relatively weaker sun and lower prevailing temperatures.

DEFENSIVE BEHAVIOR

The prime means of defense of the vast majority of snake species is flight, making for cover as soon as a would be predator is perceived. Most snakes bite as a last resort and usually only after they have been restrained in some way either deliberately or accidentally. The venom apparatus of poisonous snakes was not meant to be primarily a weapon of defense but as a means of subduing prey. It would be uneconomical for a venomous snake to use up its valuable venom by biting an aggressor that would be too large for it to eat and it would usually only do so as a last resort. Indeed some venomous snakes go out of their way to avoid biting aggressors by giving various warnings.

A typical example is the rattlesnake which, when disturbed, raises its head and draws it back in readiness to stike, coils its body for maximum acoustic effect and rapidly vibrates its tail, causing the rattle to emit a loud buzzing sound. It is almost as if the snake is saying: "take heed, I don't want to hurt you, but I am ready to do so if you don't leave me alone". The Saw-scaled vipers (*Echis* species) can make a similar buzzing warning by coiling, and grinding their rough scales against each other. The Puff Adder, *Bitis arietens*, expands and contracts its body by taking in large amounts of air, and making loud hissing noises each time the air is expelled. Many cobras warn off aggressors by raising the front of the body and expanding the neck by opening up the elongated cervical ribs. Perhaps the best example of this is the Spectacled Cobra, *Naja naja,* which has the characteristic spectacle marking on the back of its spread hood.

Many venomous snakes make use of warning coloration to warn off aggressors, a good example being the red, black and yellow or white bands of many coral snakes (*Micrurus* species). The Boomslang, one of the few rear fanged or opisthoglyphic snakes with human lethal venom, warns off aggressors by spreading the neck vertically and exposing the blue coloration between the scales. Another dangerous rear fanged snake, the Bird Snake, *Thelotornis kirtlandi,* makes a similar threat by expanding its neck into an egg shape.

Many mildly venomous and non-venomous snakes also employ various "shock" or "puzzle" tactics in order to startle or confuse would-be predators. Many species, such as the Vine Snake, *Oxybelis aeneus,* threaten by gaping their mouth wide open; the interior of the mouth is often a contrasting color to the normal color of the snake. The Copperhead Racer, *Elaphe radiata,* spreads its neck vertically and concertinas it while, at the same time, gaping its mouth. The Malayan Pipe Snake, *Cylindrophis rufus,* spreads and curls its broad tail up over its back, exposing the bright red underside, while the Ringneck Snake, *Diadophis punctatus,* rolls its tail into a spiral and turns it to expose a similarly bright red underside. In both of these cases the dorsal surfaces of the snakes are relatively sombrely colored.

Some passive defense methods are practiced by a number of snakes. The Ball Python, *Python regius,* rolls its body into a tight ball with its head protected beneath the coils. The Rubber Boa, *Charina bottae,* rolls itself into a similar ball, but leaves its fat tail exposed giving an impression of a head ready to strike. Many snakes feign death if attacked, the most famous being the North American hognosed snakes (*Heterodon* species), which turn on their backs, open their mouths and let their tongues hang out. They will stay quite still in this position until they are sure the danger has passed but, interestingly, if you turn one the right way up it will immediately roll over onto its back again!

Many snakes void the contents of their cloacas if restrained, not only does this include fecal and urinary matter but, in many cases a foul smelling substance is also released from special cloacal glands. A good example is the European Grass Snake, *Natrix natrix* ; anyone who had had the misfortune of being blessed with this snake's cloacal secretions can vouch for the fact that the smell will remain with you for some time!

FEEDING BEHAVIOR

All snakes are carnivorous and will take vegetable foods only accidentally while ingesting prey (this may include the gut contents of herbivorous prey animals). The types of prey taken will depend often on the size of the snake or its habitat. Many juvenile snakes start life feeding on invertebrates and many of the smallest species live on invertebrates throughout their lives. Most of the small, primitive burrowing snakes feed almost exclusively on termites and ants. Members of the family Leptotyphlopidae (thread snakes) suck out the contents of the bodies of their insect prey and discard the hard chitinous exoskeletons.

Some species of snakes specialize in certain types of prey. There are those that prey exclusively on snails for example. A brief rundown on the various specialists is given in the feeding section of this text.

Snakes can be conveniently divided into passive predators and active predators. Passive predators include many of the heavy, slow moving boids and viperids which lie in wait for their prey rather than actively hunt it, though they may lie close to a source of good prey such as at the edge of a permanent animal track. The prey is normally detected by a combination of the senses, including sight (the movement of prey is particularly important with this sense), heat reception in those species which have it and, most importantly, scent. The snake is is continually flickering its tongue in and out as it waits for a meal to turn up. As soon as it perceives potential prey the tongue begins to flicker more excitedly, sending scent messages to the brain via the Jacobson's organs and the snake will contract its body ready to strike. The front third of the snake is drawn back into the shape of a horizontal S and, as the prey comes into range it launches its head forward, opens its mouth and bites into it. In the case of many viperids and crotalids, the fangs are stabbed into the prey and the lower jaw is brought with a biting motion as the venom glands contract and venom is injected into the prey. In most cases, the prey is then released and, as it often is not immobilized immediately, because viperid and crotalid venom is largely cytotoxic or haemotoxic (tissue and blood destructive), it tries to make its getaway. This does not seem to worry the snake which pauses for a while as though it knows it has plenty of time. After a minute or two the snake casually and almost pensively follows the scent trail of the dying prey, tongue flickering continually. The prey may have covered quite a few yards before it becomes incapacitated and dies, but the snake will eventually track it down and proceed to swallow it. This strategy is used to protect the snake from potential bites from the prey before it has deceased.

Constricting snakes grabbed their prey with the mouth and hold on to it. As the recurved teeth bite into the prey, the snake simultaneously throws several coils of its body around it and begins to squeeze. Each time the prey struggles, the coils are tightened a little more until the prey cannot operate its lungs and soon suffocates. In spite of common belief, a constrictor does not necessarily need to have its tail anchored around a solid object in order to constrict, nor does it crush every bone in its victim's body. A constricting snake seems to have a certain intuition in being able to hold the biting parts of the prey away from its body by manipulation of its coils.

Active predators go out searching and hunting for their prey. They will follow tracks, enter burrows, hollow trees etc. in search of suitable prey, catching it by surprise. Many colubrid and elapid snakes are active predators. Some arboreal colubrid and elapid snakes search among the foliage for tree frogs, lizards and nestling birds. Fast moving terrestrial snakes such as many racers will actively chase and catch fast moving lizards and small mammals. Unlike the viperids and crotalids, the venomous elapids are less likely to release their prey after biting it. This is because elapid venom is largely neurotoxic, attacking the nervous system and immobilising the prey almost immediately, rendering it harmless to the snake. Many colubrid snakes (kingsnakes are a good example) can also constrict prey to varying degrees, even other snakes. While potentially dangerous prey (even a mouse can give a deep and painful bite) may be constricted, harmless prey such as frogs are often just grabbed and swallowed without need for any immobilising constriction.

Having captured and immobilized prey by one means or another most snakes dispatch it down the gullet in a similar manner. Snakes tend to seek prey of a convenient size to swallow, neither too large, nor too small, though most snakes are capable of swallowing relatively larger prey than almost any other predator. As snakes are incapable of tearing or chewing their prey it has to be swallowed whole. The prey is normally swallowed head first as it is more streamlined that way. Immobilized or dead prey is carefully examined by the snake with much tongue flickering. Once the snake has discovered the snout end of the prey it seems to get more excited, its tongue flickering faster than ever. Opening the mouth wide the snake engulfs as much of the prey's head as it can. The points of the chin spread widely as the mandibles separate and each mandible is capable of separate movement. A similar situation exists in the upper jaw, where the palatine and pterygoid bones are capable of independant movement. With complex muscle and bone maneuvers, the prey is progressively hooked into the snake's gullet by its numerous recurved teeth. In contrast to the moveable bones of the jaw and palate, those of the skull form a firm and rigid container, which protects the skull from damage during the rigors of swallowing.

Once the prey has passed through the buccal cavity, muscular and peristaltic action coupled with sinuous body movements move the prey down into the stomach. The time taken to digest prey depends on the type of prey and the temperature. A snake kept at too cold a temperature after it has been fed will be unable to digest the prey and it is likely to putrefy in the snake's gut and make it sick; one reason why optimum temperature is important for captive snakes. Generally, small snakes eating small prey feed more frequently than larger snakes that eat larger prey. A large boid, for example, will usually thrive on a couple of chickens or rabbits a fortnight, but a worm eating garter snake will probably feed every couple of days throughout the summer.

SOCIAL BEHAVIOR

Snakes are not generally famous for their social lives. Most snakes remain fairly solitary for most of the year, basking, feeding and sleeping and keeping much to themselves. However, the situation changes in the breeding season when females are releasing sexually attractive pheromones. Male snakes become aggressive to one another as the female scents drive them into a frenzy.

Exceptions to the solitary rule occur during hibernation when large numbers of snakes may congregate in the few available hibernating sites. A typical example of such behaviour is the Common Garter Snake, *Thamnophis sirtalis*, in which hundreds of individuals may hibernate communally. A similar situation may arise with regard to egglaying sites. When suitable sites are scarce, large numbers of females may congregate and lay their eggs in one spot. A few years ago in an area close to this author's home in southeast Queensland, a bulldozer driver uncovered a clutch of over 500 eggs of Yellow-faced Whipsnakes, *Demansia psammophis*. As the average clutch of this species is only about six, this amount would be the produce of almost 100 females!

HANDLING

There is a certain amount of controversy over the amount of handling a captive snake should receive. Snakes with a naturally nervous disposition (such as many racers and tree snakes) and those kept for breeding purposes or as part of a "natural" setup should be handled as little as possible; venomous snakes should not be handled at all, unless it is strictly necessary for venom extraction, veterinary examination or treatment, or transfer from one cage or location to another. On the other hand, "pet" snakes should be handled regularly to tame them and to keep them tame. Snakes that tame easily and can be handled regularly once they are tame include many pythons and boas, ratsnakes, kingsnakes and garter snakes.

Untame snakes of various sizes require slightly different handling techniques; venomous snakes will be discussed separately.:

Small Snakes to 60 cm (2ft): Juveniles of larger species and naturally small species are included in this category. Although many non-venomous snakes of this size will attempt to bite on being restrained the small size of the teeth will barely break the skin other than making a series of minor pinprick-like punctures. However, even such a minor bite should be wiped with an antiseptic solution or cream in case of secondary infection. To avoid bites such snakes should be grasped with thumb and forefinger, gently but firmly, just behind the head and the rest of the snake's body is restrained with the remaining fingers and the heel of the hand. Remember that small delicate snakes can easily be injured if they struggle and you apply too much pressure (one reason why small children should be allowed to handle snakes only under supervision). A certain amount of practice may be required before you become proficient in this technique. If a small snake is to be restrained for examination it is possibly, safer method for the reptile if it first coaxed into a fine-meshed net. The net material can them be moved away to examine the various parts of the snake's body, while the main part of the snake is restrained with the help of the hand and the net.

Medium Sized Snakes from 60-150 cm (2-5 ft): Some non-venomous snakes in this category are capable of giving quite a sharp, deep bite. With teeth up to 6 mm (1/4 in) in length, it is quite possible that a bite will cause minor hemorrhage. Though the bite itself is not particularly dangerous, it is recommended that the teeth punctures are bathed in an antiseptic solution and that a dressing is applied to the affected area in order to avoid possible secondary infection. Snakes of this size should, again, be gripped just behind the head, but with the thumb and all fingers of one hand, while the other hand should restrain the snake's body about half way along its length. Never suspend a snake by the neck and allow it to thrash about as this could cause irreparable damage to the reptile's vertebral column. Also, although it is common practice, a snake should not be picked up by the tail for similar reasons. However. the tail may be used to maneuver the snake when most of its body is on the substrate.

Large Snakes from 150 cm (5 ft) upwards: Large untamed snakes are often capable of inflicting deep, lacerative bites that may require medical attention so every effort should be made to handle them safely. Additionally, boids in excess of 3 m (10 feet) are capable of powerful constriction. It is recommended that two people are present when such snakes are retrained. The first person should grip the reptile just behind the head with one hand and midway along its body with the other. The second person should restrain the tail end to ensure that the snake does not get a constrictive grip, or to be ready to unwind the snake from the tail end should it manage to do so.

Large snakes are amazingly powerful and the following anecdote will serve to illustrate the purpose: I was once, on my own, attempting to transfer a feisty 4 m (13 ft) African Python, *Python sebae,* from a quarantine cage into its permanent quarters. Having gripped it behind the head, and before I had a chance to restrain its body, it got both of my arms in a constrictive grip, while it anchored its tail around my right leg just above the knee. Had I released its head, it may have bitten me and as I struggled to weaken its grip, it only pulled its coils tighter and, at the same time it pulled my right leg up so that I was effectively standing almost helplessly on my left foot. As there was nobody in hearing range, I had to hop about 50 yards through the length of the reptile house service area to a door through which I was able to attract the attention of another keeper by banging my head on the window and shouting for assistance. My colleague unwound the snake from its tail end and we then, together, carried it to its new quarters with no further problems. We looked back at this incident with amusement but I can assure you that, at the time, it was not funny at all. Since that day I have always made sure I have an assistant available when dealing with such large nasty snakes!

Handling Venomous Snakes: When it comes to handling, venomous snakes are in a category of their own. All venomous snakes, even those that are normally regarded as "mildly venomous" should be treated with the utmost respect. The reactions to snake bite vary from person to person, and even so called mildly venomous rear fanged snakes have caused bad reactions in a few people. The problem is that if you have never been bitten, you don't know exactly what your reaction is going to be like. So the answer is to be so cautious and professional that the possibility cannot occur. Venomous snakes are definately not recommended as pets for hobbyists and are perhaps best left to the devices of the professional staff of zoological collections and technical institutes. Unfortunately, however, there will always be those people who like to own a venomous snake to go along with their twelve bore pump action shot gun, pit bull terrier, and Harley Davidson motor cycle!

Anyone dealing with venomous snakes should have strict security in mind. Secure padlocked cages, restraining boxes, nets, shields and handling equipment are the order of the day and these should all be in place before the first snake arrives. A stock of up to date appropriate anti-venom for the species being kept should always be available; also ensure that professional medical attention can be acquired as soon as possible in case of a bite. Venomous snakes should be handled as little as popssible and then only when strictly necessary. A box trap, with a sliding door leading into the cage is a must, so that the snake can be coaxed into the box and locked in during cleaning or maintenance operations. A snake hook, which is a rod with a "T" or "L" shaped end is very useful for moving venomous snakes about. Large vipers, and pit vipers can usually be hooked up, midbody with the snake hook and lifted. Being reluctant to fall, the snake will normally stay on the end of the hook until you put it down again.

Elapid snakes are generally more agile and some (such as mambas) could easily crawl up the handle of the snake hook and attack you. For elapids, a snake grab, is normally used rather than a hook. This is a rod with a trigger at one end, which operates a crab's claw grab at the other. The grap should be padded with foam rubber or similar to prevent injury to the snake. The grab should be used to grip the front part of the snake as near to the head as possible (gently but firmly—you will need some practice before you get it right, but practice with a feisty non-venomous snake so that you will have some idea of the problems that may ensue). Once the snake is gripped, pull it gently towards you across the substrate and restain its body with your other hand before lifting it. Do not suspend the snake with the grab only, as you may injure it. Always hold the head end of the snake well away from you and from other people (it is best to keep spectators to a minimum when handling venomous snakes, but always make sure there is another responsible person close by just in case of emergency).

For safety reasons, if you are moving a venomous snake a short distance from one point to another, a square framed deep net can be used. Coax the snake into the net with a hook or grab, then twist the frame of the net so that the material is hanging from one side of the frame and held closed by the weight of the snake. Always keep a close eye on the snake in the net as you are moving from one point to another in case it should find an escape route. You can keep the snake in the body of the net by shaking and manipulating the handle as necessary.

Taming Non-Venomous Snakes: Burmese Pythons, *Python molurus bivittatus*, Ball Pythons, *P. regius*, Carpet Pythons, *Morelia spilota*, Rainbow Boas, *Epicrates cenchria*, Ratsnakes, *Elaphe obsoleta* complex, Corn Snakes, *E. guttata*, Kingsnakes, especially *Lampropeltis getula* complex, and Indigo Snakes, *Drymarchon corais couperi,* are some examples of species that tame readily. Most of these tame best if they are obtained as hatchlings and are handled on a regular basis. Some species are reluctant to bite at all on being handled, while oth-

ers will attempt to bite at first, but will stop doing so as soon as they are accustomed to regular handling.

The first step is to get the snake used to your hand; remember that some snakes grow to recognise your hand as the one that feeds it, so don't let it mistake one of your fingers for a mouse! Perhaps the best answer is to use tongs when you are feeding the snakes and use your hand only when you are handling it. With the snake still in its cage gently touch its body and stroke it. At first it will probably try and get away from your hand, or will hiss and behave in an unruly manner. Do this daily for several days until the snake doesn't panic when you touch it, though it will usually continue to show interest by flickering its tongue. The next stage is to place your hand in front of its face and let the snake taste it. At first it may draw back but eventually it will get to recognise your hand as friendly and not dangerous. At this stage you can try picking the snake up by gently sliding your hands under its body and lifting. You may have to restrain part of the body gently as the snake tries to get away, but eventually it will stop doing this and will rest across your hands or arms. Being naturally curious snakes will want to explore your body and other objects outside of its cage, so you will probably have to control it by it pulling it back each time it attempts to crawl off.

Once your tameable (remember that some snake species remain nervous and never become really tame—see above) snake had been handled a few times it will take it as routine and will give you few problems, though you should always make sure you know exactly where it is at all times when it is out of its cage. As long as you keep handling your snake on a regular basis (say three 20-30 minute sessions per week) it will remain tame and confiding. Even large pythons such as *P. molurus* will remain tame when they are as much as 6 m (20 ft) in length though they would normally be capable of constricting a human adult quite easily. However, never be completely complacent with a large constricting snake, as there have been a few cases where the "worm has turned".

HOUSING, HEATING AND LIGHTING

Housing arrangements must be decided before you acquire any specimens. Never buy a snake on impulse, take it home, and then have to worry about housing it. Remember that snakes are accomplished escape artists; don't believe for a moment that your snake will stay in a cardboard box overnight until you can arrange proper accommodations for it the next day!

A container in which snakes are kept may be called a cage, a vivarium or a terrarium; call it what you will they are all one and the same. However, I prefer to use the word terrarium because it means a contained landscape and most snake keepers like to landscape their display cage in one way or another.

There are no hard and fast rules for types of snake housing, except for the following:

1. It must be escape proof; snakes can get through unbelievably small holes!
2. It must be of adequate size for the specimen or specimens to be kept.
3. It must be furnished with the necessary life support systems required by the species being kept (heating, lighting, humidity control, ventilation and so on).
4. It should be easy to clean and service and, if it is for display purposes, it must be pleasant on the eye.

Purchased Terraria: Ever more sophisticated terraria for reptiles are coming onto the market and most of the larger petshops that deal in reptiles will be able to advise you on a selection. Cages may be made of fiber glass, plastic, timber, or glass but are normally a little more expensive than ordinary fish tanks.

Glass Tanks: These are the most common types of snake terrarium used by the hobbyists. Plastic tanks are not so popular for display purposes as the surface of the plastic tends to fog over with minute scratches when you clean it, though plastic tanks are very useful as stock or rearing cages. Ordinary fish tanks of the all-glass kind make excellent display terraria and you should find a range of sizes in your local petshop. You can even make your own to any shape or dimensions you wish. All you need is the correct sized sheets of glass, some silicon cement and a little patience. Use sticky tape to hold the sheets together while you are assembling them.

If you are starting off with a couple of small garter snakes or similar, a 12 gallon (52 liter) tank is adequate. For larger snakes you will require progressively larger tanks. A good rule of thumb is that the length of the tank should be not less than three quarters the length of the longest snake, for terrestrial species. If you are housing arboreal snakes, the tank need not be so long, but the space is made up with added height.

The tank must, of course, have a snug fitting lid that can preferably be locked into position. You can buy lids to fit most standard sized tanks. They have special lugs which fit under the glass strengthening strips around the top of the tank. The lid should have adequate, screened, ventilation panels. For the smallest snakes, insect screening is adequate, but you will require more substantial wire screening for snake over about 60 cm (2 ft) on length. A fairly new innovation is the heating hood which produces a vertical and horizontal heat gradient with safe heat. Your petshop should be able to advise you on the range of lids or hoods available.

Wooden Terraria: Some hobbyists like to construct wooden terraria for their snakes, but lumber should really only be used for cages that require low humidity as, however hard you try to seal it, it will eventually begin to rot if the internal atmosphere is continually moist. The easiest and most durable type of wood to use is outdoor (or marine) plywood that has been specially treated to repel moisture. A couple of coats of good quality polyurethane varnish or similar will further extend its durability. Most wooden terraria are constructed in a box shape, with a sliding, or framed glass viewing panel at the front. The timber can be glued and screwed, or tacked together for maximum strength. A small service door can be made in one of the ends of the terrarium so that you have access without opening the whole front panel, a useful device if you are keeping any flighty snakes!

Screened ventilation panels should be constructed at the ends and in the top of the cage. A sliding tray that fits in the floor area is useful to hold the bedding material and keep the actual cage floor free of moisture and dirt.

Masonry Terraria: Constructing a terrarium with concrete blocks or clay bricks cemented together may sound somewhat grand, and expensive, but these should be seriously considered if you intend to keep large boids. The main advantage of such a construction is that you can instal a permanent, concrete, drainable pool in the floor and instal some quite spectacular landcaping in the form of cliffs, rocky ledges and caves, and the whole interior can be conveniently hosed down at cleaning time. You will get some good ideas on the construction of such terraria if you visit the reptile collection in many zoological parks.

Stock Cages: Small plastic tanks with secure lids are ideal for housing juvenile stock or for use in breeding projects. Your supplier will usually have a range of such small tanks. For reasons of economy and simplicity, many reptile breeders use simple plastic shoe, or sweater boxes. Breeding rooms are kitted out with timber or metal shelving so that the boxes can be slid between two sets of shelves, the upper one doubling as a lid for the boxes. However, you must ensure a very precise fit if you don't want any escapees. Plastic boxes used in this manner should have ventilation holes drilled in their fronts and backs.

HEATING AND LIGHTING

Most snakes will require some form of supplementary heating in their cages. If you have a reptile room containing species from a similar climate, the easiest way to provide background warmth is to heat the whole room. Central heating, electrical heat fans, and electrical tubular heaters are some of the options. You should have a thermostat so that you can set the correct temperatures for the species in question. Remember that most snakes require a reduction in temperature at night, so you may need an additional thermostat and a couple of time switches if you don't want to control the temperature manually. Seasonal variations in temperature must also be taken into consideration whatever kind of heating you are using.

There are a number of options for heating terraria individually:

Household Bulbs: Ordinary household, tungsten light bulbs were once almost the only items used to heat reptile cages. Though there is a number of more sophisticated methods available today, light bulbs still have their uses and come in various sizes. A 40 watt bulb, for example is usually adequate to heat a 12 gallon tank. By experimenting with various wattages and a thermometer, you will come up with the right sized bulb(s) for your purposes. The bulb, or bulbs should be placed at one end of the tank only so that a temperature gradient is formed; the snakes will then be able to maintain their preferred temperature by thermoregulation. All bulbs should be screened to prevent terrarium inmates coming into contact with them and burning themselves. Household

Keeping an eye on the temperature and humidity of a captive snake's enclosure is an important facet of good husbandry. Fortunately, thermometers and hygrometers designed specifically for the snake-keeping hobby are now available in many pet shops. Photo courtesy of Ocean Nutrition.

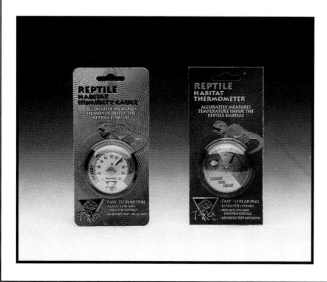

Naturalistic substrates like bark nuggets are ideal for captive snakes. They can be purchased in bulk and can be found in most pet shops that sell other herpetocultural goods. Photo courtesy of Four Paws.

bulbs emit light as well as heat, though the quality of the light is inferior to various forms of fluorescent lighting (see below). If heating is required at night, use a separate blue or red colored bulb so that the light is subdued. The subdued light does not seem to worry the snakes and nocturnal species will behave normally; the subdued lighting will give you the additional asvantage of enabling you to watch the behaviour of the terrarium inmates.

Heat Lamps: Infra-red heat lamps are useful in large terraria, less so in small terraria as the amount of heat emitted can be too intense in a small volume of space. Heat lamps are best placed outside and above the terrarium, with the reflector directing the rays through a mesh screen onto a basking area (usually a flat rock or a log). Care should be taken to ensure that the basking surface does not exceed 35° C (95° F). You can test the surface temperature by using a high range thermometer beneath the lamp, and raising or lowering the lamp until the desired temperature is maintained. Some severe infra-red burns in captive reptiles have been reported, so heat lamps should be used with the utmost caution.

Ceramic Heaters: Special ceramic heating bulbs and plates are available on the market. They come in various sizes. With reflectors they can be used in much the same way as heat lamps. As they do not emit any light they are useful for supplementary night-time heating if required.

Heating Cables, Tapes, Pads and Boards: Cables of the type used by horticulturists are useful if you want to keep the terrarium substrate warm. Most cables produce a temperature of little more than 25° C (77° F), and are relatively safe to use for background heating. To be on the safe side,

Screen tops are ideal for snakes. They are offered in a variety of sizes (to fit a variety of tanks), are relatively inexpensive, and provide a measure of ventilation through the screening. Photo courtesy of Four Paws.

bury the coiled cable under the substrate at one end of the cage only so that any danger of over-heating is avoided. Heating tapes have limited uses though they may be useful for providing background heat in batteries of rearing cages. Tapes are usually attached along the lower fronts or sides of tanks. Heating pads can be placed beneath terraria, or below the substrate. A heating board is really no more than a "stiff" heating pad, but is useful in placing up the side of a tank. Placed between two tanks it will provide warmth for both.

Special Heaters: A number of pet supply companies are producing ever more sophisticated heating appliances for reptile cages. In addition to the hoods mentioned above, there are such innova-

Providing your snakes with the correct photoperiod (day/night cycle) is very important. Photoperiod is often a factor in determining a herptile's behaviorisms. Bulbs designed specifically for the keeping of reptiles (and amphibians as well) now are available at many pet shops. Photo courtesy of Energy Savers.

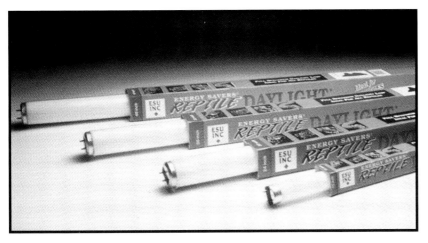

tions as hot blocks and sizzle stones. They should be used strictly to the manufacturer's instructions.

Aquarium Heaters: In cages where high humidity is required (for tropical rainforest species for example) an aquarium heater is almost essential. You can either place the heater in the pool, if you have one or, alternatively, in a jar of water concealed somewhere at the back of the cage. The aquarium heater will warm the water which, in turn, will warm the atmosphere within the terrarium. Additionally, the heater will slowly evaporate the water ensuring a moist atmosphere. Care should be taken to ensure that the water container is continually topped up.

Thermostats: Whatever kinds of heating are used in terraria, it is highly recommended that the temperature should be controlled by a thermostat. Some special heaters come already complete with a thermostat but, with bulbs, or lamps for example, you will have to buy a thermostat separately. The thermostat should be set to switch off the heater each time the maximum required temperature is reached. In colder areas, where reduced heating is required at night, you may need a second thermostat set at a lower temperature. A combination of heaters and thermostats can be controlled by time switches in case you should forget to convert at night.

Lighting: While some snakes are diurnal, others nocturnal, light cycles are necessary to all species. Biorhythms are controlled by light intensity and photoperiod and, though the importance of light quality is a gray area when applied to snakes as opposed to lizards, there is evidence to suggest that at least some snakes benefit from exposure to the blue end of the spectrum, something which is not available in normal household lighting appliances.

Natural light, at least for some of the time, should be used if you can arrange it. But remember that the heat of the sun through glass can quickly heat up the interior of a confined tank to lethal temperatures. Placing your terrarium outside on warm days and allowing unfiltered sunlight to enter through the screening on top will certainly benefit your snakes but ensure that ventilation is adequate to prevent overheating and try and shade one end of the cage so that the snake can move out of the sun if it needs to.

Artificial lighting will usually be required in terraria for most of the year. A number of electrical companies have developed types of fluorescent lamps which emit what is generally known as broad spectrum lighting. In other words they try to reproduce natural daylight. While the spectrum may be more or less complete, the intensity of artificial lights in the terrarium will never approach that of sunlight; however, this does not seem to have an adverse effect on snakes. What is more important is photoperiod, the amount of light in each 24 hour period. Lighting should be adjusted seasonally so

and installed by a qualified electrician. Electricity and moisture is a dangerous combination so don't take any unnecessary risks.

CAGE FURNISHINGS

Stock, rearing, quarantine, and isolation cages will require the minimum of furnishings, but hobbyists often want to create some kind of a natural looking landscape on their display cages.

Substrate Materials: Sometimes referred to as bedding. Some kind of floor covering is necessary in most terraria to absorb moisture from fecal matter, otherwise the snakes will be continually filthy from crawling through their own excrement. Newspaper is the simplest form of

Oriental Whipsnake, *Ahaetulla prasina*. Photo by Zoltan Takacs.

that the photoperiod in the summer is greater than that in the winter. This is especially important if you want to get your snakes into breeding condition. Use daylight type fluorescent lamps to the manufacturers instruction's. Most lighting companies will be pleased to supply you with specifications of the lamps they can supply. Never use pure ultra violet lamps in terraria, as prolonged exposure to the rays can cause severe burns.

Safety Measures: Always be safety concious when installing and using heating and lighting appliances in terraria. These are things that normally cannot be improvised unless you are an expert electrician. Always use items that have passed the necessary safety standards and any additional wiring should preferably be planned

floor covering, it is cheap, absorbant and easy to replace. While newsprint is not the most esthetic display material it is good enough for stock cages but, if you want something that looks a little better, use paper kitchen towels!

A more pleasant looking floor covering is terry towelling. Ordinary hand or bath towels in neutral colors (say brown or green rather than blue or pink!) can be folded to fit in the base of the terrarium. They are very absorbant and can be replaced and washed as necessary. Pieces of carpet cut to size also have their uses.

In display terraria, gravel or shingle is often used as a substrate. Although individual pebbles are not absorbant, the fluid content of feces sinks below the surface, but the solid material can be scooped out as necessary. Gravel should be removed and

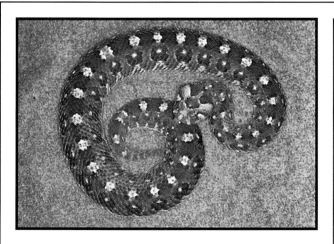

Horned Puff Adder, *Bitis caudalis*. Photo by Paul Freed.

thoroughly disinfected and washed at regular intervals (leave for 24 hours in a bucket of 10% domestic bleach solution, then hose through thoroughly and dry out in the sun before reuse). Keep spare amounts of gravel available so that the removed gravel can be replaced immediately.

Coarse sand may be used in setups for desert snakes. Never use fine sand, as it tends to stick to the snake's skin, especially if it has just crawled through the water dish. Caked sand between the scales can cause skin and shedding problems. A mixture of peat and coarse sand is useful for burrowing snakes. In most cases soiled sand and sand/peat mixtures should be discarded and replaced at cleaning time.

Orchid bark, wood chip and various other products are available as bedding from petshops. Collected and dried leaves, and wood shavings also are sometimes used. Sawdust is unsuitable as it can cause rerpiratory problems or intestinal obstruction.

Hide Boxes: Most snakes will settle down into captivity much faster and more satisfactorily if they have a hide box in which they can take refuge. Indeed, some snakes may refuse to feed if they are denied a hiding place into which they can squeeze themselves. Any type of container is satisfactory. In stock cages, simple cardboard cereal boxes or similar can be used. They are easy enough to dispose of and replace once they become soiled. Plastic ice cream tubs or similar, with access holes cut into them are more permanent as they can easily be washed and sterilized. Wooden parakeet nesting boxes may also be used. In display terraria, rock caves, or hollow logs are a more natural looking option.

Rocks and Branches: Rocks and/or logs and branches are used in display terraria for esthetic purposes as well as providing hiding places and climbing frames for active snakes. Arboreal snakes should always have a climbing branch or two, even in stock cages.

Natural and/or artificial rocks, the latter often with built-in caves can be purchased from petshops and garden centers. Alternatively you can collect natural rocks yourself. Look for interesting shapes. If using rock piles in the terrarium, make sure they are secure. Caves can be made by cementing rocks together.

You can also buy natural and artificial branches. If collecting your own, look for dead, weathered branches rather than sawing them directly from a tree. If you do take the latter course, make sure you have permission from the owner, and refrain from breaking any conservation rules. Some of the most bizarre and interesting branches and root balls can often be found along river banks or on the sea shore. They are usually well weathered, worn smooth and bleached by the action of sand, sun and water on them. All collected rocks and branches should be thoroughly scrubbed clean, disinfected, rinsed and dried before use in the terrarium. They must also receive routine cleaning at regular intervals.

Plants in the Terrarium: Living plants in the terrarium are often a challenge; sometimes they are more difficult to keep alive and healthy than the snakes themselves. With large boids and other relatively large snakes it is usually a waste of time to try and grow plants in the cages as the heavy bodies crawling over them will soon crush them. In such cases you may have to make do with some robust artificial plants, or dispense with plants altogether. However, plants in a terrarium with small snakes will enhance the display and may be a benefit to the snakes themselves, providing a more natural living environment and producing some humidity in the air space.

Try and choose plants that are compatible with the snake species. In a desert terrrarium, for example, try a couple of cacti, or desert succulant plants. In the tropical terrarium, there are several houseplants you can use, such as *Philodendron, Ficus, Peperomia, Monstera, Sansevieria* and so on. The secret of keeping terrarium plants healthy is to leave them in their

Indian Python, *Python molurus molurus*. Photo by K. H. Switak.

pots. The pots can be buried in the substrate, can be fitted into specially constructed artificial rock crevices, or can be concealed behind bark etc. Keep a spare set of plants and let each set do a tour of duty in the terrarium for say, one month, before changing it for the next set which, in the meanwhile, is kept in the greenhouse or on the window ledge. The plants must be watered regularly at all times, but any fertilising should be done outside the terrarium, at least a week before the plants are used, in case fertilizers are toxic to the snakes.

Outdoor Accommodations for Snakes: One of the most satisfying methods of snake keeping is to have them in a landscaped outdoor enclosure. Of course, if you are going to keep them outdoors all year round, and you live in a temperate climate, you will have to use snakes native to your area or those which are native to a similar climate. Some subtropical and even tropical snakes can be kept outside in temperate regions during the warmest summer months, but you must ensure that you have access to them when you need to take them indoors at the end of summer. Snakes can be difficult to find in a large lanscaped enclosure! Naturally, those of you who already live in a subtropical or tropical climate, will have a much greater scope.

The best type of outdoor enclosure for snakes is one constructed with a continuous brick wall. Sometimes referred to as a "snake pit" the wall often is built into a trench, with the earth removed from the trench placed in a mound in the centre of the enclosure, effectively bringing the proposed habitat of the snakes up to eye level. The inside of the wall should be smoothly cenent rendered and the height of the wall must be at least 30 cm (12 in) higher than the length of the longest adult snake you intend to keep. Ensure that no part of the mound comes near enough to the wall for any snake to be able to reach the top of the wall and escape. An inward overhang of about 15 cm (6 in) at the top if the wall will further enhance escape proofing.

The snake pit should be sited in a sheltered position, preferably facing south, with the protection of a building or a stand of trees to the north and east (the opposite, of course, will prevail in the southern hemisphere).

The mound can be attractively landscaped with rocks, logs and plants. Leave a few open areas with sand or gravel substrate for basking sites. Provide flood-free refuges beneath the rocks for hiding and hibernating. A built in pool even with a stream and waterfall will further enhance the effect. In some snake pits, the trench at the base of the wall is kept filled with water so that the snakes are living effectively on an island. As plants grow you must prune them to ensure their branches do not reach to the wall

Red-striped Ribbon Snake, *Thamnophis proximus rubrilineatus*. Photo by Paul Freed.

and provide escape routes. Snakes kept in outdoor enclosures will behave almost naturally and will usually breed readily. Provide them with a number of egg laying sites (plastic containers containing sphagnum miss placed under logs or rocks) and you will be able to collect the eggs up for artificial incubation.

FEEDING AND WATER REQUIREMENTS

Snakes generally have the least number of problems among the reptiles in providing them with an adequate diet. At least the commonly kept species which will gladly take food items such as mice, or day old chicks, rarely pose any nutritional problems as long as the diet items themselves have been raised on a balanced diet.

All snakes can be described as carnivores, preying only on animal foods, whether these be insects such as termites or crickets, other invertebrates such as snails, centipedes or earthworms, or various vertebrate animals such as fish, amphibians, other reptiles, birds or mammals. As far as is known, no snake voluntarily devours vegetable matter, though many may, of course, take parts of plants in accidentally while devouring prey, or as part of the undigested stomach contents of herbivorous prey animals. There are snakes which specialize in a small range of dietary items, and others which are more generalized feeders.

Southern Ringneck Snake, *Diadophis punctatus punctatus*. Photo by Paul Freed.

Rough Green Snake, *Opheodrys aestivus*. Photo by M. P. and C. Piednoir.

A balanced diet contains all of the necessary dietary constituents to maintain the bodily functions at an efficient level. The basic dietary constituents include proteins, fats, carbohydrates, vitamins and minerals. Parts of prey, especially bones, chitin, fur and feathers, also contain dietary fiber, or indigestible ash which, although not a nutrient in itself, may play an important function in digestion. Most prey animals offered to captive snakes are sufficiently nutritious to form a balanced diet. Exceptions include the types of prey offered to insectivorous or fisheating snakes. Many cultured invertebrates have been proven to contain an inadequate calcium/phosphorus ratio. In such cases a multivitamin/mineral supplement must be added to the food at regular intervals. The same goes for fisheating snakes which are trained to take strips of fish flesh. It is much better to feed them on whole fish if possible, but if fish strips must be used, they should be supplemented with additionl vitamins and minerals. Another problem that can occur with certain fish, especially marine varieties is that they contain an enzyme called thiaminase which can cause a vitamin B1 deficiency in the body by breaking it down.

Feeding Insectivorous Snakes: Here we are using the word insectivorous in its broadest sense; invertebrativorous would probably be a better choice of word if it existed! Many of these snakes eat not only insects, but spiders, centipedes, earthworms or snails. A relatively small number of snakes feed exclusively on invertebrates, but they include most of the burrowing snakes in the families Typhlopidae, Anomalepididae and Leptotyphlopidae which feed almost exclusively on ants, termites and other small burrowing invertebrates. Several members of the family Colubridae are invertebrate specialists. Examples include members of the North American genera *Opheodrys*, which feed on a variety of insects and spiders, *Gyalopion* which feed primarily on spiders, centipedes and scorpions, and *Storeria* and *Tantilla* which feed on earthworms, slugs and snails. Crayfish snakes of the genus *Regina*, as their common name suggests, feed mainly on freshwater crayfish, though they may also take large aquatic insect larvae and frogs. Almost all members of the South American colubrid subfamily Dipsadeinae and the Southeast Asian subfamily Pareinae feed exclusively on snails, which they extract from their shells with their special jaw and tooth structures.

In addition to the regular invertebrate eaters, the juveniles of many smaller vertebrate eating species begin their lives eating a variety of invertebrates but graduate to vertebrates as they mature.

Many particularly specialized invertebrate eating snakes are difficult to maintain in captivity, and indeed, should not be kept unless a constant supply of their special prey items are available. More generalized invertebrate eaters can be kept successfully on a variety of collected or cultivated invertebrates. Anyone with a garden in the moister climates can usually collect earthworms, slugs and snails on a regular basis by turning over ground debris. It is quite easy to encourage, even cultivate earthworms if you have a pile of moist organic material such as fallen leaves, grass clippings, vegetable scraps etc; but not meat scraps or manure, which can produce toxic substances in the worms' bodies. Indeed, to be on the safe side, it is best to purge your worms before feeding them to snakes by keeping them for a couple of days in clean, moist, potting mixture. Earthworms are an excellent food for some species of garter snakes, *Thamnophis*, and brown snakes, *Storeria.*

Crickets are an excellent standby item for small, insect eating snakes such as North American green snakes, *Opheodyrys* species, and Middle Eastern dwarf collared snakes, *Eirenis* species. Crickets are produced quite widely on a commercial basis. Adult crickets are about 2.5 cm (1 in) in length, but their various staged nymphs are as small as 3 mm (1/8 in), suitable for the tiniest of juvenile snakes. It is quite easy to breed your own crickets on a regular basis. Place a purchased group of crickets in a large, escape proof container such as an old aquarium tank or a plastic trash can. Provide balls of rolled up newspaper or torn up egg boxes as refuges. Rig up a platform on which you can place a dish of food; mixed cereal is ideal, plus some greens. A dish containing water soaked cotton wadding will provide additional moisture if needed. Further dishes of very lightly moistened sand will provide egg laying sites. Maintained at a temperature of 25- 30 °C (77-86° F) your cricket culture will be self sufficient for about three months. To prevent disease breaking out in the colony, remove spoiled food, keep food dishes clean and clean out the whole culture at least every six to eight weeks. Other useful cultured invertebrate foods that may be available include locusts, mealworms and king mealworms.

Feeding Vertebrate-Eating Snakes The easiest kinds of snakes to feed are those which will willingly accept laboratory mice, rats, or domestic chickens of various sizes. Other useful food animals may include rabbits, guinea pigs, hamsters, gerbils and gophers. Ducks, pigeons, geese and turkeys are suitable for many larger snakes. Quails are a useful items for smaller bird eating snakes,

Glossy Crayfish Snake, *Regina rigida.* Photo by Dr. Sherman A. Minton.

You don't necessarily need to purchase live mice for your snakes. Frozen mice are available at many pet shops and can be portioned out as needed. Photo courtesy of Ocean Nutrition.

the chicks are very small and will be eagerly taken. Quail and pigeon eggs can be used to feed smaller egg eating snakes. However, there is a number of more specialized vertebrate feeders that are often reluctant to accept anything other than their chosen natural diet. In the absence of a reliable supply of the natural diet such snakes often have to be force fed throughout their captive lives; an example of this is the King Cobra, *Ophiophagus hannah*, which feeds exclusively on other snakes. It is often better not to keep snakes that specialize in certain, difficult to obtain food items. These may include, snake eaters, lizard eaters, frog eaters and

Boa Constrictor, *Boa constrictor*. 'Hog Island' variety. Photo by W. P. Mara.

salamander eaters. Some of them can eventually be persuaded to take alternative foods, but others never seem to do so and must be force fed or they will perish.

For those species that feed mainly on frogs, salamanders or a combination of both you may be able to collect clumps of frog or toad eggs in the breeding season and allow them to hatch into tadpoles. These will be eaten by many small semi-aquatic snakes. Kept in an aerated, planted aquarium, some of the tadpoles can be reared into froglets which can be further grown on a diet of insects so that you have frogs of various sizes. If you collect wild amphibians, take those only that are common and not protected under any conservation laws; it is bad policy to endanger a species in order to feed captive snakes. Some hobbyists like to breed a supply of frogs. One species that can be bred all year round and is available commercially is the African Clawed Frog, *Xenopus laevis*. You can use the tadpoles for small snakes, or allow the frogs to metamorphose and grow into various sizes. The Mexican Axolotl, *Ambystoma mexicanum* is an aquatic salamander that also is available commercially and will breed most of the year if given the right conditions. Most frog and salamander eating snakes will take these home bred amphibians readily.

One way of getting some snakes to take say pinkies (nestling mice), rather than their natural prey of salamanders, is to rub the pinky with some of the moisture from a salamander's body so that a "salamander flavor" is imparted to the bait. Many hobbyists have found that, using this method, their snakes have eventually grown to accept mice without the salamander scent.

Some lizard and frog eating snakes, such as Long-nosed Tree Snakes (*Ahaetulla* species) can be persuaded to take small live fish, such as guppies, by offering the fish in a dish of very shallow water so that they flop about and draw the snake's attention.

Some controversy exists about whether live or dead food prey items should be fed to captive snakes. This is because some people feel sorry for the prey animals. However, most snakes kill their prey quickly and efficiently. Many hobbists try to feed dead food to their snakes as often as possible. This is because it is usually more practical to use stocks of dead frozen food rather than keep the food animals alive. However, other enthusiasts like to breed their stocks of food animals so that they have a fresh continuous supply. Remember that any animals kept for this purpose should be housed cleanly, fed well and treated kindly and not neglected just because they are snake food.

Frequency of Feeding There are no hard and fast rules about how often a snake should be fed and how much it should be given and it is often a case of trial and error. The main danger often seems to be overfeeding rather than underfeeding. In the wild there is a natural balance between the nutritional value of the prey and the amount of energy used in catching it. You will rarely see an overweight wild snake as it has to work hard for its living and will often have to fast for some considerable time between meals. Captive snakes have to work less hard for their food and are usually given it at regular intervals. This means that captive snakes sometimes are overfed and become grossly overweight with enormous amounts of fat deposited among the internal organs. Such snakes eventually become debilitated as a result of their metabolism being disturbed, making them behave abnormally and they may be of little use for breeding.

The following generalizations can be taken as guidelines. Insectivorous snakes can be more or less fed ad lib, though you should occasionally give them a fasting period for a week. Vertebrate feeders generally are fed less often. Juvenile growing snakes should be fed about twice per week until they are doubled in length (usually about six to nine months), then they should be offered food on a weekly basis. The largest snakes such as boas and pythons need to be fed a substantial meal only every two to three weeks. Any snakes that appear to be getting too fat, should be allowed to fast for a few weeks.

When more than one snake is kept in a cage you should keep close watch at feeding time. Not infrequently two snakes may grab the same prey animal and the larger of the two snakes may end up swallowing the smaller one in the process of feeding.

Adding a little calcium powder to your snakes' food items will enhance their nutritional value, which in turn will be passed along to the snakes. Such supplements can be found at many pet shops. Photo courtesy of American Reptile, Inc.

Remember that snakes usually refuse to feed at shedding time. When a snake appears to be about to shed it should not be fed, especially with live food. Mice or rats left overnight with a snake have been known to attack and feed on the body of the reptile. Live food should generally not be left with a snake for longer periods. If the snake does not feed within a few minutes of introducing the live prey it is best to remove it and try again a couple of days later. Many snakes will soon learn to take dead prey, especially if it is jiggled about in front of the snake's snout with a stick or with tongs.

Force Feeding Force feeding will have to be performed on snake's with a specialized diet when the special pray is not availabe. Other snakes, for one reason or another may steadfastedly refuse to feed and will begin to lose weight. These must also be force fed.

Before force feeding make sure the snake is not suffering from any debilitating disease which could be the cause of its loss of appetite. Treatment for disease should precede or accompany force feeding; your veterinarian will advise you. Force feeding a dead mouse to a snake is fairly easy after a little practice. Open the snake's mouth by gently but firmly pulling down on the loose skin beneath its jaw and push the mouse head first into the buccal cavity. Occasionally the snake will take the cue and start swallowing voluntarily, in which case you can release it and let it proceed. Otherwise you may have to push the prey down into the gullet. A smooth rod (the handle of a wooden spoon for example), lubricated with mineral oil or animal fat can be used to push the prey down past the neck area. Then the prey can be gently massaged with the hand down into the stomach.

Another method of force feeding is to liquify the dead prey animal first in a food processor adding a little water to make a slurry. The slurry is poured into a large syringe with a smooth ended stomach tube or nozzle attached to the nozzle. The tip of the lubricated stomach tube is passed into the snake's mouth via the labial notch and down into the stomach, about one third of the snake's length, and the contents gently squeezed out. A little extra water added to the syringe and squeezed through the tube will ensure all of the food is used up.

WASTE MANAGEMENT

Snake cages are surprisingly easy to keep clean as snakes empty their bowels infrequently, depending in how often they feed, and their feces are usually fairly solid and easy to remove. Fecal matter should generally be removed from cages as soon as it is noticed. On gravel or sand substrates use a scoop to remove the feces and a small amount of the substrate. Paper, wood shavings, or bark, substrates should be removed and freshly replaced. Launderable substrates such as artificial grass, towelling, or carpet should be removed and washed as necessary. Always ensure you have a supply of clean, dry substrate material for replacement.

Fecal matter and biodegradable substrate materials can be incinerated, placed in your garden compost heap, or buried. Large snake breeding establishments should make arrangements with their local authority or a contract refuse disposal company to remove their waste material. Dead animals should be incinerated, or preserved if they are being sent for autopsy.

REPRODUCTION AND CAPTIVE BREEDING

At one time there seemed to be a never ending supply of imported wild-caught reptiles through the pet trade and captive breeding was the exception rather than the rule.

In past couple of decades conservationists are becoming increasingly alarmed at the rate of which the natural world is being destroyed. Increasing human populations are expanding into and exploiting wildernesses that had hitherto been hardly touched. Logging, and clearing land for agricultural purposes seem to be the most damaging processes as, not only do the trees and plants go, but also the fauna which is part of the total ecology. This applies especially to areas of tropical rainforest where the biodiversity is at its most complex. In the past, logging was a relatively slow process as trees had to be cut down manually but with the advent of ever more sophisticated machinary, forests are being razed at an alarming rate. Additionally, in some countries such as Brazil, millions of acres of primeval rainforest are being literally burnt out of existance to make way for agricultural land. In Haiti and Madagascar it is estimated that 90 % of the original forests have been destroyed in the past 30 years. In Australia, about 90% of what little rainforest existed at European settlement has since been destroyed.

Many snake species are inhabitants of the forests and, as the trees go, so do they. Snakes dependent on the ecological diversity of the forests are unable to adapt to new conditions, so they just become extinct. One by-product of logging in some countries has been the collection of exotic animals for export to the pet trades of North America and Europe. Purists have always argued that the capture of wild animals for the pet trade is immoral. This may have been a fair argument at the time when there still were vast areas of habitat. But, as habitats are being systematically destroyed, surely it must be better to save what animals we can for the pet trade, rather than let them succumb to the deprivation of their natural biotope.

As natural habitats continue to be eaten up by the "expanding economies", however, imported specimens will become increasingly fewer and the supply will eventually dry up altogether. Then, the only snakes available to hobbyists will be those that have been bred in captivity. Captive breeding of substantial numbers of specimens (albeit of relatively few species) is something that has arisen only in the past few years. Studies on the reproductive biology of reptiles have shown that to reproduce successfully most species require climatic conditions similar to those of their native habitats, and application of this knowledge has led to increasing numbers of captive bred specimens available to hobbyists.

Snake breeding is one of the most satisfying and exciting aspects of keeping them. In order to perpetuate our hobby for the benefit of future generations of snake fanciers it is imperative that we make every effort to encourage our captive specimens to breed. To do this we must have details of the species' original natural habitat and climate, whether it be tropical rainforest, desert, savannah or temperate woodland, for example, and a knowledge of its reproductive behaviour.

General Reproductive Behaviour of Snakes: Breeding patterns in snakes are closely tied in with the climate. Most temperate and subtropical species mate and breed in the spring, after a winter period of hibernation. Tropical and some subtropical species often will breed at any time of the year, but may be influenced by seasonal rains. During periods of drought, when food and water are scarce, snakes will estivate until favorable conditions arrive again. It is only during periods of plenty, that such snakes are able to reproduce.

Most snakes live fairly solitary lives outside of the breeding season though some species may congregate in numbers in suitable hibernaculae. One example if this is the Common Garter Snake, *Thamnophis sirtalis,* which, in the northern part of its range, may hibernate in groups of many hundreds in suitable refuges. Increase in temperature and photoperiod in the spring triggers the release of hormones in the bodies of snakes which makes male snakes want to find a female, and female snakes to attract males. The sexually receptive female releases secretions from her vent and, as she moves along, she leaves a trail along the substrate which is "sweet smelling" to any male snake that may encounter it. The female snake also releases a pheromone called vitellogen from tiny glands in the soft skin between the scales to further enhance her attraction to males.

Male snakes of many species often seem to outnumber females by as much as five to one. In the breeding season males are out and about actively seeking females. On encountering a scent trail left by a female, the male follows the trail, tongue flickering in excitement. As the female is approached the scent obviously becomes more intense and the male snake becomes progressively more agitated. Sometimes a number of males may pick up the scent of a single female and on approaching the female a form of combat will ensue, the males writhing and twisting together, endeavouring to force their opponents into submission. Males are rarely injured in these combats, the weaker ones eventually falling out of the contests, and leaving the strongest snake to court the female, which usually shows no interest in the proceedings whatsoever!

Once a victorious male finds himself alone with a female, he then has to persuade her to mate. Although a female snake produces male attractants, she still often seems to want to play hard to get and, when a male approaches, she may at first shun his attentions and even try to make herself scarce. However, the male is quite persistent in his efforts and usually will not give up until he has reached his goal. He approaches her from the rear, first nudging and tasting her vent, then crawling beside or along her body, tongue flickering in excitement as he tastes her pheromones. Some of the more primitive species with cloacal "claws", such as the boids, use these appendages to stimulate the female's skin, especially in the area of the vent.

Eventually, the receptive female will lay still, raise her tail and allow the male to get his vent in apposition to hers and insert one of his hemipenes into her cloaca. Copulation takes anything from a few minutes to several hours. Sperm passes down a groove in the surface of the everted hemipenis and into the female cloaca, ready to fertilize her eggs.

After fertilization the eggs are stored in the female uterus. The time taken for their development varies, depending on the species and its method of reproduction. In oviparous snake species the eggs are laid relatively early, usually in the range of 25-70 days after fertilization. The eggs, which are white, round to oval in shape, and have a soft, but tough leathery shell, contain large amounts of nutritive yolk to allow further development of the embryo outside the maternal body. Of course, the eggs vary in size depending on the species. In ovoviviparous snake species the eggs are retained in the maternal body for longer periods, often for 100 days or more and the embryo develops to hatching point just as, or just after, the eggs are laid. In this case the eggs have no leathery shell but a soft translucent membrane. Because ovoviviparous snakes produce fully developed young, they are often known as livebearers.

Some snake species are able to store viable sperm in a cavity situated near to the head of the oviduct and fertilization does not then take place until conditions are right. This may be several months or even years after copulation and explains why some female snakes suddenly become gravid even if they have not been with a male for some time.

At egglaying time the oviparous female selects a spot which she instinctively knows as being ideal for the safety of the eggs and further development of the embryos. Many snakes lay their eggs in a cavity beneath rotting logs, beneath rocks, among rotting vegetation or under ground litter; termite mounds are a favored spot for many tropical species, the relatively constant temperature and humidity in the mound providing ideal conditions for incubation.

Ovoviviparous snake species generally are less selective in selecting sites for giving birth, though they generally choose a spot that is reasonably sheltered. The vast majority of snake species show little interest in their eggs, or young after they have been safely deposited. Exceptions include most python species which lay their eggs in a cone shaped mound and coil around them during their incubation. Incubating female pythons are able to increase their body temperatures by a few degrees by metabolic means not yet thoroughly understood, but muscular twitching seems to provide the energy for an increase in temperature. The Malayan Pit Viper *Agkistrodon (Calloselasma) rhodostoma*, and the King Cobra, *Ophiophagus hannah*, are other examples of snakes that guard their eggs during incubation. Once the eggs have hatched, brooding snakes show no further interest in their offspring.

CAPTIVE BREEDING

Creating A Breeding Response: Most snakes kept in conditions that are substantially different to those of their natural habitat are unlikely to breed so we must attempt to emulate or at least provide conditions as close as possible to that of the natural habitat of the species. Temperate species are most likely to breed after a period of hibernation, followed by a progressive increase in temperature and photoperiod. Species from dry subtropical climates with fairly cold winters will also require an increase in temperature

Boa Constrictor, *Boa constrictor*. Photo by R. D. Bartlett.

and photoperiod after a short rest period at reduced temperatures. Many tropical rainforest species, or species from areas with marked wet and dry seasons are most likely to breed during the wetter parts of the year, so an increase in terrarium humidity may help trigger a breeding response.

The best results often occur when sexes are kept separately outside the breeding season and only introduced when conditions are right for breeding; in some cases pairs of snakes have lived together in a cage for years without making any attempt to breed, but after a period of separation have got down to the job immediately. Success in some species will be further increased by introducing two males to a sexually ripe female. The combat ritual of the males will make the victor even more determined to mate. Close watch should be kept on suitors at this time, especially pythons, which occasionally have been known to rip deep gashes into the flesh of their rivals. If things get too hot, remove the male that seems to be losing the battle and leave the other male to mate with the female.

Leave the courting snakes together for a few days to allow for any consecutive matings, before moving the male to another cage. It is best to keep gravid females singly and to disturb them as little as possible. After a few weeks you will be able to see if the

Desert Death Adder, *Acanthophis pyrrhus*. Photo by K. H. Switak.

mating was successful. The outline of the developing eggs can be seen along the posterior part of her body.

Oviposition Oviparous snake species should be provided with an egglaying receptacle. A plastic ice cream tub loosely filled with moist sphagnum moss will be used by many species. Cut one or two snake-sized holes in the side of the tub so that the female can enter and leave comfortably. Hopefully the snake will lay her eggs in the receptacle, where they will be protected by the moist sphagnum. Some snakes, however, are never satisfied with what you have to offer and, after a period of restlessly moving about, may end up scattering the eggs over the terrarium floor, sometimes even in the water dish. It is therefore important that you keep a close watch on your gravid snakes as egglaying time approaches so that the eggs can be collected up for artificial incubation before they drown in the water dish or are desiccated by the terrarium heating.

Incubation The best breeding results are usually obtained when the eggs of oviparous snakes are removed from the laying site and placed in an incubator. The soft leathery shells of snake eggs are designed to absorb moisture during the incubation period and the eggs do indeed increase in weight during the period of incubation providing adequate moisture is present in the incubation medium. Newly laid eggs often show kinks, which soon fill out during incubation.

Various incubation media have been used by breeders over the years, ranging from damp sand, peat or sphagnum moss, to moist, absorbent paper. The material most widely used today seems to be vermiculite, a sterile, inert, highly absorbent material often used for insulation or as a horticultural additive to soils. Vermiculite comes in granules of various grades; a medium grade seems to be suitable for most cases, though you may wish to use a finer grade for the eggs of very small snakes. The vermiculite is mixed with an equal volume of water then the excess water is squeezed out. Place a thick layer of the moist material into a plastic incubation box (a food storage box, with ventilation holes drilled in the lid is ideal).

The eggs should be collected up carefully, as soon as possible after laying, and buried to about two thirds of their depth in the incubation medium leaving the top third exposed to the air. Snake eggs are moist with mucus on being laid and if you don't collect them up immediately, the mucus will dry out and the eggs will adhere together. Do not attempt to separate adhered eggs as you will be likely to damage them. Place them in a clump partially buried in the incubation medium. Most breeders advocate keeping the eggs in the same position (the right way up!) throughout incubation; if this is the case you must mark the "top" of each egg with a non-toxic marker.

There are a number of incubation options; special reptile egg incubators are available on the market and domestic fowl egg incubators or even human infant incubators can also be used if modified. Most snake eggs are incubated in the temperature range of 28-32°C (about 83-90°F) though you may have to obtain expert guidance from experienced breeders for individual species. A simple incubator can be made using a fish tank about one quarter filled with water containing a thermostatically controlled aquarium heater. A shelf placed on two bricks emerging from the water surface will hold the incubation boxes. You will have to set the thermostat (which may have to be modified to higher temperatures) to the correct temperature and monitor it with a thermometer for a few days before the incubator is used. The water in the incubator will help maintain a high humidity in the air which for incubation of most species should be in the range of 75-100%.

If using an incubator without permanent water you should gently spray the eggs and incubation medium every two to three days with a fine mist sprayer. The sprayer should be kept in the incubator so that the spray water is always the same temperature as the interior. Hatching times vary from about 40 to as much as 100 days but it is usually in the region of 60 days for most species. Disturbance of the eggs should be kept to a minimum during incubation but you should inspect them daily and check the incubation temperature. You can remove the eggs occasionally to see how they are developing. After a while blood vessels may be seen through the walls of healthy developing eggs and, if you hold them up to the light you will see the shadow of the developing embryo.

Some snake eggs tend to discolor during incubation and may even become moldy. However, don't be in too much of a hurry to discard bad looking eggs; some of the most awful looking ones often hatch quite normally! There is also no evidence to suggest that dead eggs in a clutch are in any way detrimental to the development of others.

At hatching time, all viable eggs from a single clutch start to hatch usually within 48 hours. The young snake possesses the so called egg-tooth, a sharp spine in the snout which allows it to slit open the egg shell when it is ready to hatch. After making a slit in the egg the snake often pokes out its head and rests for several hours while it is practicing the respiration of atmospheric air and absorbing the remains of its yolk sac.

Rearing Once the snakes leave their eggs and become free moving, you can transfer them to their nursery cages. Small snakes can be reared in plastic tanks or boxes. Optimum climatic conditions should be provided for the species in question and it is advisable to maintain a high humidity for a couple of weeks as neonate snakes are very susceptible to des-

Pueblan Milk Snake, *Lampropeltis triangulum campbelli*. **'Apricot' variety. Photo by Paul Freed.**

iccation. Keep furnishings in the nursery cages to a minimum. A paper towel substrate can be changed as it becomes soiled. Provide a shallow water dish, a small hide box and perhaps a rock or a climbing branch.

Neonates normally refuse all food until after the first shedding which occurs usually within a few days after birth. Specialized feeders may have to be given their natural food until they begin to grow, as it is very difficult to force feed very small snakes. Many commonly bred snakes start off on pinky mice, graduating to larger mice as they grow. To give the snake a good start over the first few weeks allow it to feed as much as it will take, but thereafter you should reduce feeding to about once per week if obesity is to be avoided.

PREVENTIVE HEALTH CARE

In the past, many reptile fanciers eventually gave up their hobby in despair after losing a number of specimens to various diseases. In the last couple of decades, however, the joint efforts of many other hobbyists, veterinarians and professional herpetologists have brought snake keeping to a fine art. By studying the needs of wild snakes and providing these to captive specimens the prospects of keeping snakes alive and healthy to a ripe old age are increasing.

Texas Rat Snake, *Elaphe obsoleta lindheimeri*. **Leucistic specimen. Photo by R. D. Bartlett.**

Stress: One of the major problems in snakes had been stress, especially in newly captured specimens. The trauma of being captured and kept in alien, often grossly overcrowded conditions, leads to stress-related loss of resistance to disease, allowing new pathogens to invade the body, or those that are already present, to be activated. This phenomenon may be called trauma- related immunosuppression. An exotic snake often has to go through a whole gauntlet of stressful situations before it eventually reaches its new permanent home. Numbers of snakes, often of different species may be stored by collectors in dirty rice sacks or similar. They may be kept for several weeks, unfed, unwatered and certainly not cleaned before they are finally sold to an exporter who makes arrangements for them to be flown to a dealer in their country of destination. At this stage they may be sorted, cleaned, and watered, though they are not usually fed. The importer often had a tough time keeping all of the specimens alive. Some of them may already be emaciated and debilitated beyond saving.

It seems that most importers in developed countries today have a much more positive attitude to the snakes in their care than many may have had in the past. At one time a large portion of a shipment was lost in transit or shortly after arrival and this had to be reflected in the retail price of specimens. Today, much improved international regulations regarding transport of animals means that far fewer specimens are lost. Additionally importers and retailers, are not prepared to lose valuable specimens which are far more difficult to replace now, than they would have been in past booms in the trade. This means that imported specimens are considerably less subject to stress now, than they would have been in the past, but the situation still requires to be carefully monitored.

We know more about optimum conditions for snake keeping now than we have done at any time in the past. The secret is to make the snake "feel" that it is still free in its natural habitat; stress, and stress related diseases, will then not pose a problem.

Quarantine: As we have already discussed in the selection of specimens, it is of utmost importance to ensure, as far as possible, that we do not acquire sick specimens that could bring infectious diseases into our collections. If you acquire a new specimen and want to introduce it to any existing stock you may have, say for breeding purposes, it is highly recommended that the newcomer is first subjected to a period of quarantine. Although the word quarantine, originally meant 40 days, a period of three weeks is normally acceptable though, realistically "the longer the better". The quarantine cage should be set up as simply as possible though the necessary life support systems must, of course, be provided. The cage must also be kept as far away as possible from those housing existing specimens, preferably in a separate room or outhouse. It is best to collect fecal samples from the new specimens and have them examined in a veterinary laboratory for signs of internal parasites. Keep close observation on the new animal during its period of isolation and, if any symptoms of disease appear, you should seek veterinary advice. If, after the three week quarantine period the animal is still apparently healthy, then you should be safely able to place it in its permanent cage.

General Prophylactic Measures: In many cases, hobbyists keep a number of specimens and cages in a so called reptile room. Outbreaks of infectious disease can be difficult to control if they occur in areas with a concentration of reptiles, so careful prophylactic practices should be adhered to. The following list of elementary rules will help lessen the transmission of diseases considerably:

1. Any snake that shows symptoms of infectious disease should be isolated immediately; placed in a simple cage well away from the rest of the stock. Seek veterinary advice as soon as possible.
2. Do not transfer cage furnishings, food dishes, or other items from one cage to the next, without first disinfecting them, even if no disease is apparent.
3. Do not move uneaten food from one cage into the next one, it is best to discard it.
4. Do not allow fecal matter or uneaten food to accumulate in cages.
5. Always insure that clean, fresh water is available. Some snakes have a habit of defecating in their water dish; clean this out as often as necessary.
6. The interior of cages and furnishings should be disinfected each time they are cleaned. A 10% solution of household bleach is ideal for general disinfection purposes; soak all surfaces in the solution for a few minutes and rinse off well before reusing. Never use phenol, coal-tar, or so-called "pine" disinfectants as they can be toxic to snakes. Temporary accommodations for a snake while you are cleaning out its permanent cage should also be disinfected before using it for the next reptile. Wash your hands thoroughly and disinfect all cleaning equipment before moving to the next cage.
7. Disposable soiled furnishings, uneaten food and dead snakes should be placed in a plastic bag and removed from the room as soon as possible. Such items are best incinerated (unless dead snakes are going to be autopsied).
8. For personal hygiene, it is best to wear an overall when dealing with your snakes. Keep it in the snake room, put it on when you enter, and remove it when you leave. Some hobbyists like to use rubber or plastic gloves during cleaning sessions. These must, of course, be disinfected each time you progress from one cage to the next.

Above: Eastern Hognose, *Heterodon platirhinos*. Feigning death to fool a cat. Below: Gaboon Viper, *Bitis gabonica*. Eating a rabbit. Both photos by Paul Freed.

HUSBANDRY OF TURTLES, TORTOISES AND TERRAPINS

BY: JOHN COBORN

GENERAL INFORMATION

Chelonian is an anglicized collective name used to describe any member of the reptilian order Chelonia which includes the turtles, tortoises, and terrapins. The English names applied to the various kinds of chelonians can be confusing, so let's try and clear that up first.

In American English, the word turtle is often used to describe any kind of chelonian, though the word tortoise may be used for some of the land dwelling forms. Most Americans also usually use the plural "turtles" when collectively referring to chelonians. The word terrapin (which is derived from an American Indian language) is almost never used today in the USA, except sometimes for one species, the Diamondback Terrapin, *Malaclemys terrapin*.

In British English, the word turtle is usually reserved only for the saltwater or marine species, plus a few large freshwater species such as the snappers. Most of the smaller freshwater turtles are called terrapins (including cooters, sliders etc.), while all land dwelling forms are referred to as tortoises.

To further complicate the issue, in Australia, where there are no native terrestrial chelonians, they call their freshwater turtles, tortoises, as in Long-necked Tortoise (*Chelodina longicollis*). In this work we will favor the American usage of words.

How turtles evolved is only partially understood. To date insufficient fossil evidence has been found to link turtles to any definite pre-turtle ancestors, though one or two possibilities such as *Eunotosaurus*, a turtle-like "lizard" have been found. The oldest positive kinds of fossil turtles discovered belong to an extinct suborder, the Amphichelydia, which evolved during the late Triassic period about 200 million years ago, and died out in the Pleistocene period about three million years ago. However, there is much evidence to assume that our two modern sub-

Diamondback Terrapin, *Malaclemys terrapin*. Photo by Paul Freed.

Blanding's Turtle, *Emydoidea blandingi*. Photo by W. P. Mara.

orders of turtles, the Cryptodira and the Pleurodira, evolved from, or with, the Amphichelydia. Since their first appearance on earth, chelonians have barely altered in their physical makeup, a fact that makes them relatively successful vertebrates.

LIFESPAN

Chelonians are often noted for their longevity and many stories, both authenticated, and dubious, exist about aged specimens. One fairly well documented story concerns an Indian Ocean Giant Tortoise collected from the Seychelles islands in 1776 and taken to Mauritius, where it survived for 152 years. As it was apparently adult when it was collected this specimen could have been in excess of 200 years old. There have been many reports of pet Mediterranean tortoises, *(Testudo)* and North American box turtles (*Terrapene*) living for over 100 years. An Alligator Snapping Turtle, *Macroclemys temmincki*, has lived in captivity for more than 60 years. In general, most turtles can be expected to live in captive conditions for twenty years or more providing they are given optimum conditions.

HABITAT PREFERENCES

Different turtle species have evolved in various environments, though most species occur in the tropics and subtropics. Species habitats range from cool mountain streams to wide murky rivers; from deep clear lakes, to muddy roadside ditches; from green temperate meadows, to sparsely vegetated semi-deserts; from windy Savannah grasslands, to humid tropical rainforests; plus all those places in between. Certain species have developed in fairly limited ranges in a single habitat, while other species have been able to adapt to a range of habitats. Most marine turtles are pandemic in subtropical and tropical oceans, but may occasionally turn up on temperate shores (probably accidentally). The only places where turtles do not survive, are those places where the average annual temperature is too low for them to complete their annual breeding cycles; such places include the polar regions and the higher altitudes of mountain ranges. The fossil record shows that, even where turtles do not live today (due to human development), they would almost certainly have lived there at some time in the past.

Turtles occur on all continents except Antarctica. Most species are not especially cold tolerant, though Blanding's Turtle, *Emydoidea blandingi*, has been observed swimming below ice in the Great Lakes region of North America. Most turtles hibernate during the winter months in sub-tropical to temperate areas. Aquatic species often burrow into the mud of the substrate and, as they reduce their metabolism considerably, are able to survive on minimal oxygen. Terrestrial species bury themselves below ground, often among thick leaf litter or in the burrows of other animals.

North America is fairly rich in numbers of species of freshwater turtles. They occur in rivers, lakes, irrigation dams, ditches and indeed any suitable stretch of water. Most turtles prefer to live in areas protected by adequate vegetation and where there is water deep enough for them to take instant refuge if disturbed. Similar numbers of species occur in South America.

Compared to North America, Europe is sparse in native turtles; there being only two species of freshwater turtle and three species of land tortoise. The most northerly European turtle, *Emys orbicularis*, is rapidly losing ground in the northern part of its range due, it is said, to deteriorating seasonal weather patterns over the past few decades, the summers being too cold and short to allow satisfactory development of embryos. However, loss of habitat, pollution, and collection by hobbyists will also have contributed to its disappearances from many of its old haunts.

In Africa, north of the Sahara, turtle populations more or less follow the European pattern, whereas the rest of Africa has an interesting mixture of species of land tortoises, softshells, and sidenecks.

No sidenecks occur in Asia, but numbers of species of softshells, emydid turtles and land tortoises increase from the temperate regions to the tropics, with the greatest diversity occurring in Southeast Asia.

Australia and New Guinea are home only to aquatic sidenecked turtles, with the exception of one Asian species of softshell, *Pelochelys bibroni*, which has made its way to New Guinea.

PHYSICAL CHARACTERISTICS

From the fossil record we know that turtles appeared on earth over 200 million years ago. That was before the crocodiles, lizards, and snakes evolved, let alone the birds and mammals. Although these turtle fossils possessed teeth, and were unable to withdraw their heads, they are positively identified as turtles by the character of their shells, which are similar to those of modern turtles.

The Shell: The shell is the first physical characteristic that comes to mind when we think of a typical turtle. This protective armor is unique among vertebrate animals and comprises about 60 bones. The top, domed part of the shell is known as the carapace, while the flat part of the shell below the body is called the plastron. The bones that form the shell are derived from modified parts of the pectoral and pelvic girdles, plus dermal bone. The shell bones are all fused together with one another, and with the ribs and vertebrae. The functional part of the pectoral girdle has found its way inside the rib cage, a unique feature in the vertebrate world.

The outer part of the bony shell is further protected with large horny scutes, or plates, which have arisen from the epidermal layer of the skin and correspond to the scales in other reptiles. Though arranged symmetrically the joints of the scutes do not correspond with the joints in the bony plates beneath, and thus contribute further to the overall strength of the shell. Numbers of scutes vary slightly between genera and indeed, the number, size, shape and position of the scutes are fairly simple guidelines to identification of species.

The various scutes have been given special names. The most common arrangement is as follows. The scutes around the edge of the carapace are known as the marginals, with the exception of the one above the neck (nuchal), and the one or two above the tail (supracaudal), the next row of larger scutes adjoining the marginals are the pleurals and the row of scutes along the center of the back are the vertebrals. The plastron scutes are paired. Starting at the anterior end below the neck we have the gulars; working back, the next pair, below the forelimbs, are the humerals, then we have the pectorals, the abdominals, the femorals and the anals. There are a few exceptions which have additional kinds of scutes (for example: supramarginals, intergulars and interanals).

The carapace and plastron are securely joined at the edges, along the lower flanks of the body. The joined part is known as the bridge. The limbs emerge laterally through apertures in the shell front (axillary aperture) and rear (inguinal aperture), which also allow emergence of the head and the tail respectively.

In many modern groups of chelonians the shell has become much reduced, and no modern species have such massive shells as their prehistoric ancestors. In large land tortoises, the shell has been dramatically reduced in weight by the thinning of the bony plates, though strength remains due to the shape of the shell and the arrangement of the bones and scutes. Many aquatic species have vastly reduced shells. Softshelled turtles (Trionychidae) no longer have surface scutes while, in certain marine species, the bony plates of the shell have reduced in area, leaving spaces between them filled with tough, leathery skin (for example, *Dermochelys coriacea*). In other aquatic turtles, the whole shell

Above: Pancake Tortoise, *Malacochersus tornieri*. Photo by R. D. Bartlett. Below: Eastern Box Turtle, *Terrapene carolina*. Photo by M. P. and C. Piednoir.

has been reduced so much in size that the reptile can no longer withdraw its head for protection. In such examples as snapping turtles and large-headed turtles, lack of complete protection by the shell is more than compensated for by fight and aggression!

Shell morphology varies considerably among the various chelonian groups. Most land tortoises have high domed carapaces that give them maximum protection from the snapping jaws of terrestrial predators. An exception is the Pancake Tortoise, *Malachocercus tornieri,* of East Africa which, when threatened, can scuttle along at a quite remarkable pace before jamming its flat, relatively soft, yielding shell into a rock crevice. Once in position it takes in air which allows its shell to expand making it almost impossible to remove from its refuge. Many freshwater species have fairly low carapaces, allowing streamlining against water resistance. Exceptions in this area include certain river turtles that share their habitats with crocodilians, and have high domed carapaces to protect them from the powerful jaws of these leviathans. Some turtles have one or two so-called hinges (elastic joints) across their plastrons which allow them to close up like a box, protecting the head and limbs completely when they are withdrawn.

These include species of mud turtles, box turtles and a few land tortoises. One African genus of land tortoises, *Kinixys,* has evolved a hinge in the rear part of the carapace, which may protect the rear part of the body, but the exact function is open to speculation.

The Limbs: The forelimbs of land tortoises are strongly built with the feet oriented slightly away from the body, making them ideally adapted for grubbing and burrowing. The limbs are usually covered with more or less conventional reptilian scales. Both fore and rear feet are furnished with strong claws. Most turtle species have five clawed toes on each foot (exceptions include *Agrionomys horsefieldi,* and *Terrapene carolina,* which have only four digits on each rear foot; one subspecies of the latter, *T. carolina triunguis,* has only three!). In freshwater turtles, the rear feet have become extremely flattened and in some cases webbed, to aid swimming. In marine turtles the forelimbs are flattened and have become flippers that are ideal for swimming over long distances.

The Head: The shape of the head varies from species to species. Most land tortoises have a broad head and blunt snout, while many aquatic turtles have a narrower head and a rounded or even pointed snout. The jaws are toothless in all turtles, but are formed somewhat in the manner of a short, blunt beak with sharp edges. In many species the edges of the jaws are serrated to allow more precise biting of food. Many herbivorous species possess a row of hard, chewing ridges on the palate. In most species the tongue is thick and fleshy. The skull is simple when compared to other reptilian orders; unlike the jaws of snakes the lower mandibles are fused at the chin, and unlike all other reptilian orders, temporal fossae (openings at the upper posterior aspect of the skull) are quite absent.

The Tail: Most turtle species have a rather short tail. That of the male is often thicker and somewhat longer than that of the female. Species with a relatively long tail include the snappers and the Big-headed Turtle (*Platysternon*).

The Senses: As far as we know, most turtles have a reasonably good eyesight, and quite an efficient sense of smell. Hearing is thought to be fairly efficient but nowhere near as keen as that of the higher vertebrates. The sense of touch is good and even the shell is equipped with nerve endings.

Respiration: Due to the inflexibility of the armored shell, Chelonians respire somewhat differently to other vertebrates. A turtle is unable to expand and contract its thorax by movements of the diaphragm, so has special abdominal muscles which push and pull air into the large spongy lungs that are situated high in the carapace. Pumping of the throat, and movements of the head and limbs also aid respiration. If you have ever been close to a giant tortoise as it withdraws its head and limbs, you will hear a loud hissing as the air is driven out of its lungs. Some aquatic turtles are known to be able to absorb oxygen through mucus membranes in other parts of the body including the throat and the lining if the cloaca. These membranes are richly supplied with blood vessels which allow extraction of oxygen from water passing over them.

Turtles are one of the oldest and most primitive groups of reptiles and, during their history, have seen many other groups of animals come and go. Can it be the protective efficiency of the shell that has allowed the turtle line to outlive so many other groups of animals? Although primitive by modern reptilian standards, the chelonians can be considered a very successful group.

PHYSICAL DIAGNOSTIC CHARACTERISTICS OF TURTLE SUBORDERS AND FAMILIES

It is not within the scope of this book to give formal identification keys for taxa. However, a few simple group diagnostic features will give the reader an idea of the great diversity of species.

Big-headed Turtle, *Platysternon megacephalum.* **Photo by K. T. Nemuras.**

Suborder	Family	Common Designation	Characteristics
Pleurodira		Side-necked Turtles	The neck is bent sideways on a horizontal plain when the head is withdrawn, and is tucked into a niche between the carapace and the plastron. There is a complete bone (tympanic ring) around the ear aperture in the skull. A condyle, which inserts into an aperture in the quadrate, is situated on the lower jaw. The pelvis is fused to the shell.
Pleurodira	Pelomedusidae	Afro-American Side-necked Turtles	Mostly omnivorous freshwater turtles, which can retract the neck completely within the shell. They do not possess nasal bones. All are relatively short necked. Genera include *Erymnochelys* (Madagascar), *Pelomedusa* (Africa, Madagascar), *Pelusios* (Africa, Madagascar), *Peltocephalus* (South America), and *Podocnemis* (South America). Species length range: from 12 cm (5 in) to 90 cm (36 in).
Pleurodira	Chelidae	Austro-American Side-necked Turtles	Mostly carnivorous freshwater turtles, which, on retracting the neck leave part of it exposed. They possess nasal bones. Some genera have extremely long necks. Genera include *Chelodina* (Australia, New Guinea), *Chelus* (South America), *Emydura* (Australia, New Guinea), *Hydromedusa* (South America), *Platemys* (South America), *Rheodytes* (Australia). Species length range: 14 cm (5.5 in) to 48 cm (19 in).
Cryptodira		Straight-necked Turtles	The neck is bent vertically in an S shape when the head is withdrawn (though in many genera the head cannot be, or can only be partially withdrawn). The bone (tympanic ring) around the ear aperture in the skull is incomplete. In most cases a condyle situated on the quadrate fits into an aperture in the lower jaw. The pelvis is not fused to the shell.
Cryptodira	Carettochelydae	Pig-nosed Soft-shelled Turtle	The plastron is very short. There are no hard scutes, the shell being covered with leathery skin. The forelimbs are developed as flippers, reminiscent of those of marine turtles, each possessing only two claws. *Carettochelys insculpta* (Australia, New Guinea). Length: to 70 cm (28 in).
Cryptodira	Chelydridae	Snapping Turtles	Carnivorous river turtles. Large, non-retractile head. Temporal region of skull is covered anteriorly. The shell is relatively small. The plastron is cross-shaped and inframarginal plates are present in the bridge. The tail is relatively long. The two monotypic genera are *Chelydra* and *Macroclemys* (North America). Species length range: 48 cm (22 in) to 65 cm (26 in).

Florida Snapping Turtle, *Chelydra serpentina osceola*. Photo by K. H. Switak.

Cryptodira	Dermatemydidae	Central American River Turtle	Omnivorous juveniles; adults mainly herbivorous. Retractile head. The temporal region of the skull is not covered. Wide, low carapace; large plastron. Marginals and pectorals separated by large inframarginal scutes. Single genus and species, *Dermatemys mawii* (Central America). Length: to 61 cm (24 in).
Cryptodira	Cheloniidae	Marine Turtles	Pelagic inhabitants of the tropical and subtropical oceans. May be carnivorous, omnivorous or herbivorous. Head not retractile. Only one or two claws on flipper-like limbs. Reduced, streamlined shell. The backbone and ribs are fused to the carapace. Genera include *Chelonia*, *Caretta*, *Eretmochelys*, and *Lepidochelys*. All pan-tropical. Species length range: 75 cm (30 in) to 113 cm (45 in).
Cryptodira	Dermochelyidae	Leathery Turtle	Largest of all turtles. Carnivorous sea dweller. Skin leathery, scutes replaced by small bony platelets. No claws on flipper-like limbs. The vertebrae and ribs are not fused to the carapace. Single species, *Dermochelys coriacea*. Pantropical. Length: to 185 cm (74 in).
Cryptodira	Emydidae	Pond and River Turtles	Largest chelonian family with 85 species in 31 genera. Mostly freshwater, some estuarine, some mostly terrestrial. The various species may be carnivorous, herbivorous or omnivorous. The head can be retracted in most species. The shell is well developed. There are no inframarginal scutes. The feet are usually webbed and fully clawed. Most turtles kept as pets are members of this family. Genera include: *Chinemys* (Southeast Asia), *Chrysemys* (North to South America), *Clemmys* (North America), *Cuora* (Southeast Asia), *Cyclemys* (Southeast Asia), *Emydoidea* (North America), *Emys* (Europe, North Africa, Middle East), *Geomyda* (Southeast Asia), *Graptemys* (North America), *Heosemys* (Southeast Asia), *Kachuga* (India to Indo-China), *Mauremys* (Europe, North Africa to eastern Asia), *Pseudemys* (North America), *Rhinoclemmys* (Central and South America), *Terrapene* (North America). Species length range: 12 cm (5 in) to 80 cm (32 in).

Above: Wood Turtle, *Clemmys insculpta*. Photo by K. T. Nemuras. Below: Red-eared Slider, *Trachemys scripta elegans*. Photo by W. P. Mara.

Cryptodira	Kinosternidae	Mud and Musk Turtles	Carnivorous freshwater turtles. The relatively large head is retractile. The temporal region of the head is not covered. There are inframarginal scutes in the bridge. The plastron is hinged so that the head, limbs and tail can be completely enclosed. The two genera are *Kinosternon* (North, Central and South America) and *Sternotherus* (North America). Species length range: 12 cm (5 in) to 27 cm (11 in).
Cryptodira	Staurotypidae	Mexican Musk Turtles	Carnivorous freshwater turtles. The relatively large head can be retracted. The carapace is three keeled, and the plastron is reduced and cross shaped. The two genera are *Claudius* and *Staurotypus* (both Central America).
Cryptodira	Testudinidae	Land Tortoises	Mainly herbivorous terrestrial tortoises. The head is retractile. The carapace is relatively high domed (except in *Malachocercus*). The rear limbs are columnar, the forelimbs somewhat flattened, with well developed claws. Genera include *Geochelone* (Galapagos Islands, Africa, southern Asia), *Homopus* (Africa), *Malachocercus* (Africa), *Pyxis* (Madagascar), *Testudo* (Eurasia, North Africa), *Gopherus* (North America). Species length range: 10 cm (4 in) to140 cm (56 in).
Cryptodira	Trionychidae	Soft-shelled Turtles	Mainly carnivorous, freshwater dwelling turtles (though one species, *Pelochelys bibroni* occasionally enters estuaries and even the open sea). The head is retractile. The snout often is elongated. The temporal region of the skull is not covered. The carapace is relatively flattened and there are no horny scutes, these being replaced by soft, leathery skin. The limbs are paddle-like but claws are present. Genera include *Chitra* (India, Indo-China), *Cyclanorbis* (Central Africa), *Cycloderma* (southern Africa), *Lissemys* (India, Indo-China), *Pelochelys* (India to Southeast Asia and New Guinea), *Trionyx* (Africa, Asia, North America).
Cryptodira	Platysternidae	Big-headed Turtle	Inhabits cool mountain streams. The relatively large head cannot be withdrawn into shell. It has a powerful hooklike beak. The temporal area of skull is completely covered. Inframarginal scutes are present. It has a long tail. The single species is *Platysternon megacephalum* (Southeast Asia). Length: to 20 cm (8 in).

Loggerhead, *Caretta caretta*. Photo by K. Gillett.

411

Redbelly Shortneck Turtle, *Emydura subglossa*. Photo by R. D. Bartlett.

GROWTH AND DEVELOPMENT

The vast majority of turtle species rarely reach a maximum carapace length of 30 cm (12 in). Two of the smallest species are the Bog Turtle, *Clemmys muhlenbergi*, and the Flattened Musk Turtle, *Sternotherus depressus*, both of which are native to North America and which barely reach a length of 11 cm (4.5 in). As far as land tortoises go, the smallest species is probably *Homopus boulengeri*, or its close relative *H. signata*, both of South Africa, and both rarely attaining a length of more than 10 cm (4 in).

In contrast, there are several species that can be described as giants. The largest living turtle, and the heaviest of all reptiles, with the possible exception of the Salt-water Crocodile, *Crocodylus porosus*, is the sea dwelling Leathery Turtle, or Luth, *Dermochelys coriacea* which reaches up to 1.8 m (6 ft) in length. A large specimen has a weight of up to 680 kg (about 1500 lbs), remarkable for an animal that is less than 5 cm (2in) long with a weight of less than an ounce when it hatches from its egg. Most other marine chelonians reach an impressive size.

Large sized fresh water turtles include the North American Alligator Snapping Turtle, *Macroclemys temmincki*, with a maximum length of 30 in, but with a record weight of 99.5 kg (219 lbs); and the Arrau River Turtle, *Podocnemis expansa*, at 90 cm (35 in) and weighing up to 100 kg (220 lbs). The largest soft-shelled turtle is the Indian Narrow-headed Softshell with a length of 120 cm (4 ft) and a weight of 120 kg (about 265 lb). There are unconfirmed reports of specimens with a length in excess of 180 cm (6 ft).

The largest land tortoise is the Aldabra Giant Tortoise, with a maximum recorded length of 140 cm (4ft 7in) and a weight of 254 kg (560 lbs). The Giant Tortoises of the Galapagos Islands also reach impressive sizes. It is interesting to note here that the largest fossil turtle found was a land tortoise that lived about three million years ago in India. This *Collosochelys atlas*, as it has been named, would have been more than 2.4 m (8 ft) in length. A specimen this size would probably have weighed as much as 1.5 tons.

Growth rates among turtles vary markedly from species to species, and even among members of a single clutch depending on prevailing climatic factors and availability of food. In general, most species grow relatively rapidly in order to reach sexual maturity after which the rate is substantially reduced. Most small turtle species stop growing, or grow very slowly indeed at a certain stage but large species may continue to grow slowly throughout their lives. A fairly typical growth record for a captive bred batch of five Hermann's Mediterranean Tortoise (*Testudo hermannii*) siblings gave the following results:

At one day old the heaviest hatchling weighed 8.0 grams, the lightest 6.0 grams with a mean weight of 7.3 grams. At one year of age the heaviest in the batch weighed 70.0 grams, the lightest 25.0 grams, with a mean weight of 48.4 grams. At two years of age the heaviest in the batch weighed 225.0 grams, the lightest 48.0 grams, with a mean weight of 129.5 grams. Though all raised under

the scute, much as can be seen in the annual growth rings in tree trunks. The system is not, however, totally reliable. In many aged specimens, the surface of the shell is worn smooth and the growth rings are difficult to discern. Climatic conditions in some years may result in two or more growth/rest periods. Of course the system cannot be used for soft-shelled turtles, or those species that shed the surface of their scutes at regular intervals.

SEXING

The determination of the sexes of captive chelonians is important. Not only is it nice to know whether you should name a specimen Abel or Mable, it is quite obviously essential to have one of each sex if you intend to breed them. Unfortu-

Hermann's Tortoise, *Testudo hermanni*. Photo by R. D. Bartlett.

identical conditions there was a great variance in growth rates among these five specimens. Surprisingly, the lightest hatchling ended up as the heaviest specimen at two years of age! Growth rate records of various species in tabular form can be found in the herpetological journals.

It is possible to make a fairly accurate estimate of the ages of many turtle species by counting the growth rings at the edges of the horny scutes of the shell, each ring corresponding to approximately one year of life. In wild specimens, growth is seasonal, most of it occurring during the parts of the year when suitable temperatures and food supplies are most abundant. During periods of hibernation in cold climates, or aestivation in hot, dry climates growth will virtually stop. During each period of minimal growth, a depressed ring forms in

nately sexing of many species is rather difficult as there is little or no external sexual dimorphism.

Some of the more general characteristics used in distinguishing sexes are as follows:

Size: In many species of aquatic turtle the adult female is often much larger than the male. In some species, such as the Diamondback Terrapin, *Malaclemys terrapin*, she may be up to twice the size. However, size variation does not help when dealing with immature specimens. In many land tortoises and box turtles the opposite situation occurs; the adult male growing considerably larger than corresponding females.

The Shell: In many species the male's plastron is concave, while that of the female is flat or slightly convex. The concavity of the male is a device which helps stop him slipping off the female's back when he mounts her for copulation. In some species the rearmost part of the male's carapace is curved sharply downward and inward; a device which helps the male hold position under the slightly upward flared portion of the corresponding part of the female's carapace during copulation.

The Tail: In males, the tail is often longer and thicker than that of the female, especially at the base, where the penis is inverted. In fact the male's vent is situated under the tail, a little distance from the tail base, rather than at the base of the tail as in the female. During copulation the male's tail is inserted under that of the

Head Size: In some genera, *Kinosternon* and *Sternotherus*, for example, the male's head is much wider than that of the female. The opposite occurs is genera such as *Graptemys* in which the head of the female is wider.

Claws: In the males of some *Chrysemys* (*Trachemys*)(*Pseudemys*) species the foreclaws are especially long and used to caress the females face during courtship.

Mental Glands: In some genera,*Gopherus* (*Xerobates*), for example, sexually mature males possess large, paired, mental glands situated on the lower side of the mandibles (under the chin). These glands are thought to produce pheromones that are sexually attractive to females and may also

Florida Redbelly Turtle, *Pseudemys nelsoni*. Photo by R. D. Bartlett.

female so that the erect penis can easily enter her cloaca.

Color: Sexes are similarly colored and patterned in most species, but a few exceptions include the Spotted Turtle, *Clemmys guttata*, in which the female has orange eyes and a yellow chin, while the male has brown eyes and a tan chin. In another example, The Red-eared Slider, *Chrysemys* (*Trachemys*) *scripta elegans*, the male has ear patches that are larger and much brighter red than those of the female. Eye color differs in the Eastern and Western box Turtles, *Terrapene carolina* and *T. ornata*, those of the males being red, while those of the females are yellowish brown. In some genera of tropical Asian river turtles, *Kachuga* for example, the male takes on colorful patterns, especially on the head and neck, during the breeding season.

be used for territory marking against rival males.

Behavior: Courtship and mating behavior are often a sure sign that you have a pair of turtles. The claw caressing of *Chrysemys* (*Pseudemys*) mentioned above is a good example. In many land tortoises, courting males make amorous advances to females by butting them sharply with their shells, and biting them on the limbs.

Feces and Blood Testing: Hormonal testing of blood samples has been an expensive, but reliable veterinary method of sex determination for some time. A new veterinary technique for sexing reptiles involves hormonal examination of feces samples. This is also reliable and less drastic than blood sampling, but probably no less expensive.

SELECTION AND ACQUISITION

The prospective turtle keeper may obtain his/her turtles from a petshop or from a specialist dealer. Those on sale may be imported wild captured specimens or may have been bred in captivity. The latter are more desirable as they will most probably adapt better to a new home. Additionally, as a measure of conservation, every captive bred turtle means one less being taken from the wild.

You may have thoughts of collecting your prospective pet turtles(s) directly from the wild. This option should be regarded with the greatest of caution. Not only are most turtles in most countries protected by law (you could end up with a hefty fine or even jail!), modern ethics really make it taboo to get specimens other than from a licensed collector/dealer, petshop, or breeder.

It is highly recommended that specimens are obtained from reliable suppliers. Happily, most petshops and dealers today have attractive, clean, well maintained premises and their livestock is kept in optimum conditions. However, there may still be a few unscrupulous traders about who care more about making a fast buck than for the welfare of their stock. It is in your own interests to avoid buying unhealthy stock from such dealers, whose premises often reflect their characters. Dozens of specimens kept in overcrowded, dirty conditions are hallmarks to be avoided. If you are not happy with the hygiene or the attitude, simply go elsewhere.

Novice turtle fanciers are advised to take a more experienced friend or acquaintance with them the first time they acquire specimens. It is recommended that they start off with fairly "easy" species, such as sliders to begin with. Larger, feistier specimens like snappers, and more "difficult" tropical species are best left until you have more experience.

It is suggested that you buy only a single pair of specimens initially. Indeed, many turtle keepers are quite content with a single pair, period; though there are many others that like to have a broad cross section of groups of species. The number of turtles you may want to keep is all a matter of the time you can spare to care for them and the expense of keeping them in optimum conditions. Anyway, even if you intend to keep a lot of specimens in the future it is advisable to get just have a pair to "practice on" initially.

All prospective purchases should be inspected carefully before you make a decision to buy. Most dealers will allow prospective customers to handle

Loggerhead Musk Turtle, *Sternotherus minor*. **Photo by Aaron Norman.**

Bog Turtle, *Clemmys muhlenbergi*. Photo by R. D. Bartlett.

the stock before making a decision to purchase. Check all parts of the shell for signs of damage which may be an entry point for fungus or bacteria (especially in aquatic turtles). However, well-healed previous shell wounds are usually of little concern other than that of esthetics. What is more of a concern is abnormally shaped shells, brought about by an improper diet. Such abnormal shells are an indication that the internal organs may also be abnormal, may interfere with the functioning of the organs anyway, and could prevent normal reproductive behavior. Look closely at the skin of the head, neck, limbs and tail for signs of parasites (mites or ticks), for skin blemishes, wounds or lumps which could indicate infections, abscesses or growths of one form or another.

Examine the eyes, which should be clear, bright and alert. The eyelids should be clean and unswollen. The turtle should be lively and have a "heavy" feel about it. Unlike other pet animals it can be hard to see if a turtle is underweight but, with practice, you will know if a turtle is heavy enough as soon as you pick it up. Check the mouth, nostrils and vent for signs of inflammation or unpleasant discharges which could indicate an internal disease.

Taking Them Home: Once you have made a decision on what specimens to buy, your next step will be to get them safely home. Remember that the turtle's accommodations should be ready before you acquire any specimens. For short journeys by car or public transport most turtles can be simply placed in a strong carton with a bedding of straw.

Delicate aquatic species are perhaps placed on a bed of damp sphagnum moss so that they don't lose too much moisture. If transporting in very cold weather the carry box should be insulated (Styrofoam veggie boxes are ideal). Always get your turtles home as quickly as possible and, for obvious reasons, never leave them for long in a vehicle on very cold or very hot days.

Get your new pets into their quarantine or permanent cages as soon as possible and leave them undisturbed, other than feeding them, for a couple of days so that they can get accustomed to their new surroundings. Moving to a new home can be a stressful time for most animals, so we must make it as easy as possible for them by keeping handling and disturbance to a minimum. In the case of particularly nervous specimens it is best to cover the cage viewing panel for a few days so that the ani-

Testudo **sp. Photo by Mark Smith.**

mals are not continually disturbed by movements outside the cage.

BEHAVIOR

The behavior of turtles mainly concerns those aspects of their lives that cover locomotion, feeding, thermoregulating, aestivating, hibernating and social reaction. Reproductive behavior is discussed in the section on reproduction.

LOCOMOTION

Due to the relatively unconventional body shape governed by the presence of the unwieldy shell, turtles, especially when moving on land, have had to overcome certain locomotory problems that are not experienced by most other animals. Most land tortoises move slowly with, what to us seems an awkward and ungainly gait. However, this does not seem to worry most tortoises, which have been walking like that for millions of years and still continue to do so. One problem is that the limbs are oriented out of the sides of the shell, meaning that they have to support the often heavy body and shell

Southern Painted Turtle, *Chrysemys picta dorsalis*. **Juvenile specimen. Photo by W. P. Mara.**

at an angle. That this is exhausting to the limb muscles of a turtle can be seen by the frequency in which the turtle lowers its body to the ground to rest. The larger and heavier the turtles, the greater the problem seems to be. A typical example can be seen in the gravid female marine turtle that must laboriously drag itself up a tropical beach in order to lay its eggs above the high water mark. Then, after excavating a hole, laying its eggs, and covering them up, it has the return journey back to the surf. Most of this is done at night so that the hot sun of the day can be avoided. Turtles that loiter on the beach and return to the water too late may perish from overheating.

In the water however, aquatic turtles are different creatures. Marine turtles move gracefully through the sea, beating their flippers in unison like the wings of a bird, and using their rear limbs as rudders for steering and braking. Most freshwater dwelling turtles swim with alternating beats of the limbs of either side of the body in a sort of paddling motion; not as elegant as the marine turtle, but nevertheless quite efficiently and sometimes with an amazing turn of speed.

FEEDING BEHAVIOR

As turtles are relatively slow moving reptiles, most do not have the ability to catch fast-moving prey. The majority of turtle species either feed on vegetation, or on fairly sedentary creatures such as worms, crustaceans, mollusks, insect larvae and so on. Carrion also forms a fair part of the diet of most carnivorous turtles. Even land tortoises which are primarily herbivorous will eagerly consume carrion. Aldabran Giant Tortoises have been reliably reported to feed on the carcasses of beached whales when these are available!

Herbivorous land tortoises use a combination of sight and smell to find their food items. While abundant plants such as grasses, may be eaten without ceremony, scarcer or less familiar plants will first be sniffed with the nose before the reptile makes a decision whether to eat it or not. Most herbivorous turtles are relatively clumsy feeders. Their jaws are made for tearing rather than cutting, so the counter leverage of living plants anchored in the ground is important as the turtle tears pieces away from it. This is why it is often important to cut up the food of your captive turtles into bite-sized pieces. As turtles have no teeth, chewing is kept to a minimum, though food may be masticated somewhat with the special linings of the mouth and jaws.

Most carnivorous turtles have a fairly simple method of feeding; finding their prey by grubbing around in the substrate and using a combination of touch and smell for prey recognition. Some turtles have developed special techniques for catching prey. Most of these methods rely on some kind of stealth, or ambush, rather than in active hunting. Many aquatic turtles lay in wait just submerged at the water's edge, with just the eyes and snout above the water, waiting for small animals to come down to drink. Small mammals and birds may be caught in this manner. Once an animal has been seized by one turtle, this signals the start of a feeding frenzy in which several turtles all get a grip on the carcass and pull in all directions, soon separating the carcass into bite-sized pieces. This strategy is a useful one for all turtles concerned as a single turtle has a difficult time dismantling a carcass by itself. The method is also used when dealing with large items of carrion. You can easily observe this behavior if you keep several aquatic turtles together in a tank. Just give them a whole dead mouse and see how they deal with it.

Snapping turtles and many softshells are largely ambush feeders. The Common Snapper, *Chelydra serpentina*, of North America simply lies in wait on the river bed, waiting for a suitable fish to come within striking distance. The Snapper is well camouflaged, with its muddy color, and its shell often covered with algae, and goes unnoticed by any fish that swims by. Once the fish is close enough, the turtle stretches out its muscular neck, opens its cavernous mouth and sucks the fish into oblivion. In many such turtles, the opening of the mouth is combined with a muscular action in the throat which creates a vacuum, sucking in a large volume of water with all of its edible contents. The water can be discharged back out of the mouth, but the food remains inside the turtle.

The Matamata Turtle, *Chelus fimbriata*, of tropical South America has developed its camouflage to an even finer art than the Snapper. Not only is it cryptically colored, its head is leaf shaped and its neck is festooned with filamental growths designed to look like river bed detritus. These filaments may even wave about in the water currents, causing fish to investigate the possibility of a meal; only to be suddenly engulfed by the Matamata's enormous jaws.

The Alligator Snapping Turtle, *Macroclemys temmincki*, has an even more sinister means of catching its prey. Like the Common Snapper it lays, camouflaged, in wait on the river bed. However one part of it is not camouflaged. This Snapper has a pink, wormlike appendage attached to the top of its tongue. This appendage looks so much like a worm, that it even has segments. By laying with its mouth open the wriggling "worm" is presented as bait for any unsuspecting fish that may care to investigate. The size of the fish seems not to matter to the Alligator Snapper; if it is too large to swallow whole, it just bites a big chunk out of it with its scissors like jaw edges.

Flour Beetle, *Tenebrio molitor*. **Photo by Michael Gilroy.**

THERMOREGULATION

Like all reptiles, turtles are ectothermic, or cold-blooded as is the lay term used to describe this condition. Unlike the higher vertebrates, the birds and the mammals, which are able to maintain a normal average body temperature by metabolic means, reptiles, including turtles, rely on external influences to regulate their body temperatures.

Turtles from tropical regions have little difficulty in maintaining a preferred body temperature as the prevailing ambient temperature around them is usually sufficiently high. Indeed some tropical species have more trouble keeping cool than keeping warm. The Aldabra Giant Tortoise, *Geochelone gigantea*, for example, has a problem in that shaded areas (stands of trees and shrubs) on its island habitat are somewhat sparse, which limits the distance the reptiles can travel to forage for food. If they were to travel too far, the hot midday sun beating on their shells would cause them to overheat and perish before they were able to get back to the shade.

Most subtropical and temperate turtles and tortoises sunbask at certain times of the year in order to get their bodies to a temperature suitable for

Domestic Cricket, *Achetus domesticus*. **Photo by Isabelle Francais.**

normal activity. Many species can maintain their bodies at an almost constant temperature for much of the summer season, by moving in and out of the sun as necessary. Land turtles shelter from the sun under vegetation, or ground litter, while aquatic turtles simply have to get back in the water to cool down. Most turtles can operate efficiently with a body temperature somewhere between 22-30°C (71-86°F). In areas where cooler winters mean that turtles are unable to maintain an optimum body temperature, then they hibernate until the warmer weather returns in the spring.

HIBERNATION

In temperate regions, turtles hibernate during the winter months. The gradual reduction in the length of daylight and lowering temperatures as winter approaches causes the turtles to become ever less active. During the warmer months the turtle has been feeding frequently in order to build up its body reserves ready for the demanding period of hibernation. Most hibernating terrestrial turtles seek out an area of loose soil and vegetation and burrow themselves to a depth great enough to avoid any surface frost. Some North American Gopher Tortoises, *Gopherus (Xerobates)*, species, hibernate or aestivate in their self excavated sloping burrows that may be 10 m (30 ft) or more in length, with a sleeping chamber at the end about 1 m (3ft) below the surface. Many aquatic turtles from temperate regions hibernate in mud below the water level. Reduced temperatures cause the metabolism if the turtles to slow down to the extent that very little oxygen is required. The small amount of oxygen needed to support life is absorbed from the water through the turtles' mucus membranes. Hibernation ends with increasing photoperiod and temperature in the spring. In many species, a period of hibernation seems to be essential for successful reproduction.

SOCIAL BEHAVIOR

Other than reproductive behavior during the breeding season, turtles show relatively little interest in each other socially. While many aquatic turtle species may assemble to bask, even stacked up on top of each other, it is more likely it is the suitability of the basking site that causes them to do this rather than any degree of gregariousness. Numbers of turtles will also assemble to devour carrion. Counter leverage of several turtles pulling at a large carcass is of benefit to all individuals, though this is an accidental form of social cooperation as each individual tries to out-eat its colleagues. One example of mutual cooperation is the action of certain tropical American river turtles which apparently clean each other's shells by biting off algae, parasites, and old loose scutes. Territorial behavior also seems to be largely lacking among most species, though in certain land tortoise species some males may try to outdomineer others by butting them with the edges of the carapace.

HANDLING, TAMING AND TRAINING

Although most chelonians are not the type of pets to be cuddled and petted like the standard dog, cat or bunny, there are times when it becomes necessary to handle them or restrain them. One of these times is when you are making your initial inspection before purchase. Other times are when you are moving them from their cages for routine cleaning chores, moving them for mating purposes, or to inspect them for ailments. Indeed it is highly recommended that turtles are not handled for the pure sake of handling. They can be admired, they can be hand fed and scratched on the head, but really not petted and cuddled. Such actions are more likely to stress them out and put them off their food rather than make them love you.

Most of the smaller, less aggressive turtles and land tortoises are quite easy to handle. They just need to be picked up, depending on their size, in one or two hands, gripping by the edges of the shell. Remember that turtles can be fragile if dropped, so it is always best to hold them near the floor, or over a table, preferably with a cushioned surface, rather than high over the ground; just in case of mishap.

Snappers, some of the mud and musk turtles, and soft-shelled turtles can be quite aggressive and many species will not hesitate to take a bite at your fingers. Their sharp, horny beaks can give you a painful wound if you are not careful, and a very large snapper is indeed capable of rendering you digit free. The answer is to get hold of them around the shell at a point where they can't reach you with their mouths. Some softshells have quite long necks, so you will need to catch them near the back of the shell. As softshells are quite slippery, and struggly, you will have to make sure you get a good hold on them. A pair of cloth gloves, or a piece of toweling material between your fingers and the shell will help you get a better grip, and may give your hands some added protection.

Really large land tortoises, river turtles, and marine turtles may be so heavy that they will be a real struggle, or impossible, for a single person to lift. Two people may have to carry them, one either side, with their hands below the edges of the shell. Beware of possible injury if your fingers are trapped beneath the shell should the turtle (especially ap-

Spiny Softshell, *Trionyx spinifera*. **Photo by K. T. Nemuras.**

plicable to giant land tortoises) suddenly withdraw its limbs. I can personally vouch for the fact that such an incident is extremely painful! In zoological collections, staff often use a trolley to move large tortoises and turtles about.

TAMING AND TRAINING

Turtles are generally not the best subjects for taming and training, though you will eventually get some limited interactive responses between you and your turtles especially at feeding times. Most turtles are initially shy, and will withdraw their head and limbs into the shell when disturbed. A sudden looming shape at the cage door will no doubt scare the living daylights out of them so they cannot be blamed for hiding.

When you acquire new specimens you should put them in their cage or tank, supply them with some food and leave them completely to their own devices for a couple of days so that they get accustomed to their new accommodations. When approaching them, always do so slowly and quietly. Try and make your interactions with your turtles at the same times every day; they will get used to routine times more quickly than to erratic ones. Do not touch or handle them for the first week if at all possible, but feed them daily and clean out any mess in the cage. Some species, indeed some individuals, will settle in faster than others but, in a few weeks most pet turtles will stop withdrawing into their shells on your routine visits.

As soon as they stop withdrawing into their shells you can start hand feeding them. With land tortoises you can offer a succulent treat, like a strawberry or a slice of tomato; just reach it slowly towards the reptile's nose and let him/her smell it. After a few tries the tortoise will stretch out his neck and take a bite out of the proffered item. Once past this stage you can give the tortoise a regular scratch on his head, neck or limbs. You can even take him out of his cage and give him a run on the floor or, in warm sunny weather, out in the backyard (but keep a good eye on him), where he will no doubt enjoy foraging out some tasty weeds.

With aquatic turtles you will initially be feeding them by dropping food items on the water surface. Eventually the turtles will associate your approaching hand with a deposit of food and, many species will soon be more or less begging, stretching their heads right out of the water to take a proffered mealworm, cricket or pellet. It is not recommended that aquatic turtles are handled frequently just for the sake of handling them, or taken out of the water and placed on the floor. Such turtles are totally dependent on their watery home and, even when they come out to bask in the sun they always make sure they have a quick route back into the water the moment danger should threaten. Being removed from their escape route back into the water must be a stressful time for an aquatic turtle, so leave it in the water; it will probably let you scratch its head there, or while basking, eventually.

Some of the turtles such as snappers, and most softshells remain mean and nasty however kind you may be to them and will almost never become tame, though they may learn to snatch food from your hand. In such cases you must take great care that one or two of your fingers don't become used by the turtles for gastronomic experiments.

many turtles may be quite small when you get them but can soon outgrow their accommodations. You should ensure that you select a species for which you will have adequate space to house it, even when it grows up. Fortunately, there is a good choice of turtle species that never grow much beyond 30 cm (12 in) in total length.

Southern Painted Turtle, *Chrysemys picta dorsalis*. Photo by Aaron Norman.

HOUSING, HEATING AND LIGHTING

The types of housing required for turtles will depend on the particular species natural habitats. Although all turtles lay their eggs on land, there are some species that are otherwise totally aquatic. Others are semi-aquatic and, of course we have the totally terrestrial land tortoises.

AQUATIC TURTLES INDOORS

Most aquatic turtles can be kept in aquaria much the same way as fish. However, turtles are generally more violent with their surroundings than fish and because of their digging and grubbing activities, it would be difficult to set up the type of planted, decorative display favored by many fishkeepers.

Aquarium tanks come in a great range of dimensions and there will be one available for almost any size of turtle. Remember, however, that

In relation to size of accommodations it should be said that turtles require the largest area of swimming space you can provide. Young turtles especially will do better if they are able to exercise easily. Their muscles will become strong, they will have a healthier appetite and will grow faster. As a rough guide, I would say that the absolute minimum water surface area for each turtle with a 15 cm (6 in) carapace length should be 900 sq. cm (1 sq. ft), but preferably more!

Water depth in an indoor tank may vary depending on the species being kept. For semi-aquatic turtles the depth is really immaterial as long as the turtles have easy access to a land area, but should of course be deep enough for them to be able to swim freely. For those turtles such as snappers and softshells, which hardly ever leave the water, the water should be just shallow enough for them to reach the surface with their snouts when they are standing on the substrate.

Unfortunately, the water in a turtle tank quickly becomes fouled. This is due partly to the nature of a mainly carnivorous diet, and partly to the copious droppings produced by the turtles. Unless the water is changed frequently, you will have a stench in your house that would make even that of a sewage treatment plant pale into insignificance. Though the water can be siphoned out, it is much more useful to have a tank with a drain in the base, controlled by a valve, that will allow you to drain the water out into a bucket, or more conveniently, directly into the sewage system. After draining and rinsing the tank,to avoid giving your turtles thermal shock, it should be refilled with water of a similar temperature to that which was removed.

For reasons of hygiene it is best to avoid having gravel or other substrate material on the floor of a turtle tank. However, with turtles such as softshells, which naturally conceal themselves below the substrate it will be necessary to provide a layer of coarse river sand or fine gravel. Although such turtles conceal themselves in mud, in wild conditions, sand or gravel makes a cleaner substitute in the tank.

The use of a good, powerful water filter will help keep the water clean in your turtle tank. You will still have to change the water from time to time but not so often as when you don't have a filter. With a filter you will perhaps only have to change the water once or twice a month rather than two or three times per week. The frequency with which you have to change the water will be a matter of trial and error at first but your nose will soon guide you into a routine. You will be able to see a range of aquarium power filters at most pet stores. For a turtle tank it is best to choose a filter that is at least two size grades up from that recommended for a fish tank of the same size.

As semi-aquatic turtles like to sun bask frequently, it is important to provide a "land" area with a heat lamp suspended over it, in their tank, so that they can leave the water to bask when they want to. There are several ways you can provide land. You can use a simple large rock, or pile of rocks which breaks the surface of the water. You can divide the tank into water and land areas by siliconing a sheet of glass across the width of the tank or across one corner; the "land" area is filled with gravel. You can rig up a shelf, just above the water surface across the width of the tank, with a sloping platform entering the water. An advantage of such a shelf over the other mentioned methods is that you lose no water volume and the turtles have a larger area of water to swim in.

Egyptian Tortoise, *Testudo kleinmanni.* **Photo by W. P. Mara.**

LAND TORTOISES INDOORS

Small land tortoises and box turtles may also be kept in aquarium tanks, but will eventually outgrow them. Thus more specialized housing is often required for such species. One such method is to construct a tortoise table. Any old table will do, but the larger the better. A standard 240 cm x 120 cm (8 ft x 4 ft) sheet of plywood can be used as a top for a smaller table if necessary, but make sure the table legs are strong enough to take the weight of the finished article. You will need to build some walls around the edge of the table top. The height of these walls will have to be such that a tortoise cannot reach the top, even when it climbs on another tortoise; the risk of three tortoises climbing on top of each other is very minimal to say the least! For the average Mediterranean tortoise, or box turtle a height of 30 cm (12 in) will be adequate. To facilitate viewing of the tortoises you can make one or more of the sides from glass. The home handyperson will be able to make an extremely attractive setup. One or two piles of rocks can be used to surround and protect some potted plants so that they are out of reach of the tortoises. Do not place any solid objects near to the sides which could help allow the tortoises to scale the walls.

Some people like to give their land tortoises the run of their own room, shed or greenhouse. It is easy to set up a room for tortoises but it is advisable to use one with a floor that can be thoroughly washed and/or hosed down at regular intervals. It is also important that the room can easily be heated to the tortoises preferred temperatures (see below). If want you keep numbers of tortoises in breeding groups you can divide the floor up into a number of separate pens, using plywood sheets or similar. Each pen should be provided with its own water bath and basking facility (a suspended heat lamp for example).

You can use gravel, coarse sand, bark chippings and so on as bedding, but these will have to be removed and washed or discarded and replaced at

Matamata, *Chelus fimbriatus.*
Photo by R. D. Bartlett.

regular intervals. In smaller setups, artificial grass matting, or pieces of carpet can be used. These can be washed, or changed as they become soiled.

CAGE HEATING

Most species of turtles kept in indoor enclosures will require some kind of a supplementary heating. Both freshwater turtles and land tortoises will require basking facilities but must have the opportunity to move to a cooler area if necessary.

Aquatic turtles native to temperate areas will not normally require water heating but should be provided with a basking lamp. There are several types of lamp that can be used. A simple household tungsten light bulbs with a reflector can be useful. This is simply suspended over a basking area, preferably at one end of the tank so that the turtles can move to the cool of the other end if they want respite from the heat. I have found a long stemmed desk lamp which can be directed into the top of the tank to be very practical. Various kinds of lamps specially made for heating reptile cages are available. Again these should only be used at one end of the tank.

Tropical aquatic turtles will require some form of water heating in addition to a basking lamp. The water should be maintained at about 25 C (77 F). The best way to achieve this is to use a thermo-statically controlled electric aquarium heater. There are many patterns and sizes available and you will have to select the size depending on the amount of water you have to hear. Most aquarium heaters consist of a heat resistant glass tube with a thermostatically controlled element sealed and waterproofed inside it. Most have a dial, with which you can adjust to the desired temperature. The heater should be placed in the water and the cable plugged into the mains; be sure to read carefully the safety instructions before use. For large turtles, it is best to protect the glass casing from damage by inserting it inside a narrow piece of PVC pipe which is secured in position below the water level.

Land tortoises also require basking areas, which can be set up much in the way as described for aquatic turtles above, ensuring that the reptiles can get to a cooler area if they want to. For tropical species it will probably be necessary to maintain some form of background heat. Air temperature should not drop below 22°C (71°F) but it is recommended that part of the cage area does not exceed 25°C (77°F). In more or less enclosed cages, the heat lamp may be adequate to heat the whole interior, but for more open or larger cages you may have to use other options such as heat pads, boards, or cables. A heat pad placed under a flat slab in the cage will provide a good warming site for tor-

Painted Wood Turtle, *Rhinoclemmys pulcherrima*. Photo by K. H. Switak.

toises and will also help maintain the air temperature. A heat board is useful for placing against the end of a tank so that one wall is warmed. One heat board can be used between two tanks to provide warmth for both.

For all kinds of accommodations it is important to reduce temperatures by a few degrees at night, as is a natural occurrence in all native habitats.

LIGHTING

Turtles kept indoors will require some kind of artificial lighting in order to bring light intensity and quality up during the day. We must not ignore the possibility that turtles subjected to low or inadequate lighting levels for protracted periods may be susceptible to stress and the possibility of stress related debilities. Although domestic lighting indoors may be adequate for us, we must realize that even the strongest wattages of ordinary light bulbs provide only a fraction of the light intensity provided by the sun outside, and do not offer certain beneficial rays from the blue end of the spectrum at all. Fortunately, ongoing research into lighting apparatus for indoor terraria has resulted in the availability of a range of full spectrum fluorescent lamps which emit good quality, healthy light. Fluorescent tubes come in various sizes; there will be a size to fit most terraria, and for very large enclosures a number of lamps are recommended.

A final word about both heating and lighting. For optimum health, natural living, and breeding successes, captive turtles should be subjected to climates and seasons as they would experience in their native habitats. To do this, it will be necessary to manipulate temperature and photoperiod depending on the seasons you need to replicate. As long as you know the geographical range of the species you keep, it will be quite easy to find climatic and seasonal facts and figures about the area from a good quality world geographical atlas.

SAFETY MEASURES

As many terrarium installations are operated electrically, often are made exclusively for certain applications, or may be experimental, it is most important that safety measures are adhered to. If possible use only appliances that have certified standards, and use them only to the manufacturer's instructions. Unless you are qualified or extremely proficient in electrical work, do not attempt to modify apparatus or install systems without consulting an expert. Remember that electrical currents and water together comprise a lethal mixture!

KEEPING LAND TURTLES OUTDOORS

Many species of turtle will thrive if kept in an outdoor enclosure. Indeed, some are more likely to breed if kept in almost natural conditions out-

Aldabra Tortoise, *Geochelone gigantea*. Photo by M. P. and C. Piednoir.

doors, where they will have the benefit of real sunlight, normal temperature and humidity fluctuations, and the reduced possibility of "confined space syndrome". If you keep species that are indigenous to the actual area in which you live, or those from areas with a similar climate to your own you should have no problems whatsoever, providing the enclosure is sited correctly. In some cases you can even keep species that are not native to your area, outdoors, all year round. A good example of this is the testudinarium of Prof. Dr. Walter Kirsche who lives close to Berlin, Germany. Over many years he has bred numerous specimens, over several generations, of tortoises of various species from southern Europe and Asia, especially those of the genus *Testudo*. The tortoises are kept all year round in spacious outdoor enclosures. The only unnatural sequence in their lifestyles is that Prof. Kirsche has to collect up the eggs after they are laid, and incubate them artificially, the Berlin summer being too short, and sometimes too cold for complete incubation to succeed outdoors. In

Reeves's Turtle, *Chinemys reevesi*. Photo by M. P. and C. Piednoir.

most cases the hatchling tortoises are kept indoors for their first year and introduced to the outdoor enclosures in their second year.

There is a number of options for creating an outdoor pen for turtles. The simplest form of enclosure for land tortoises and box turtles can be made with wire mesh. The height of the mesh need not be greater than 60 cm (2 ft) and an area about 2m x 2m (appx. 6 ft x 6 ft) will be adequate for a pair of turtles. It is best to use an area with natural grass and weeds for the turtles to forage in. A small shrub in the enclosure will provide some shade and added interest. As some turtles are adept burrowers, it is advisable to bury the bottom of the mesh below the ground. Alternatively you can lay wide-gauge mesh all over the floor area, which will stop any burrowing out, but the turtles will still be able to browse on the grass and weeds growing through the mesh.

For a more permanent outdoor enclosure you could construct a wall with concrete blocks or bricks. Another good option is to make a wall with 60 cm (2 ft) concrete paving slabs buried in the soil to about one third of their width.

The site you choose should be one that receives a good amount of sunlight and, if possible should include a south-facing slope. If there is no natural slope you can make one with a mound of soil. The more natural vegetation in the enclosure the better, but also ensure that there are adequate basking sites that receive lots of sunlight, and some sunny areas of loose soil or sand for egg laying sites.

All outdoor enclosures for land turtles should be provided with retreat hutches so that the turtles have somewhere to escape the hot sun, cold winds, or rain, and to sleep in at night. It is advisable to loosely pack the interior of the hutches with hay or straw so that the tortoises can completely conceal themselves when resting. Prof. Kirsche provides his tortoises with little huts made from timber with thatched straw roofs. As winter approaches the huts are stuffed with increasing amounts of straw and, when the tortoises are ready to hibernate the huts and entrances are completely covered with mounded straw. The tortoises hibernate safely in their hibernaculae even if, on occasions, they are covered with snow. Whatever type of hutch you construct for your tortoises, it must be rain and draft proof, and frost proof if it is to double as a hibernaculum.

KEEPING AQUATIC TURTLES OUTDOORS

Aquatic turtles can also be satisfactorily kept outdoors in most areas. They can be provided with an enclosure similar to any of those described for land turtles, but these must, of course, include a pool of sufficient depth. Unfortunately, liner pools are not suitable for turtles, especially large specimens, as they are likely to damage the liner and cause the pool to leak. Pre-fabricated fiber glass fish ponds are much tougher and quite easy to install. You need to dig a hole to take the pond so that the edges are flush with the surrounding soil. You then have to pack soil tightly down the sides of the pool to fill all cavities.

The best type of pool is one constructed from concrete. This will be permanent and can be constructed to any size or depth you require. If turtles are to spend the winter in an outdoor pool in a temperate area, it must be at least 60 cm (2 ft) deep at its deepest part so that the turtles can get down well below the ice level. It is not within the scope of this volume to go into details of concrete pool construction but you will find much useful information on outdoor pools (usually described for fish, but perfectly suitable for turtles) in one of several books available on water gardening or garden ponds. One such book, also published by T.F.H., and highly recommended, is the *Atlas of Garden Ponds,* by Dr. Herbert R. Axelrod, Albert Spalding Benoist, and Dennis Kelsey-Wood.

FEEDING AND WATER REQUIREMENTS

Modern veterinary food technology has revolutionized our thoughts on the nutrition of captive reptiles. In the past, many reptile ailments arose directly or indirectly as a result of suboptimal diets. Today, if we follow the general rules of reptile nutrition, there should never be any need for any turtle to have an unbalanced diet. The main difference between reptile nutrition and that of the higher vertebrates (mammals and birds) is that the former require a more precise ratio of some nutrients to others, and may be adversely affected by a dearth of nutrients such as animal proteins and certain vitamins.

For the purposes of nutritional studies chelonians can be loosely divided into two groups; one group including those which are largely herbivorous and the other those which are largely carnivorous.

A herbivore is an animal that lives on plant material. Although many chelonians are classed as herbivores, few of them feed completely or exclusively on plant material. Animal matter may be also taken opportunistically (most so-called herbivorous land tortoises will take carrion eagerly, and will occasionally catch live invertebrates) or small animals may be accidentally consumed during grazing activities.

Most herbivorous turtles are general herbivores, eating a whole range of foliage, buds, flowers, or

Vitamin sprays are available at many pet shops and can be used in a number of ways to improve the life of your captive reptiles, including being sprayed on their food or right on their skin. Photo courtesy of Four Paws.

fruits, rather than specialist herbivores subsisting on fruits, or leaves, or particular plant species exclusively. An exception is the Green Turtle, *Chelonia mydas* which, as an adult, feeds almost exclusively on sea grass. Juveniles, however, start life being largely carnivorous, feeding on a variety of small marine animals including jellyfish, crustaceans and fish.

A carnivore is an animal that feeds on animal material. This can include living prey of various types, or carrion. Plant material may be taken opportunistically by some carnivores; it may be ingested accidentally while eating prey, or may form part of the undigested content of the prey's gut. Some turtles start life being primarily carnivorous (some *Chrysemys* species for example), but may be more herbivorous as adults. Most carnivorous turtles are general carnivores, feeding on a variety of prey ranging from small invertebrates, to amphibians, fish, small reptiles and even occasional birds and mammals (see feeding behavior).

A BALANCED DIET

Whatever kind of food is eaten it is important that turtles, like all animals, get a nutritionally balanced diet. A balanced diet is one that contains all of the essential nutrients in suitable ratios. In the wild, in various habitats, animals and their foodstuffs have evolved together over millions of years, and a situation had arisen where each species is able to collect the variety of foodstuffs required for a nutritionally balanced diet over a relatively small area. These essential nutrients, in simplest terms, include proteins, carbohydrates, fats, vitamins and minerals (see also water below).

A lack or poor supply of one or more of these essential nutrients will result in a nutritional deficiency disease, which not only is debilitating itself, it opens the door for other infections. In most cases a balanced diet can be achieved in captive feeding regimes by giving the animals as great a variety of food items (of the type they eat) as possible.

Food items will depend on the species, size (and age) but can be divided roughly into four groups.

1. Juvenile aquatic freshwater turtles (especially in the genera *Chrysemys* and *Pseudemys*: Tubifex, bloodworms, water snails, freshwater shrimps, other freshwater invertebrates, fly maggots (in moderation), mealworms (in moderation), crickets, earthworms, tiny fish, tadpoles, tiny strips of lean, raw, beef, chicken, liver or heart (in moderation), finely chopped greenfood or, especially algae and water plants.

2. General freshwater turtles, including adults of genera mentioned in 1 (above) and Asian box turtles (*Cuora*): Similar to 1 (above), but larger sized items and portions, plus a greater amount of plant material (algae and water plants especially). May be given whole (dead) fish, whole (dead) mice or whole (dead) day old chicks which will be pulled apart by two or more turtles.

3. American box turtles (*Terrapene*): Snails, slugs, earthworms, mealworms (in moderation), strips of lean beef, chicken, liver or heart (in moderation), greenfood, fruits (especially berries), and mushrooms.

4. Land Tortoises: A vast variety of plant food may be given including grass, lettuce, dandelion (leaves and flowers), cabbage, broccoli, cauliflower, Brussels sprouts, bean sprouts, alfalfa sprouts, grated carrots, various fruits including tomatoes, cucumbers, melons, zucchinis, squash, apples, pears, plums, strawberries, plus almost any other plant related material you may want to try. Many land tortoises will take a small amount of animal based food. Small pieces of lean red meat, chicken, liver or heart can be mixed in with the greenfood. Most carnivorous turtles can be given canned dog or cat food, but only occasionally and in small quantities. These products contain high amounts of the vitamins A and D, too much of which can contribute to severe mineralization of the soft body tissues.

Eastern Box Turtle, *Terrapene carolina*. Photo by Aaron Norman.

A FEEDING STRATEGY

Remember that not all turtles will run to a standard feeding pattern. You may have an individual of one species that wouldn't eat a piece of tomato even if it was starving to death, while another of the same species would eat tomato until it "came out of its ears". You may have to experiment until you come up with a successful feeding strategy.

Once you have developed a successful regime for your particular turtles you will usually find that the best policy is to stick to it, though it may take a while to get there. Trial and error is one of the interesting parts of herpetoculture!

ACQUISITION OF FOOD ITEMS

Invertebrate Foods: These can be collected, purchased on a regular basis, or cultured at home so that you have a continuing supply. Many aquatic turtles prefer aquatic invertebrates. You can collect such animals from streams and ponds. By turning over stones in shallow water you will find a range of freshwater crustaceans such as freshwater shrimps, small crays and so on. Aquatic larvae of various insects such as dragonflies may also be used. You can often find quantities of water snails attached to clumps of waterplants that you can fish out of the water with a hook or fork.

Many terrestrial invertebrates also are good food for freshwater turtles. Earthworms can be simply dug up from the garden of you have the time, but you can get an almost permanent supply of earthworms together by digging a large amount of organic material (dead leaves, kitchen waste etc.) into a patch in the garden and keeping it moist. Covering it with more dead leaves or some hessian sacking will help to retain moisture. Worms will soon seek out this area to consume the organic matter and will breed in situ. As long as you don't take out too many worms at a time you will have a continuing supply. Slug and snails can be searched out in shady, moist parts of the garden under fallen logs or other ground litter. Many beetles, pill-bugs, grubs and so on can also be found in such situations.

Many petshops and specialist companies now supply a range of invertebrate live foods. Tubifex worms and water snails are often available in tropical fish stores. A clump of tubifex will be relished by many aquatic turtles.

Many specialty products are now being made specifically for the ambitious reptile keeper. Most are affordable and can be found at pet shops that stock other herpetocultural goods. Photo courtesy of Energy Savers Unlimited, Inc.

Mealworms are also readily available and can be used as a standby item when other live foods are not available. However, as mealworms are not considered to be a balanced diet in themselves they should only be given as part of a more varied diet. Mealworms are the larvae of a kind of flour beetle (*Tenebrio molitor*). It is quite easy to get your own mealworm culture going. All you need is three or four shallow boxes (each about 30 cm x 20 cm - 12 x 8 in) with ventilated lids. A 5 cm (2 in) layer of bran mixed with some rolled oats is placed in the first box. Put about 50 purchased mealworms on the mixture and cover with a piece of cotton or hessian cloth cut to size. Place a couple of pieces of carrot or apple on top of the cloth to provide moisture (these should be changed regularly before they spoil). The box should be placed where the temperature can be maintained at 20 - 25°C (68 - 77°F).

The mealworms will feed on the mixture, grow, and eventually pupate. The adult male and female beetles hatch from the pupae and, after mating, the females each will lay up to 180 eggs which will hatch after 18-22 days as a new generation of tiny mealworms. At 22°C the complete life cycle will take about four months, at 25°C a little less. You can progressively start a new culture after each four month period until you have three or four cultures going. The oldest culture is then discarded (you can use the remaining larvae, pupae or beetles to start another culture, or feed them directly to your turtles). If you keep three or four cultures going in various stages you will have a permanent supply of mealworms.

Crickets (usually of the genera *Acheta* or *Gryllus*) are a live food item for terrarium animals which have grown enormously in popularity during the past few years. This is not surprising as crickets are highly nutritious food items that are eaten eagerly by many small carnivores; they are also relatively inexpensive to buy and quite easy to breed. I have found a plastic trash can to be very useful for breeding or storing crickets. Alternatively you can use any other kind of escape proof plastic, metal or wooden container. A plastic trash can have a large hole cut in its lid and this is covered with standard insect screening. The can is about half filled with old egg boxes, rolls of corrugated cardboard or balls of newspaper. A narrow plank is placed across the top of the bedding (can be jammed in or screwed firmly from outside the can); this will take the dishes for food and water.

Food for crickets consists of bran mash, plus any kind of cereal (muesli is very nutritious for crickets and the goodness will be passed on to your turtles when they eat the crickets). Some fresh green food or chopped fruit should also be given daily to provide moisture. The food should be given in dishes placed on the plank mentioned above. The crickets will hide in the bedding and come out at night to feed.

Other invertebrate foods that may be bred on a commercial basis may include various cockroach species (if you use these mind they don't escape in your house) and grasshoppers, especially migratory locusts (*Schistocercus migratoria*). Larger specimens of these insects are ideal for larger turtles.

VERTEBRATE FOODS

Turtles will fare better on whole food animals rather than on pieces of raw meat. Though they will eat the latter eagerly, it does not contain the bone, organs, skin, fur, scale or feather of the whole prey animal. Most aquatic turtles will eagerly accept dead mice or young domestic chickens. A mouse or chick placed in a tank full of hungry turtles will soon be dismembered and devoured, not only do the turtles get a nutritious meal, they get quite a bit of exercise at the same time.

Most petshops that sell herptiles will be able to supply you with mice or chicks. Dead, frozen examples of these two food items can also be purchased in bulk. These can be kept frozen until required for use. However, they must be thoroughly thawed out before being fed to your turtles. Allow natural thawing (preferably overnight) and not in the oven or microwave.

Fish will also be taken by turtles, dead or alive. Pieces of fish should have the bone and scales left on. Small cheap, common fish such as guppies or goldfish can be used. If you live near a trout farm or other kind of fish farm you may be able to get cheap reject fingerlings or similar. Tadpoles will be accepted eagerly by many small turtles but as tadpoles are also herptiles most herpetologists do not like to use them (which is a good thing because many amphibians are on the decline in the wild), though if the tadpoles are captive produced maybe the moral connotations are not quite so bad.

MANUFACTURED FOODS

Several pet food companies offer foods manufactured especially for turtles and other reptiles and are usually described under the name of turtle pellets. These contain a mixture of items which together constitute a balanced diet for turtles and the manufacturers claim that an exclusive diet of such pellets is all that your turtles require to keep them in top health. I am not entirely convinced that this is the case and would recommend that pellets should constitute no more than half of the diet, the rest being made up of a mixture of the various natural foods described above. Without intending to anthropomorphize turtles, I would believe that any individual chelonian with its minute amount of reasoning power, would prefer to occasionally share in the dismemberment of a mouse or fish, rather than forever stuff its mouth full of dry pellets, an exercise that could be likened to one of us humans being forced to live for eternity on a diet of muesli!

VITAMIN/MINERAL SUPPLEMENTS

Although turtles receiving a variety of foods should theoretically receive a balanced diet, most hobbyists like to give their reptiles a regular dose of a vitamin/mineral supplement, just in case there is a deficiency of certain micronutrients in their regular diet. A number of proprietary preparations are available on the market. Your veterinarian or supplier will be able to advise you on the product most suitable for your purposes. For most turtles a product in powder form is best as it can be simply sprinkled over food items once or twice per week. Always follow the manufacturer's instructions and take care not to overdose your animals. Some vitamins given in excess can be as damaging as a lack of them.

WATER REQUIREMENTS

Aquatic turtles obviously require water in which they spend most of their lives. Most aquatic turtles will quickly dehydrate and die if kept in a dry situation for a protracted period. As aquatic turtles live mainly in water, it is not necessary to provide them with any additional drinking facilities.

The amount of drinking water required by terrestrial species will depend on the amount of moisture contained in their food. Although some species and individuals will hardly ever be seen to drink, fresh drinking water should always be available just in case. Additionally, some terrestrial species are fond of a water bath. A shallow container with easy access and egress should be provided.

WASTE MANAGEMENT

The management of waste is usually no great problem when small numbers of chelonians are kept. Soiled water from aquatic turtle accommodations can be used to irrigate the garden if you have one, an added advantage is that the feces content is a good nitrogenous fertilizer. If you vary your points of disposal each time, you will never have any problems of smell or pollution. If you live in an apartment, your waste water can be flushed down the toilet—never down the kitchen waste.

With terrestrial species, soiled organic bedding and feces can be used on the compost heap in the garden, or dug directly into the garden itself. It makes excellent compost or manure. If you don't have a garden, you may have to get rid of the waste via the refuse collection. However, you should make yourself familiar with the your local authority's regulations, before using garbage chutes etc. for this purpose

REPRODUCTION AND CAPTIVE BREEDING

GENERAL REMARKS:

As many wild habitats are rapidly on the decline, many turtle species are in danger of extinction unless specific parts of these habitats are preserved and managed. Concern by conservationists has led to international legislation being passed to protect many species. While this legislation may stop many species being collected from the wild and sold to hobbyists, it does not seem to be working in many countries which seem to be systematically wiping out their wilderness areas - natural habitats for many species. Many concerned naturalists are therefore now taking the opinion that numerous species are likely to be saved from total extinction only by the initiation of serious captive breeding programs. A knowledge of particular species reproductive habits and requirements are essential for such breeding programs to be successful.

COURTSHIP AND MATING BEHAVIOR

In most species reproduction is seasonal. In temperate areas breeding takes place in the spring, while in tropical areas it may take place at any time of the year, but most usually during the wet seasons. Many species breed once per annum, some several times per annum; others (especially marine turtles) may breed only every second or third year. Most land and freshwater turtles have relatively small areas of territory and breed in their immediate foraging areas. Marine turtles, and some river turtles, however, may migrate some considerable distances at breeding time. Many Green Turtles, *Chelonia mydas*, for example, that spend most of their time living near the coast of Brazil, migrate as much as 4500 kilometers (2800 miles) so that they can mate near the mid-Atlantic Island of Ascension, the females laying their eggs on the sandy beaches of that island. It is assumed that these migrations occur so that the eggs can laid in relatively safe areas, rather in places where predators are common.

In view of the migratory behavior of sea turtles it is doubtful that complete captive breeding will ever be successful. However, management of breeding beaches, and the captive rearing of hatchlings to a less vulnerable size before release into the sea is a viable proposition. In some countries, the Cayman Islands for example, this process is being successfully carried out.

Freshwater turtles have a range of courtship and mating behaviors ranging from the simple to the quite elaborate. Male mud turtles and snappers simply overpower the females before copulating, while certain male emydid turtles may spend hours courting the females with elaborate swimming and stroking procedures. Male *Chrysemys* (*Pseudemys*) species, for example, are well known for their long foreclaws. Swimming backwards in front of the female, the male continually strokes her face with his claws until, overcome by his caresses, she sinks to the bottom and submits to copulation. The male mounts her from above, gripping the edge of her carapace with his claws and passing his tail beneath hers so that he is able to insert his single, erect penis into her cloaca. As copulation may take an hour or more, the pair may have to surface several times for air during this time.

Land Tortoises often have violent and noisy courtship procedures, a fact that has indirectly led to the demise of many species. In some southern Mediterranean countries, the sound of male tortoises battering the shells of the females during courtship once was a signal for the local population to go out and collect them for the food or pet markets. Guided by the noise, the mating tortoises were easy to find. Fortunately, these tortoises are now protected by strong legislation in most of these countries. In many land tortoises and especially box turtles the male has to get into an almost vertical position to satisfactorily achieve intromission and copulation. Some male tortoises are tremendously vocal during copulation, often letting out a series of loud bellows and grunts.

Egg of the Snapping Turtle, *Chelydra serpentina*, incubating in both vermiculite and sphagnum moss. Photo by W. P. Mara.

SPERM RETENTION:

The females of some species are able to retain viable sperm in their cloacas and can successfully fertilize two or more successful clutches, often more than a year after copulation.

EGGLAYING:

All turtles, whether marine, freshwater or terrestrial, lay their eggs on land, in burrows or beneath ground litter. Marine turtles typically have specific nesting beaches which, in many cases, are now protected to prevent the collection of eggs by people who regard them as a delicacy. Mass nesting occurs on various tropical beaches. Some beaches may be very popular with turtles, while others, with apparently similar qualities are ignored or only sparsely used. How the turtles decide what are the best beaches is a mystery. Female marine turtles and some of the larger river turtles only leave the water in order to lay their eggs and have to drag their enormous weight laboriously up the beaches in order to reach suitable sites above the high water mark. Nesting usually takes place at night, for secrecy and to avoid the hot sun. Most of these turtles excavate flask shaped burrows with their hind limbs. After depositing the eggs the nests are carefully filled in. Some species disturb an area of substrate around the nest in order to confuse predators. Others may dig one or more false nests, or deposit their clutch in two or three sites for similar reasons. After egglaying and concealing the nest, the turtles return to the water.

There is no parental care in most species, the eggs being left to their own devices as soon as they are covered. One exception to this rule is the female Phayre's Tortoise, *Geochelone emys*, who lays her eggs in a mound nest constructed from decaying vegetation and mounts guard on it for several days before finally leaving it. Some small freshwater turtles lay their eggs under ground litter with little or no attempt at burrowing, others such as the Florida Red-bellied Turtle, *Chrysemys nelsoni*, often utilize the burrows of other animals in which to lay their eggs.

SOME EGG DATA:

Turtle eggs are either spherical or elongated. Those laying spherical eggs include the sea turtles, the snappers, and the softshells. Those laying elongated eggs include the mud turtles and many of the emydid turtles, while land tortoises and sidenecked turtles may lay either spherical or elongated eggs depending on the species. In general those species that lay large numbers of eggs usually lay spherical eggs. Eggshells are white to off-white in color and may be "soft" or "hard". Though there are some exceptions, most temperate emydid turtles, the snappers, the softshells, the sea turtles, and some sidenecks lay eggs with a soft, flexible, leathery shell. Such a shell is easily able to absorb and lose moisture. Most tropical emydid turtles, mud turtles, some sidenecks, and most land tortoises lay eggs with a hard, but brittle shell, which protects against moisture loss.

Egg dimensions vary from species to species. The largest spherical eggs, up to 6 cm (2.5 in) in diameter, are laid by Galapagos Giant Tortoises, *Geochelone elephantopus*, while the largest elongated eggs, up to over 7.5 cm (3 in) in length are laid by the Borneo River Turtle, *Orlitia borneensis*. Generally, the size of the eggs is related to the size of the turtle species, but there are exceptions such as the Black Wood Turtle, *Rhinoclemmys funerea*, which although only averaging about 30 cm (12 in) in carapace length, lays eggs up to 7 cm (2.8 in) long.

There is also much variation in numbers of eggs laid by turtles. Most sea turtles lay relatively large numbers of eggs but the most prolific is the Green Turtle, *Chelonia mydas*, which regularly lays clutches in excess of one hundred eggs and a single clutch of 226 has been recorded. However most turtles lay much smaller numbers, generally the smaller the turtle the less eggs it lays per clutch. An extreme example is the Pancake Tortoise, *Malacochercus tornieri*, which usually lays but a single egg, very occasionally two.

Eggs are laid in sites carefully selected by the turtles for safety and for warmth. Most sites are exposed to sunlight for much of the day so that the temperature is sufficient to incubate the eggs successfully. Some species void the fluid contents of their cloacas in or over the nest cavity. This may help conserve moisture in the nest, as the surface of the excavated soil soon dries out and becomes quite hard, but remains moist beneath.

Incubation times vary among the species and may be as little as two months in some temperate species, but often as much as eight or nine months in tropical species. In some species from colder temperate regions, embryological development may be suspended during the winter, the eggs

Black Wood Turtle, *Rhinoclemmys funerea*. Photo by Dr. Peter Pritchard.

hatching in the following spring. In other species hatchlings may have to wait, sometimes for a considerable period, until seasonal rains soften the hardened plug over the nest sufficiently for them to escape.

On hatching the turtles burrow their way to the surface, where they must make for cover and protection as quickly as they can. Marine turtle hatchlings in particular are very vulnerable at this time and large numbers of them are picked off by predators (mainly sea birds) during their perilous journey down the beach. Even after the hatchlings have reached the relative safety of the sea, further marine predators will be waiting for their share of the booty. The huge casualty rate (as much as 99 percent) among hatchling marine turtles is one reason why so many eggs are laid in the first place. Hatchling freshwater turtles and land tortoises are somewhat less vulnerable so smaller numbers of eggs may be laid.

TEMPERATURE RELATED SEX DETERMINATION:

Eggs develop more quickly at the higher end of the optimum range. However, in several species, incubation temperatures have been found to be correlated with the sexes of the hatchlings. While similar amounts of males and females will emerge from nests incubated at an average optimum temperature, mostly males, or mostly females will hatch at the upper, or lower optimum temperature ranges. This phenomenon has been proven in eggs artificially incubated at various constant temperatures, but as eggs developing in the wild are normally subjected to natural temperature fluctuations within the optimum range, more or less equal numbers of the sexes usually hatch.

CAPTIVE BREEDING

Creating A Breeding Response: In the past the successful breeding of captive turtles has been fraught with difficulties. However, over the past couple of decades, our knowledge of the captive reproductive husbandry of many species has led to many species being bred in increasing numbers. Much of our knowledge in this field must be attributed to a few dedicated herpetoculturists who have spent many painstaking years of research and experienced many disappointments. Most of these herpetoculturists have passed on the results of their failures and successes to other herpetologists through the various herpetological journals and, today, most hobbyists are in the position to successfully breed their animals thanks to those pioneering spirits.

After the obvious necessity of having a male and a female of the species to be bred, the most important aspect of successful captive breeding seems to be the provision of a suitable seasonal regime. As already discussed, most turtles breed seasonally. In temperate species, a period of hibernation, followed by an increase in photoperiod and temperature seems to be the major trigger in producing a breeding response. Specimens kept outdoors and allowed to hibernate more or less naturally, will be influenced by the natural progress of the seasons, but those kept indoors under artificial conditions will have to have those conditions seasonally manipulated if breeding is to be successful.

A knowledge of the prevailing seasons in the natural habitats of certain species is essential. It is necessary to produce a facsimile of those particular seasons. In some cases compromise situations will be successful; for example a dramatically reduced period of hibernation is better than no hibernation at all and will often lead to good breeding results. Compromise periods of hibernation are often used for turtles kept indoors.

Most species, even those from tropical areas, are influenced by changes in photoperiod and temperature. Indeed, there always is a summer and winter seasonal change in photoperiod, however slight, with the exception of those areas situated right on the equator. So manipulation of photoperiod and temperature is the first consideration.

A typical regime for subtropical and tropical turtles (in which hibernation is not required) kept indoors is to keep them throughout the summer with 14 hours lighting during the day, and ten hours darkness at night, with a maximum daytime air temperature of 28°C (82°F) (but warmer basking areas may be provided) reduced at night to around 22°C (71 °F). During the fall, decrease the photoperiod gradually (say by 10 minutes each day over a period of 24 days) until you arrive at the winter regime of 10 hours lighting during the day and 14 hours darkness at night. At the same time, the temperature should be reduced a little daily, until the maximum daytime air temperature is 24°C (75°F) (basking reduced to 2 hours per day), reduced at night to 18°C (64 °F). During the cooling off period turtles should become relatively inactive and need reduced quantities of food.

You can artificially reduce the "winter" by a couple of months if you wish and start the reverse procedure in late winter/early spring, by gradually bringing the photoperiod and temperature back to summer levels. Introduction of the sexes and an increase in humidity (for terrestrial species) at this time should trigger a breeding response.

The Gravid Female: Turtles should be disturbed as little as possible at breeding time. Once copulation has taken place it takes from 4-8 weeks before the female lays her eggs, depending on the species. As egglaying time approaches, the female

Eggs of the Peninsula Cooter, *Pseudemys floridana peninsularis*. Photo by Isabelle Francais.

Egg of the Peninsula Cooter, *Pseudemys floridana peninsularis*. Photo by Isabelle Francais.

becomes ever more restless. Aquatic turtles will leave the water at this time and search for a laying site in the land section of their accommodations. It is important to provide an area of moist sand at least 15 cm (6 in) deep for the smaller turtle species; larger species will, of course, require larger accommodations and deeper substrates. After excavating a hole in the sand, the female will lay her eggs.

Artificial Incubation: As the conditions in most terraria are unsuitable for natural incubation to take place, the eggs must be removed for artificial incubation. Whatever kind of accommodations you keep your turtles in, from small indoor terraria, to large outdoor enclosures, you must keep a close eye on gravid females at egg laying time so that you do not miss any eggs. Turtles are remarkably clever at concealing their nesting sites, even in relatively small terraria! Allow the female to complete her laying, cover the clutch and leave the site, before removing the eggs. They should be dug out very carefully so as not to damage them. Most hobbyists advocate marking the eggs "on top" with a non toxic marker and this remains the top throughout the period of incubation. Reptile eggs should not be turned as one would the eggs of birds.

The eggs are placed in plastic containers packed with moistened sphagnum moss, clean sand, or vermiculite. The latter is becoming ever more used as an incubation medium. It is clean, inert, and holds a large amount of moisture. The usual method is to mix the vermiculite with its equal volume of water. Any excess water should be pressed out through a fine sieve. The eggs are buried to about three quarters their depth in the moist medium with just the tops showing. The containers should then be placed in an incubator and maintained at about 30°C for the duration of incubation.

There are some commercially made incubators available, but it is quite simple to make your own. A glass or plastic tank with a thermostatically controlled aquarium heater set in a few inches of water is quite suitable. A couple of bricks are placed in the water so that a shelf can be installed just above the water surface. The egg containers are placed on the shelf and the thermostat is set to 30°C. The warmed water will maintain high humidity in the air which will, in turn, keep the incubation medium moist (moist only, it must never be allowed to become waterlogged). A piece of sloping glass set above the incubation chambers will stop excessive condensed water dripping onto the medium. Incubation times vary from species to species and may be anything from two months to nine months or more. The following table provides a sample of breeding data for a number of selected species:

Species	No. of Eggs Laid/ Clutch	Incubation Time*
Chelonoidis carbonaria	6-8	100-200 days
Chinemys reevesi	2-5	70-100 days
Chrysemys picta	2-20	70-100 days
Clemmys guttata	2-8	80-120 days
Emydoidea blandingi	4-10	80-90 days
Emys orbicularis	6-18	60-80 days
Graptemys geographica	12-14	80-90 days
Geochelone elegans	1-4	90-130 days
Kinosternon subrubrum	1-6	90-120 days
Macroclemys temmincki	10-50	80-120 days
Sternothorus odoratus	1-9	65-90 days
Terrapene carolina	3-8	65-100 days
Testudo graeca	2-8	75-100 days

* based on incubation temperature of 25-30°C (77-86°F)

HATCHING AND REARING

When ready to hatch the young turtle slits open the eggshell with an egg tooth, a hard, sharp projection situated on the snout. The egg tooth is shed after hatching. Most turtles do not leave the eggshell immediately after slitting it, but spend one or two days absorbing the contents of the egg sac. Do not be tempted to "help" the hatchling; let nature take its course. Once the neonates have completely left the shell and are free moving, they can be transferred to rearing cages or tanks. Carnivorous species should be fed initially on small invertebrates plus finely chopped lean meat. Herbivorous species should be provided with a variety of finely chopped greenfood, fruit and vegetables. Vitamin/mineral supplements should be given with the food twice per week. As the young turtles grow they can be gradually introduced to the adult diets as described in the chapter on feeding.

PREVENTIVE HEALTH CARE

The old proverb, "prevention is better than cure", applies very much to turtle husbandry. As treatment of reptilian diseases can often still be a hit or miss affair, as well as being expensive, it is better to apply prophylactic methods of husbandry from the outset.

STRESS CONTROL

Stress is one of the biggest bugbears in animal husbandry. Although stress cannot really be defined as a disease in its own right, it is a condition that is disease conducive. Newly captured wild turtles often are extremely stressed. Firstly any animal is stressed to some extent after being removed from its natural environment; without trying to be anthropomorphic, it can be compared to a human being forcibly removed from his/her home and locked up in strange premises. While a turtle may not be able to think about the situation in the way we can, its body chemistry will certainly be knocked about.

Stress causes malfunctions in normal metabolism; not only is the animal's resistance to disease reduced by failure to produce antibodies to fight disease, the situation is further exacerbated by reluctance to feed, refusal to thermoregulate and so on; in other words, a stressed animal often seems to give up the ghost and, unless we can offer some kind of relief, the animal will eventually die.

The secret of getting captive wild animals stress-free is to fool them into thinking that they are not captive. That is, we must give them housing of adequate size, provide optimum temperatures and other climatic factors, and feed them on a balanced diet (which may not be the same as it would get in the wild but is a fair substitute).

To summarize: a stress-free turtle is least likely to succumb to disease so we must make ever effort to keep our turtles in optimum anti-stress conditions.

QUARANTINE

One of the most important disease control factors in a collection of turtles is to ascertain that disease is not brought in from outside, especially with newly acquired specimens. The acquisition of healthy specimens is discussed elsewhere in the text, but to be doubly sure that the new specimen(s) are not suffering from a disease still in its undetectable stages, it is highly recommended that they are kept in a period of quarantine before being introduced to any existing specimens you may have.

Quarantine cages should have exactly the same necessary life support systems as permanent cages, though furnishings can be on the simpler rather than on the more decorative side. Quarantine cages should preferably be in a separate room from the rest of the collection; better even, in a separate building. Turtles in quarantine are best kept singly for a period of not less than six weeks. If there are no symptoms of disease after this period, you can almost certainly be assured that the animals are not infected with pathogens. If symptoms occur, the period of isolation must be lengthened and attempts made to diagnose and treat the malady.

GENERAL HYGIENE

Both personal and general hygiene is of prime importance in animal husbandry, both for the sake of the animals and for their human caregivers. Enthusiasts with numbers of specimens should deal with each cage individually (here take "cage" to mean any form of enclosure in which turtles may be kept). Always wash your hands and any equipment you use before moving onto the next cage.

While cage cleaning should be carried out as and when necessary, and anyway at least twice per week, complete disinfection of cage interiors and furnishings are recommended at regular intervals. Monthly would deem a suitable regime. Remove turtles to a suitable spare container (plastic trash bins kept for this purpose are ideal; they can easily be cleaned and disinfected between uses), take out all furnishings, and discard the perishables.

The cages and furnishings should be scrubbed clean with a mild detergent, then rinsed and placed in a solution of household bleach, a cheap but efficient disinfectant, for about 30 minutes. After bleaching, cages and equipment should be thoroughly rinsed with clear water and dried before reassembling the accommodations and returning the turtles.

Tanks for aquatic turtles should have all water completely discarded. The interior of the tank should be cleaned and disinfected as described above, then refilled with clean water.

REFERENCES AND RECOMMENDED READING
BY TFH PUBLICATIONS

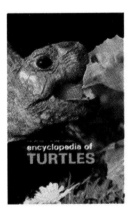

H-1011

RE-101

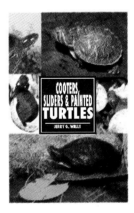

RE-146

RE-141

KW-051

RE-135

ASIAN BIG-HEADED TURTLES (PLATYSTERNIDAE)

David T. Kirkpatrick, PhD
Department of Biology
University of North Carolina - Chapel Hill
Chapel Hill, NC 27599-3280

David T. Kirkpatrick received his Bachelor of Science degree in biology from Carnegie-Mellon University in Pittsburgh, and his Doctorate in molecular genetics from MIT in Boston. Currently, he is a postdoctoral researcher at the University of North Carolina at Chapel Hill, where he is working on the molecular basis for the initiation of recombination in meiosis. While in graduate school, he was Secretary of the New England Herpetological Society. Other reptile-related activities included organizing and teaching a short course on herpetoculture at MIT, and participating in a program to help the recovery of the federally-protected Plymouth Redbelly turtle. He is the author of over a dozen articles on turtle species, focusing primarily on their husbandry and natural history. He and his wife Catherine maintain a moderate collection of turtles, focusing on captive reproduction of less common Asian, North American and Central American semi-aquatic turtles.

BASIC TAXONOMY

Platysternon megacephalum is a monotypic turtle, meaning that it is unique enough to be placed in its own family, the Platysternidae, and has no close relatives. However, the exact placement of Big-headed turtles has been the subject of some controversy over the years. Agassiz originally grouped this turtle with the snapping turtles, but subsequent authors placed *Platysternon* in its own group. More recently, Eugene Gaffney grouped *Platysternon* with the Chelydridae (snapping turtles) based on a number of morphological features of the skull (Gaffney, 1975).

Evidence gathered from examining chromosomes of various species indicates that the Big-headed turtle most closely resembles the batagurine group of turtles, the Old World pond turtles, including such turtles as *Chinemys* and *Cuora* (Haiduk and Bickman, 1982). The evidence indicated that chromosomes vary more between *Platysternon* and the chelydrids than they do between *Platysternon* and the batagurines.

Although portions of the Big-headed turtle's anatomy resemble portions of other turtles, these

An adult male Big-headed turtle (*Platysternon megacephalum*). Note the long, scaled tail and the heavy plating on the head. Photo by David Kirkpatrick.

are only superficial resemblances and do not indicate an underlying relationship. Peter C. H. Pritchard, in his book on Alligator Snapping turtles (*Macroclemys temminckii*) discusses these differences in form between Alligator Snappers and Big-headed turtles (Pritchard, 1989).

SPECIES STATUS

Currently there are five subspecies of *P. megacephalum* recognized:
—*P. m. megacephalum*
—*P. m. peguense*
—*P. m. vogeli*
—*P. m. tristernalis*
—*P. m. shiui*

Big-headed turtles were first described in 1831 by J. E. Gray, with various subspecies advanced in 1870, 1969, and 1984. Ernst and McCord described the most recent subspecies, *P. m. shiui*, in 1987. Some subspecies may be invalid, as the diagnostic characteristics used to separate them might be too variable to adequately differentiate between subspecies. Carl Ernst is investigating the relationships between the subspecies (Ernst and McCord, 1987).

Currently the subspecies are designated based on differences in a number of characteristics, including:

Big-headed Turtle, *Platysternon megacephalum.* **Photo by K. T. Nemuras.**

—patterns on the plastron and carapace
—presence of growth annuli and posterior serrations on the carapace
—shape and coloration of the head and jaws

Various subspecies are found in different parts of the turtle's range: *P. m. megacephalum* is found in southern China, while *P. m. peguense* occurs in southern Thailand and Burma. The most colorful subspecies, *P. m. shiui*, is located in northern Vietnam (Iverson, 1992).

Platysternon megacephalum megacephalum. *P. m. megacephalum* is the nominate subspecies. This turtle can be distinguished by its unpatterned plastron, lack of growth annuli and posterior serrations on the carapace, and radiating pattern of narrow lines on the head, with yellow mottling of the jaws.

P. m. tristernalis. This turtle is similar to *P. m. megacephalum* except for the presence of three small scales at the intersection of the gular and humural scutes.

P. m. peguense. This turtle is readily distinguished from the previous two subspecies, as it has a dark pattern along the seams of the plastron. In addition, this turtle has pronounced growth rings on the carapace, while the poste-

rior portion is serrated. The head of this chelonian has a dark stripe behind the eyes and an unpatterned jaw.

P. m. vogeli. The subspecies *P. m. vogeli* also has a dark plastral figure, but the carapace is smooth and lacks serrations.

P. m. shiui. This turtle is the most recently described subspecies. It is distinguished by its coloration; it is heavy spotted with pink, orange or yellow on its limbs, head, shell and tail. It has a smooth carapace with respect to both growth annuli and posterior serrations (Pritchard, 1979, and Ernst and Barbour, 1989).

LIFESPAN

As with many semi-aquatic turtles, *Platysternon megacephalum* is moderately long-lived in captivity. Slavens' Reptiles and Amphibians in Captivity (1994), mentions a male *P. m. megacephalum* acquired by the Chicago Zoological Park in 1959 as an adult that died over 25 years later. The Columbus Zoological Park has a male that has been in captivity over 27 years (Snider and Bowler, 1992). With reasonable care, wild-caught big-headed turtles are capable of surviving decades in captivity.

HABITAT

Platysternon megacephalum hails from Southeast Asia. Specimens have been obtained as far south and west as Burma, and as far north and east as southern China. In all of these locales, the primary habitat of the big- headed turtle remains the same. It prefers to live in fast-moving mountain streams filled with boulders and broken rock. Although big-heads are located in countries considered to be tropical, water temperature in the mountain streams favored by the turtles can reach lows of 53 degrees F (12° C) and generally doesn't exceed 72 degrees F (23° C).

PHYSICAL CHARACTERISTICS

In appearance, big-headed turtles look as if they have been assembled using mismatched and poorly sized parts left over from other turtles. The most distinctive characteristic is an oversized triangular head—it can be up to half the width of the carapace itself.

Body Part	Characteristics
Head	Due to the size of its head, the turtle is incapable of withdrawing the head into its shell. To make up for this lack of protection, the top and sides of the turtle's head are covered with a large horny scute, similar to the scutes on the carapace and plastron. As further protection, the turtle's skull is solid bone; unlike many turtles, big-heads have no openings in the roof of their skull. Their jaws have a wide but sharp beak, while the edges of both jaws are lined with another tough horny sheath. Only a narrow band of unprotected skin remains on the cheeks, extending from the turtle's eyes to the corner of its mouth. The head of *P. megacephalum* gives the impression, at least superficially, of a snapping-turtle head; it is not surprising that they have been regarded as close relatives.
Eyes	The eyes themselves are not particularly recessed, although they appear so because of the surrounding horny shielding. Each eye has a black pupil and a golden iris, occasionally with a brownish bar running through it horizontally, depending on the specific subspecies.

Big-headed Turtle, *Platysternon megacephalum*. Photo by R. D. Bartlett.

Carapace The carapace of the big-headed turtle is roughly rectangular with a squared-off front and a more rounded and notched—even serrated—posterior. It is not highly domed; in fact it can be quite flattened, especially when compared to the size of the turtle's head. The plastron, unlike that of snapping turtles or mud turtles, is well-developed and lacks a hinge. While the carapace can range from yellow to a dark brown, occasionally with a darker radiating pattern, the plastron is generally yellow. Some subspecies (*P. m. peguense*, *P. m. vogeli*) have a dark edging to the seams on the plastron. *P. m. shiui* is the most strikingly marked of the subspecies, with traces of red or pink on its shell and head.

Big-headed Turtle, *Platysternon megacephalum* viewed from above. Photo by David Kirkpatrick.

Legs and Toes Big-headed turtles have slightly webbed toes with strong claws. Their feet resemble those of wood turtles or spotted turtles (*Clemmys insculpta* or *C. guttata*) in appearance. The legs are covered with large scales, as is the very long and muscular tail.

Tail The tail itself is not very heavily built; instead it is thin and whiplike. It is capable of a large range of motions, and seems quite useful to the turtle. Individuals have been observed using their tails as counterweights when in the water; this allows them to balance on two back legs only. When swimming, big-heads will occasionally curl their tail up in an arc over their back, almost coming to resemble a scorpion. Big-heads can use their well-armored tail as a prop; while attempting to climb a smooth vertical wall a turtle was seen to support its own weight entirely with its tail.

GROWTH AND DEVELOPMENT

Juvenile big-heads are more brightly marked than adults. Also, juveniles have more pronounced serrations at the rear of the carapace; while the tail is proportionately longer than in the adults.

SEXING

There is no marked difference between the sexes in *Platysternon*. The plastron of male turtles tends to be more concave than that of females. Also, the vent is located posterior to the edge of the cara-

imported from their country of origin. Turtles should be examined for the presence of fresh wounds, abrasions or scute infections. The head plates also are a potential site for infection, and should be examined closely. Imported turtles may have old wounds, including (but not limited to) missing toes or the tip of the tail.

Locality data are usually unavailable from reptile importers, and this makes subspecies identification more difficult. If at all possible, try to ascertain the country of origin, as this information will help in determining the identity of the turtle. If your goal is to breed *P. megacephalum,* you should consider purchasing a number of turtles at the

Two *P. megacephalum* in the author's collection. These turtles, originally housed together, had to be separated, as the turtle on the left continually harassed the turtle on the right. (Note the healing wound on the rear leg of the right turtle.) At the time of this photograph, the two turtles had not seen each other for more than a month. The harassed turtle reacted immediately to the presence of the other, and would have bitten him if allowed. Note the size of the mouth and the length of the neck in big-headed turtles. Photo by David Kirkpatrick.

pace. However, these differences are rather slight, and you should examine a series of turtles to correctly identify the sexes, especially you are planning a breeding program.

SELECTION AND ACQUISITION

Big-headed turtles are relatively uncommon in captivity. Slavens' 1994 Inventory lists only 14 institutions and individuals possessing specimens. This figure undoubtedly is low, as many individual turtle keepers do not contribute to the inventory. *Platysternon megacephalum* is available occasionally from importers or secondary reptile dealers. Even more rarely they may be encountered in pet stores. Virtually all big-headed turtles offered for sale are

same time from the same shipment. Making multiple purchases will increase your chances of obtaining turtles from the same geographic region.

BEHAVIOR

Captive individuals appear to be fairly intelligent. They adapt quickly to feeding routines, for example. Specimens observed by the author generally demonstrate an interest in their surroundings. They even seem capable of recognizing the existence of glass walls, a capacity beyond that of many other semi-aquatic turtles.

In their natural environment, turtles spend the day underwater, burrowed into gravel deposits or hidden in crevices in the rocks. In the evening they emerge to search for food along the stream bottom and out of water along the sides of the stream.

Big-heads are not well-equipped for swimming; instead they are much more adept at walking and climbing. The rapid water flow in the streams they frequent makes the ability to cling to rocks more advantageous than skill in swimming.

The climbing ability of the big-headed turtle should not be underestimated. The bridge between their carapace and plastron is somewhat reduced, allowing the turtle a large range of motion with its feet. The heavy head of *P. megacephalum* places the turtle's center of gravity well forward compared to other turtles. This shift, coupled with the wide range of motion in its legs, allows the turtle to climb over anything it can reach with its claws. As noted previously, big-heads are capable of using their tail as a prop, greatly extending their reach. Reports indicate that they also use their beaks in climbing (Obst, 1988). Given all these adaptations, it is not surprising that big-headed turtles have been reported to climb trees and bushes. Their climbing ability is reminiscent of that of Pancake tortoises (*Malacochersus tornieri*), as are a number of the big-headed turtle's habits and some features of its anatomy.

HANDLING

Be careful when handling big-headed turtles. When threatened, their normal defensive reaction is to retract their legs and to move their heavily scaled tail under the rim of the carapace. They also drop their chin down, guarding the unprotected throat area and presenting the armored top of their head to the threat. However, they are capable of delivering a severe bite with their heavy jaws and hooked beak. Some individuals are quite apt to bite when provoked. However, a big-head's neck is only of moderate length, and so cannot reach as far as a snapping turtle (*Chelydra serpentina*), especially directly back over the carapace.

P. megacephalum's claws are sharp. This species also has powerful leg muscles befitting a rock-climbing turtle. *P. megacephalum* can deliver a scratch or launch itself from an unwary handler's grip, effectively attacking or escaping the handler.

HOUSING

Captive maintenance of *P. megacephalum* requires consideration of their normal ecological

A minimal aquarium setup for a single big-headed turtle. The turtle is in a hiding space under the suspended land area. A rock-encrusted ramp leads up to the dirt-filled section. A submersible filter provides filtration and movement of the water. The whole aquarium is screened to prevent escapes; this turtle is quite capable of escaping this tank if the screen is not present. Finally, a light on a 24-hour timer is provided, although the wattage has been increased specifically for the photograph. Photo by David Kirkpatrick.

Big-headed Turtle, *Platysternon megacephalum*. Photo by K. H. Switak.

niche and the adaptations they have made to that environment. As stream-dwellers, big-headed turtles should be maintained in an enclosure that allows access to both land and water. The water section cannot be too deep: big-headed turtles are ill-equipped for swimming and can drown in the wrong environment.

You must also consider their climbing abilities when designing the land area. If possible, screen the top of the enclosure to prevent escapes.

As the water area cannot be too deep, the total area of the cage should be as large as possible to give the turtles adequate room. Often you can accomplish this by building a multi-layered habitat. For example, you can design an aquarium with a suspended land section in the middle. This would permit the turtle to use the whole tank as a water area, yet still allow it access to a land area. Arrangements of this type allow the turtles to utilize all of the space in the container.

One more consideration about the land area is that it must be deep enough to allow sufficient space for the burial of eggs by females, if captive reproduction is possible or desired.

A minimum size for an enclosure containing a single big-headed turtle is 1' wide by 2' long by 1' high, if a screened top is used to prevent escapes and the land area is a suspended one as described above. If you are maintaining more than one turtle together, you must provide a larger area for the turtles.

Separate underwater hiding places must be provided for each turtle in a multiple-turtle habitat. Each turtle will select a spot in which to sleep during the day. You must also make provisions for housing turtles individually, as individual animals may be incompatible and require separation.

Platysternon megacephalum is crepuscular or nocturnal in habits, but you should still provide a light source for them. Also, attach the light source to a timer to provide a normal day/night cycle for the turtle. The light source does not need to be a heat source; in fact, do not allow the temperature in the enclosure to rise too high. Although *P. megacephalum* originates from tropical countries, it lives in water that ranges from 53 to 72 degrees F (12-23°C). If allowed to get too warm, the turtle can overheat.

FEEDING/WATER REQUIREMENTS

Big-headed turtles in their natural environment are almost entirely carnivorous. Their strong beaks and hard-edged jaws allow them to consume crustaceans and mollusks. These prey items form a large portion of *P. megacephalum*'s diet, although big-head turtles will feed on a number of other items. In captivity they will eat most meats, fishes, and insects with which they are presented. Also, big-heads can be trained to take commercial turtle foods such as Tetra's Reptomin®, Wardley's

ReptileTen®, and Purina Trout Chow®. Captive individuals are quite capable of capturing prey on land. However, they prefer to enter the water before consuming captured prey, and so should be fed in water.

WASTE MANAGEMENT

The accustomed habitat for *Platysternon megacephalum* is rushing mountain streams. In captivity, water cleanliness must be maintained for the health of the animal. For adequate water filtration, use a large canister filter. In addition to providing the maximum filtering capacity, large units also discharge the water with some force, mimicking a mountain stream.

Big-headed Turtle, *Platysternon megacephalum*. Photo by Zoltan Takacs.

Big-headed turtles benefit from having rocks on which to climb, however, these rocks often interfere with aquarium upkeep. Piles of rocks provide areas in the tank where dirt can accumulate. You should consider feeding the turtles outside of the tank in a secondary container to prevent uneaten food debris from collecting among the rocks in the aquarium. As turtles often will defecate after eating, external feeding also helps reduce the accumulation of fecal material in the aquarium rocks.

REPRODUCTION

The behavior of *P. megacephalum* in its natural environment, especially details concerning mating and reproduction, is almost totally unknown. Captive individuals in the author's collection have been observed mating. Apart from momentary nudging of the bridge and vent areas, courtship rituals were not apparent. Mating itself was a violent affair, similar to that reported for snapping turtles, with a great deal of agitated motion by both turtles. The male repeatedly attempted to bite the female on her large cranial scute presumably to subdue her. No eggs have as yet been laid, so it is unclear if the observed matings were successful.

In general, one or two white eggs are laid at a time. Unlike most turtle eggs, they are not spherical or lozenge-shaped. Instead, the eggs are ellipsoidal and resemble bird eggs. Eggs measure approximately 37 mm by 22 mm (Ernst and Barbour, 1989). Incubation times for the eggs have not been reported. Similarly, it is unclear if the sex of the hatchling turtle is determined by the incubation temperature, or if it is temperature-insensitive.

PREVENTIVE HEALTH CARE

Most specimens of *Platysternon megacephalum* will be imported, wild-caught individuals. Because of this, all newly acquired turtles should be examined for the presence of internal and external parasites. Treatments, if necessary, are dependent on the nature of the parasites detected; these treatments follow the usual protocols for semi-aquatic turtles. If you are inexperienced in dealing with chelonian parasites, you should insist on a veterinary examination. Regardless of the result of the examination, all new arrivals should be quarantined for at least a month to prevent the potentially lethal spread of disease to other turtles.

Turtles should be examined periodically for the presence of cuts, bites, or abrasions, especially if more than one individual is kept in a single enclosure. Minor wounds can be treated with topical antibiotic ointments or gels. Over-the-counter Polysporin® ointments can also work well on mild cuts.

Imported individuals may develop infections under the scutes, including the horny layers around the jaw and on top of the head. Routine monitoring will detect these infections before they become life-threatening.

Periodic supplementation of the turtle's food with vitamins and calcium may help prevent deficiencies due to undetected inadequacies in diet. Captive turtles in the author's collection are fond of calcium blocks made of plaster of Paris with added vitamin and calcium powder. The turtles use their powerful jaws to break the blocks apart and rapidly consume them. In addition to the benefits from the calcium and vitamins, the blocks also help keep a turtle's jaws worn down.

COMMON PROBLEMS

Platysternon megacephalum appears to be a relatively easy turtle to maintain in captivity, as long as the basic environment of the turtle is kept in mind. Most problems arise from a failure to provide an appropriate environment. For example, if the area is kept too warm, or the water quality and cleanliness are not adequate, the health of the turtle may suffer.

Another problematic area involves interactions between turtles. Although they have been reported to be unaggressive towards turtles kept in the same enclosure (Ernst and Barbour, 1989), fights have occurred between three juvenile big-heads maintained by the author. The level of aggression necessitated separation of the three into individual aquaria. The powerful jaws of *P. megacephalum* make any fight potentially injurious to the animals involved. Careful monitoring of specimens will prevent most difficulties.

REFERENCES AND RECOMMENDED READING

—**Ernst, CH; Barbour, RW:**
Turtles of the World. Smithsonian Institution Press, Washington, DC, 1989, 313pp.

—**Ernst, CH; McCord, WP:**
Two new turtles from southeast Asia. *Proc. Biol. Soc. Wash.*, 1987; 100(3): 624-628.

—**Haiduk, MW; Bickman, JW:**
Chromosomal homologies and evolution of testudinoid turtles with emphasis on the systematic placement of *Platysternon. Copeia*, 1982(1): 60-66.

—**Gaffney, ES:**
Phylogeny of the chelydrid turtles: a study of shared derived characters in the skull. *Fieldiana:Geol.* 1975; 33(9): 157-178.

—**Iverson, JB:**
A Revised Checklist with Distribution Maps of the Turtles of the World. 1992, Privately printed, Richmond, IN, 363pp.

—**Obst, FJ:**
Turtles, Tortoises and Terrapins. St. Martin's Press, New York, NY, 1988, 231pp.

—**Pritchard, PCH:**
Encyclopedia of Turtles. T.F.H. Publications, Neptune City, NJ, 1979, 895pp.

—**Pritchard, PCH:**
The Alligator Snapping Turtle: Biology and Conservation. Milwaukee Public Museum, Milwaukee, WI, 1989.

—**Slavens, FL; Slavens, K:**
Reptiles and Amphibians in Captivity: Breeding, Longevity and Inventory. 1994, Slaveware, Seattle, WA, 534pp.

—**Snider, AT; Bowler, JK:**
Longevity of Reptiles and Amphibians in North American Collections. 1992, Herpetological Circular No. 21, series editor: Collins, JT; Society for the Study of Amphibians and Reptiles, 40pp.

MUD AND MUSK TURTLE (KINOSTERNIDAE)

David T. Kirkpatrick, Ph. D.
Department of Biology
UNC, Chapel Hill, Coker Hall, CB 3280
Chapel Hill, NC 27599-3280

David T. Kirkpatrick received his Bachelor of Science degree in biology from Carnegie-Mellon University in Pittsburgh, and his Doctorate in molecular genetics from MIT in Boston. Currently, he is a postdoctoral researcher at the University of North Carolina at Chapel Hill, where he works on the molecular basis for the initiation of recombination in meiosis. While in graduate school, he was Secretary of the New England Herpetological Society. Other reptile-related activities included organizing and teaching a short course on herpetoculture at MIT, and participating in a program to help the recovery of the Federally-protected Plymouth Red-belly turtle. He is the author of over a dozen articles on turtle species, focusing primarily on their husbandry and natural history. He and his wife Catherine maintain a moderate collection of turtles, focusing on captive reproduction of less-common Asian, North American, and Central American semi-aquatic turtles.

Striped Mud Turtle, *Kinosternon bauri*. Photo by R. D. Bartlett.

BASIC TAXONOMY

THE FAMILY KINOSTERNIDAE

The family Kinosternidae is a moderately sized family of chelonians. There are two subfamilies: the Staurotypinae and the Kinosterninae. Each subfamily has two genera. The genera of the Staurotypinae, which consists of *Claudius* and *Staurotypus*, are endemic to central Mexico and range south into northern Central America. The Kinosterninae genera consist of *Kinosternon* and *Sternotherus*. These chelonians range more widely, occurring from southern Canada through much of South America.

THE SUBFAMILY STAUROTYPINAE

The turtles in the subfamily Staurotypinae are all moderately large musk turtles. All three types

An adult male Common musk turtle (*Sternotherus odoratus*) from Massachusetts. This individual has a lightly colored carapace and thin but vivid head markings. Photo by David Kirkpatrick.

of turtles have three keels which run the length of the carapace. Their plastron is small and narrow, cruciform in shape, with seven or eight scutes. Some researchers regard the Staurotypinae as distinct enough from the Kinosterninae to warrant elevation to full family status, as the family Staurotypidae (Bickham et al., 1983). They base this elevation on chromosomal variations. However, a number of other studies on morphological variation within the Kinosternidae support the current system.

The genus *Claudius* contains only one turtle, *Claudius angustatus*. The plastron of the Narrow-bridged Musk Turtle has seven bones, unlike any other turtle. Another unique feature of *C. angustatus* is the presence of two cusps on the turtle's upper jaw.

Two species, *Staurotypus salvinii* and *Staurotypus triporcatus*, make up the genus *Staurotypus*. These turtles are the largest in the family. *S. salvinii* (the Pacific Coast Giant Musk Turtle) can reach a length of 25 cm. *S. triporcatus* (the Mexican Giant Musk Turtle) grows to almost 40 cm. Both turtles can be distinguished from any other member of the Kinosternidae by their size.

THE SUBFAMILY KINOSTERNINAE

The subfamily Kinosterninae is a much larger and more varied group than the Staurotypinae. Turtles in the Kinosterninae subfamily can be distinguished from Staurotypinae chelonians by the number of plastral scutes. Turtles in the Kinosterninae have ten or eleven scutes, compared to the seven or eight in Staurotypinae. Another diagnostic feature of the subfamily is the absence of the entoplastral bone present in the Staurotypinae, although this characteristic is less useful when comparing living turtles.

Two genera are present in the subfamily. One genus is *Kinosternon* (mud turtles), which has at least fifteen species and a number of subspecies. The other genus is *Sternotherus* (musk turtles), with four species, one of which has two subspecies. Musk turtles are native to the United States, with one species (*S. odoratus*) ranging up into Canada. Mud turtles are more widely dispersed, with species found from Connecticut (*K. subrubrum*) south through the southern and central portions of the United States, through Mexico and Central America, and entering South America as far as northern Argentina (*K. scorpioides*).

In recent years there has been a large amount of scientific debate over the degree of separation within the Kinosterninae. Some researchers believe that the two genera should be combined into one genus, *Kinosternon*. Others favor maintaining

Yellow Mud Turtle, *Kinosternon flavescens*. Photo by K. H. Switak.

the split. The most recent controversy arose in 1986 when Seidel et al. published a report on a detailed comparison of the variation in 13 protein complexes in 18 species within the family Kinosternidae. The variation among the 13 proteins was not great, and analysis of the data supported many of the conclusions of other researchers based on morphological data (such as Bramble et al., 1984) and karyotyping (Sites et al., 1979). However, based on their data, Seidel et al. argued that two members of *Kinosternon*, *K. baurii* and *K. subrubrum*, were more similar to members of *Sternotherus* than to species of *Kinosternon* located in Central and South America. Sites et al. had noted a similar result based solely on karyotypes of the various species, but did not suggest any revisions in taxonomy. Based on this relationship, Seidel et al. relegated *Sternotherus* to subgeneric status (i.e. *Sternotherus odoratus* becomes *Kinosternon odoratum*, etc.).

A few years later, John Iverson published a work using a very large data set of variable morphological features (Iverson, 1991) to resolve phylogenies within *Kinosternon* and the possibly suspect *Sternotherus*. As he could find no unique character diagnostic for *Sternotherus* turtles, Iverson followed the taxonomy suggested by Seidel et al. Some authors also adopted the revised *Kinosternon* genus;

others have remained unconvinced. In Ernst and Barbour's 1989 edition of Turtles of the World, they included *Sternotherus* in *Kinosternon*. However, with the publication of the 1994 volume *Turtles of the United States and Canada*, Ernst, Lovich and Barbour question the split, wondering "why not relegate *K. baurii* and *K. subrubrum* to the genus *Sternotherus*, rather than the four *Sternotherus* species to *Kinosternon*?" (pg 138). Currently, the status of *Sternotherus* has not yet been resolved.

HABITAT

Habitat for mud and musk turtles varies depending on the species, but in general, they prefer slow-moving or still bodies of water. Preferred locations often have soft-bodied beds (which consist of sand or mud) and support a large amount of aquatic vegetation. Utilization of specific habitats can be the result of a complex interaction of factors, even among turtles within a particular species or subspecies. Intrinsic properties of the location (including type of substrate, presence of vegetation, and water flow) interact with other factors, such as abundance of local predators, alteration in the habitat (either naturally or by human intervention), and variable local climatic conditions. Some research has been done to evaluate the relative importance of these factors (see, for example, Webster, 1986, Christiansen et al., 1989, and Stone et al. 1993).

Basking sites are not essential, but some species will take advantage of spots if they are available. *Sternotherus odoratus* has been reported to climb trees. This turtle edges out on branches meters above the water, and drops into the water below when disturbed. The loggerhead musk turtle, *S. m. minor*, shows similar tendencies (Pritchard, 1979). Some species, especially those located in drier regions, inhabit temporary bodies of water. In the dry season the turtles will estivate in the dried mud, waiting for rainfall to replenish the water supply.

PHYSICAL CHARACTERISTICS

The three turtles in the Staurotypinae subfamily (*S. salvinii*, *S. triporcatus* and *C. angustatus*) are distinguished by their size (in *Staurotypus*), their aggressive disposition, and the presence of three keels running the length of the carapace. *C. angustatus* also has two distinct cusps on its upper jaws that help identify it. *S. salvinii* can be distinguished from *S. triporcatus* by its smaller size and also by its wider and more flattened carapace.

Four species of *Sternotherus* are recognized. *Sternotherus carinatus*, the Razor-backed musk turtle, deserves its name. This turtle has a very sharply sloping carapace; when viewed from the front, the turtle appears to be triangular. The plastron only has ten scutes, unlike the rest of the species of *Sternotherus* and *Kinosternon*. The Flattened musk turtle, *S. depressus*, also is aptly named. Its carapace is very flattened and wide. It has been considered a subspecies of *S. minor* in the past. The Loggerhead musk turtle, *S. m. minor*, has a carapacial shape that is intermediate between *S. depressus* and *S. carinatus*. Like the rest of the genus, *S. minor* species have a single weak hinge between the abdominal and pectoral scutes of the plastron. *S. minor peltifer* differs from the Loggerhead musk by the presence of strong stripes on its neck. The most commonly known musk turtle, *S. odoratus*, the Common musk turtle, or Stinkpot as it is occasionally called, has a small plastron and two distinctive stripes on each side of the face which run back from the snout and go to either side of the eyes.

Five species of *Kinosternon* are found in the United States. Possibly the most easily recognized is *K. baurii*. This chelonian is small, even for mud turtles, and has three light stripes running the length of the carapace. As with all mud turtles, it has two strong plastral hinges. Overlapping geographically with the Striped mud turtle is the Common mud turtle, *K. subrubrum*. This turtle is also

Plastral views of a male and female mud turtle. The male is on the left. Notice the heavier, longer tail, with a terminal tip, as compared to the female turtle's tail. Also evident in this photograph are the hinges on the plastron at either side of bridge. Photo by David Kirkpatrick.

Two different turtles from the same clutch of eggs. The eggs were laid by a wild-caught female in a pet store and given to the author for incubation. Both turtles have carapacial stripes reminiscent of *Kinosternon baurii*, but the facial markings are quite different. These animals may represent an intergrade or hybrid. Photos by David Kirkpatrick.

small, but lacks the carapacial striping. It is rather nondescript, with only occasional markings on some specimens; the markings are usually in the form of yellow mottling or faint stripes on the head, especially in *K. s. hippocrepis*. This subspecies is sometimes confused with *K. baurii*, which it greatly resembles except for the carapacial striping. Further west, one encounters the Yellow mud turtle, *K. flavescens*. The carapace is a drab olive or brown, while the skin is yellow, ranging to grey. Two other species just enter the United States: *K. hirtipes* and *K. sonoriense*. The Sonoran mud turtle is a medium-sized mud turtle, somewhat elongated, with an olive-brown carapace and grey skin with darker mottlings. Only one subspecies of the Mexican mud turtle, *K. hirtipes murrayi*, enters the United States, down in Texas. This species has three carapacial keels, while the skin is dark with a fine reticulated pattern on the head.

The majority of mud turtles are located in Mexico, Central and South America. A number of these, including *K. herrerai, K. angustipons, K. dunni,* and *K. creaseri*, have only been cursorily described, especially with regards to the details of their natural history. Other species may also exist; Iverson (1992) indicates that *K. integrum* actually harbors a second, undescribed species.

Some of the more distinguished species of mud turtles are *K. leucostomum*, the White-lipped mud turtle, and *K. scorpioides*, the Scorpion mud turtle. The White-lipped mud turtle has a dark carapace, with a yellow plastron. Befitting its name, the edges of the jaws are cream, sometimes interrupted by dark smudges. The Scorpion mud turtle group (there are six recognized subspecies) contains the Red-cheeked mud turtle, *K. s. cruentatum*. Individuals of this species are moderately large, with carapaces bearing three keels. The carapace itself is yellowish and the plastron shades into an orange cast. Most strikingly, the sides of the turtle's head can be red or orange, giving the turtle its common name.

To the untrained eye, many of the mud and musk turtle species appear very similar. This similarity is complicated by the presence in wild populations of individuals that are intergrades or hybrids between differing populations and species. Without a positive identification, obtaining information on a specific turtle can be almost impossible. Fortunately, two keys have been published in the last few years that are of enormous utility in distinguishing the species of *Kinosternon* (and *Sternotherus*, although both keys place *Sternotherus* in *Kinosternon*). The first key is in Ernst and Barbour's *Turtles of the World* (page 73). The second key is in John Iverson's *A Revised Checklist with Distribution Maps of Turtles of the World* (pages 214-215).

A Common Musk turtle (*S. odoratus*) with a thick coating of algae. Wild-caught individuals are often colonized by algae. It can be allowed to remain, but may spread to start growing in the enclosure, and will make detection of shell injuries and infections much more difficult. Photograph by Tom Spadaro.

SEXING

In the genus *Staurotypus*, the males have longer, thicker tails than the females, and also possess rough scales called vinculae on their thighs (Ernst et al., 1989, Platt, 1993). Males of *Claudius angustatus* have similar differences, and also have a horny tip on their tails (Ernst et al., 1989, Platt, in press). *Staurotypus* turtles have heteromorphic sex chromosomes: males are XY, while females are XX. However, unlike other species with similar arrangements, the X chromosome is more evolutionarily derived than the Y chromosome, and so the XY male is an intermediate between the ancestral form and the more divergent XX female (Sites et al., 1979).

In the subfamily Kinosterninae the males of all species possess a longer, thicker tail than the females (Ernst et al., 1989. Many also have vinculae and horny tips on their tails. However, some species lack these tips, or both females and males possess them (for example: *K. flavescens, K. herrarai,* and *K. oaxacae*). In a number of species (*K. dunni, K. alamosae, K. hirtipes, K. integrum,* and *K. leucostomum*) the male turtle is larger than the female. However, in *K. acutum, K. angustipons* and *K. sonoriense*, females are larger than males. Some species have other sexually dimorphic characteristics. For example, the male Narrow-bridged mud turtle (*K. angustipons*) has an enlarged snout. Finally, in a few species, the plastron of the male has a slight concavity.

REPRODUCTION

Very little has been published on the reproduction of either *Staurotypus* or *Claudius*. Details of mating behavior in the wild are undescribed. Elke

Eastern Mud Turtle, *Kinosternon subrubrum.* **Albino specimen. Photo by R. D. Bartlett.**

Zimmermann, in her book *Breeding Terrarium Animals* (Zimmermann, 1986) gives a detailed description of mating observed in captive *Staurotypus salvinii*. Many of the motions are similar to those exhibited by *Kinosternon* and *Sternotherus* turtles. From observation of captive breeding at the Columbus Zoo, it appears that male-to-male combat helps ensure fertilization (Platt, 1993).

In *Staurotypus triporcatus*, an average clutch size is nine eggs, with more than one clutch possible in a season. As might be expected from the presence of sex chromosomes in *Staurotypus,* these turtles do not seem to exhibit temperature-dependent sex determination, or TSD. (However, refer to Ewert et al., 1991, for some potential complications.) *Claudius angustatus* also exhibits no TSD (Vogt et al., 1992). This species probably lays multiple clutches during the year, although the number of eggs deposited is lower (Flores-Villela et al., 1995).

Eggs are deposited in nests in mats of vegetation, rather than being buried. Although incubation times in the wild are unknown, captive incubation is variable but long, ranging from 95 to 229 days (Flores-Villela et al., 1995). *Staurotypus* eggs will hatch after 145 days at 25 - 30 degrees C. *Claudius* eggs only take approximately 90 days (Zimmermann, 1986).

Courting and mating has been described in detail for a number of species in the subfamily Kinosterninae, especially the North American forms. For details on courting and mating, refer to Ernst et al., 1994 and references therein, and also refer to Mahmoud, 1967 and Bels et al., 1994. In general, kinosternids do not have an elaborate courtship procedure, although there are a number of variations dependent on species. Typical events include a phase where the male follows the female, sniffing at her cloaca and sometimes the bridge between the carapace and plastron. This is occasionally accompanied by a head-to-head confrontation or nudging by the male. If the female moves away, the male will give chase, repeating the sniffing and nudging until the female remains stationary. The male then mounts the female from the side or rear, using all four feet to grasp the shell. When actual copulation takes place, the male may move backward or up at an angle to the female's carapace. These motions can depend on the relative size of the individual turtles and on the specific species involved, since tail length and location of the vents may contribute to positioning.

Egg deposition varies between the species and even among individuals within a particular species. Some choose to bury their eggs, while others deposit them under vegetation or in other enclosed areas. Most species of mud or musk turtles lay multiple clutches of eggs during a single season, with a relatively low number of eggs deposited each time (from one to five, on average). Incubation times are dependent on local conditions and the exact species, but eggs seem to take from three to five months to hatch.

Mud and musk turtles exhibit TSD. Eggs incubated at an intermediate temperature range generate predominantly males; while females are produced at temperatures above or below this temperature interval (Ewert et al., 1991). For artificial incubation, incubate eggs in damp medium (both sphagnum moss or a dirt/vermiculite mixture hold water well, for example) at temperatures ranging from 25 - 30° C. In *Sternotherus odoratus*, for example, almost all eggs incubated at 25° C result in male turtles; while almost all eggs incubated at 30° C result in females (Ewert et al., 1991). Incubation times range from three months to over six months, depending on the temperature and the species of turtle (Zimmermann, 1986).

GROWTH AND DEVELOPMENT

Hatchlings of some of the smaller mud turtle species are among the smallest in the world (see Figure 7A and B). For example, hatchling *S. odoratus* are only approximately 20 mm in length, while hatchling *K. baurii* can be as small as 16.5 mm (Ernst et al., 1994). The size of the hatchlings is dependent on the size of the eggs, which in turn is dependent on the size of the female laying the eggs.

Although mud and musk turtle hatchlings resemble their adult counterparts, some differences are demonstrable. In particular, some species have more dramatic markings as hatchlings. The Loggerhead musk turtle (*S. m. minor*) has a pinkish plastron, while the other subspecies, *S. m. peltifer*, has a yellow-orange cast to the plastron and a striped neck. The head stripes on hatchling *S. odoratus* are very noticeable, also. Intriguingly, Britson and Gutzke speculate that these colorations may be warning signs to predatory fish. In experiments with largemouth bass, fish initially

An overview of a Common musk turtle *(Sternotherus odoratus)*, **gives a dramatic demonstration of the size of these hatchlings. Photograph by Tom Spadaro.**

Mexican Giant Musk Turtle, *Staurotypus triporcatus*. Photo by Jim Merli.

attempted to eat hatchling turtles, but quickly learned to reject them. Apparently the violent motions of the ingested hatchlings were harmful to the gills or digestive tract of the fish (Britson et al., 1993).

Growth rates of hatchlings and juveniles are dependent on local conditions, including the available amount of food, the length of the year (based on climate) available for feeding, and other variables. It may take up to a decade for some individuals to reach breeding size, especially in regions where activity is limited by adverse conditions. However, mud and musk turtles can live to an advanced age. Ages in excess of two decades are not uncommon, and one *S. odoratus* lived over 54 years at the Philadelphia Zoo.

BEHAVIOR

Staurotypus, *Claudius*, and a number of the species of *Kinosternon* and *Sternotherus* are nocturnal or crepuscular in habit. This tendency may make it harder to observe behaviors in captivity. However, some species, such as *K. flavescens*, are primarily diurnal.

Activity patterns may also change over the course of the year, depending on environmental conditions. Turtles from the northern part of the family's range usually hibernate for a portion of the year. In contrast, turtles in hot, dry regions may estivate during the hottest portion of the year, especially if the local water sources dry up. Although kinosternids usually are considered to be chiefly aquatic in nature, some species spend a reasonable amount of time out of water. For example, *S. carinatus* is active in the afternoon and can be found basking (Ernst et al., 1994). *K. subrubrum* and *K. baurii* are often found moving around on land.

In temperment many of the kinosternids are generally shy and retiring turtles. Exceptions to this are *S. triporcatus* and *S. salvinii*. *C. angustatus* has also been known to be aggressive (Platt, in press) when handled. Newly caught individuals of other species may also bite: Pritchard reports a particularly painful bite from the Florida mud turtle, *K. subrubrum steindachneri* (Pritchard, 1979).

Detailed life histories for a number of members of the family Kinosternidae have been published. If you intend to keep any of these chelonians, these publications are invaluable starting point. Careful attention to the data given therein will greatly improve the husbandry of your turtles. A number of these publications are listed in the references section.

SELECTION AND ACQUISITION

Selection of mud and musk turtles will depend on one of the three purposes for which the turtle has been acquired: as a pet, for short-term observation in captivity, or for long-term maintenance to investigate details of the turtle's lifestyle, including breeding. If the turtle is to be a pet, try to locate a breeder of mud and musk turtles. Breeders do exist, and more herpetoculturists are working with kinosternids each year. Captive-born chelonians are the most likely to be disease-free and to acclimate to captive maintenance with a minimum of problems. If you cannot locate captive-born turtles, purchase a turtle from the local area, or at least within the United States. Much more is known concerning the natural history of North

455

American kinosternids than of the Central and South American forms. Knowing the natural history of the animal makes it easier to design an appropriate enclosure and provide an adequate diet.

A few things should be mentioned when keeping mud or musk turtles to observe details of the turtle's life cycle for a short term, as this generally involves collecting local specimens. First, try not to stress them, as even short captive periods can conceivably cause a potentially fatal buildup of internal parasites. Second, don't mix specimens from different locales. This increases the chance of disease spread, and it might also mix up differing genetic pools. Finally, do not release a turtle if it appears to be suffering from an illness acquired in captivity.

For long-term studies or breeding purposes, try to acquire turtles from the same area, to lessen the chances of accidentally mixing up unknown subspecies. If the turtles are imported, get as much data as possible from the importer (if you are not acquiring the animals yourself). Specific collection sites, habitat at the collection site, and similar data can be invaluable in setting up an appropriate captive environment. If possible, check the health of the turtles before purchase. Examine them for injuries, overall appearance, and sex. After acquisition, examine all animals, whether captive-born, locally collected, or imported, for parasites (both internal and external) and quarantine the turtles appropriately before housing them with other animals.

HANDLING

Mud and musk turtles are easy turtles to handle, in general. Newly captured or extremely stressed musk turtles will exude a yellowish compound from glands under the rim of their shell. This liquid has a rather pungent odor, thus the common name for the group (although all kinosternids possess the glands). Captive individuals usually lose this habit quickly. Even newly-hatched turtles are ca-

A twenty gallon aquarium designed to hold a pair of Striped mud turtles *(K. baurii)*. This setup includes a land area, a basking rock (rarely used), an underwater heater, and an in-tank filter. Photo by David Kirkpatrick.

pable of producing musk and will do so readily if disturbed. Some of the larger species in the family Kinosternidae are capable of delivering a strong bite, and should be handled with care. In particular, the two species of *Staurotypus* are known for their tendency to bite, in addition to a rather fierce temper that does not diminish with length of time in captivity. For these reasons, handling of these two turtles in particular should be kept to a minimum.

HOUSING

Mud and musk turtles can be maintained in captivity if care is taken to address their environmental needs. Depending on the species of kinosternid and the local environment, outdoor maintenance can be considered for part or all of the year. Outdoor maintenance has the advantage of giving the turtle a more natural environment, but often does not allow the keeper to closely observe the turtle, for signs of illness for example.

Animals kept outside will require a water area and a land area. The areas should be enclosed by a fence, and the fence should be constructed so that the turtles cannot get through or under it. As mud and musk turtles are occasionally preyed upon by large birds or climbing animals such as raccoons, it might be necessary to cover the whole enclosure to prevent loss of turtles.

Indoor maintenance most likely will be the norm. As the majority of the kinosternids are relatively small animals, suitable environments can be created with commonly-available aquariums. Smaller mud turtles, such as *K. baurii* or *K. subrubrum*, will do well in a 20- or 30-gallon aquarium; the larger species require more spacious accomodations. The Giant Musk Turtles can grow large enough to require specially constructed enclosures. Although generally considered to be mainly aquatic in nature, many of the mud and musk turtles will roam on land, and will benefit from the presence of a land section in their enclosure. An area of sandy dirt of sufficient depth to permit egg deposition is a necessity if breeding is planned or might occur. Land areas can be constructed in aquariums by walling off a section of the tank with silicone aquarium sealant and appropriately sized pieces of glass or plastic.

A thirty gallon aquarium with a suspended land area. This tank holds four juvenile Common musk turtles (*S. odoratus*). Photo by David Kirkpatrick.

As in the previous figure, this tank has a heater, a filter, a basking area, and an overhead light. Photo by David Kirkpatrick.

A more economical use of the space is to make a suspended 'island' in the tank with three pieces of plastic: two positioned vertically and one running horizontally, parallel to the tank bottom but suspended a few inches above it. Access to the land area can be provided by conveniently placed rocks, wooden cork floats, or ramps constructed of plastic. Depending on the setup, the land area can be made accessible from both sides, but animals can still pass underneath it. If the land 'island' is placed at one end of the tank, an underwater 'cave' is created. Many kinosternids take advantage of naturally occurring underwater shelters created by rocks or tree roots, and will use the artificially created cave in a similar manner.

Tank decorations can range from minimal to elaborate, depending on the desires of the turtle-keeper. However, you should keep in mind the natural environment of the species. If one of the goals is to observe natural behaviors of the turtle, a setup that duplicates the native habitat as closely as possible might be necessary. At the other extreme, a minimalistic setup might be used for its ease of maintenance. Depending on the species, the bottom substrate could consist of sand, gravel, or a layer of silt, or be left bare. You can provide piles of rocks, wooden logs, or cork-bark floats. Broken clay pots often make suitable underwater caves.

Tank decorations will increase the maintenance required to keep the water clean, as they provide inaccessible areas where dirt can accumulate. They must also be arranged carefully; if a turtle becomes trapped underwater by poorly designed cage decorations the turtle can drown before its plight is noticed. Plants, both aquatic and terrestrial, may need to be replaced periodically if provided, as they may become sources of food for the turtles. Finally, most, if not all, of the mud and musk turtles are active foragers, and will dig up or otherwise disturb aquarium decorations or plants while hunting for food.

Filtration of the water is a necessity for most aquatic turtle setups. In general, the larger the filtering unit, the easier it will be to achieve and maintain water cleanliness. Canister filters, either submerged or placed outside the tank, generally work well. Undergravel filters may be overloaded by waste material, especially in smaller aquariums. Make sure you consider the rate of water exchange when constructing the enclosure. Some species of kinosternid chelonians prefer still or slow-moving water, and may suffer if placed in a setup with a high volume of water flow.

The temperature of the water will depend once again on the exact species of mud turtle. Those from the northern part of the family's range, such as *S. odoratus* or *K. subrubrum*, may not require

Loggerhead Musk Turtle, *Sternotherus minor*. Photo by R. D. Bartlett.

much heating and might benefit from a cooling off or hibernation period in the winter, while those from the southern part of the range may require supplemental heating all year. Submersible heaters that can be set to maintain a desired temperature work well in mud and musk turtle enclosures. Be careful to ensure that the heater is protected from accidental breakage, but is not blocked off to such a degree that water flow around the heater is impaired. You must also consider the rooting and digging tendencies of most mud and musk turtles before placing a heater in the enclosure.

Lighting will depend on the type of mud or musk turtle being maintained. Many of the kinosternids are nocturnal or crepuscular. Of those that are not, many do not bask and so will not use basking lamps very often. For similar reasons, the use of full-spectrum bulbs may not be required. However, if any plants are kept in the enclosure, they will benefit from the full-spectrum lighting, and it certainly won't hurt the turtle if such lighting is provided.

The turtle will still require a normal day/night cycle. Because of this, you should use lights with a cycle keyed to either the outside environment (especially if the turtle is kept in a room with windows) or to the day length in their native environment. The amount of seasonal variation in day length is also dependent on the specific species of turtle being kept.

FEEDING

Kinosternids are opportunistic omnivores or carnivores. They will eat many different types of food, depending on what is available in the local environment. The members of the subfamily Staurotypinae are almost entirely carnivorous. Staurotypinae feed on aquatic insects, snails, clams, fish, worms, crustaceans, and possibly amphibians (in *Claudius*) and other turtles (in *Staurotypus*). It has been speculated that the upper jaw cusps in *C. angustatus* may be used to grasp soft-bodied prey, such as frogs (Platt, 1995). Platt (1993) reported that captive *S. triporcatus* take fruit in captivity.

Food items in the subfamily Kinosterninae vary depending on the local environment and the species. If other turtles are present, competition for food items may alter what the turtles will consume. For example, studies in Belize with *K. leucostomum*, *K. scorpioides*, *S. triporcatus*, and *Trachemys scripta*, showed that diets altered as relative densities of turtles changed (Vogt et al., 1988 and Moll, 1990). Many of the items listed for *Staurotypus* and *Claudius* are consumed by *Kinosternon* and *Sternotherus* species, and some will also eat aquatic vegetation of various types.

In captivity, kinosternids will eat many of the items that they eat in their natural habitats. Various insects, earthworms, and fish are all readily consumed. For those species that are omnivorous, vegetable matter should be offered on a routine basis. Commercial turtle foods and trout chows will be accepted by most kinosternids, although it may take a period of acclimation. Turtles should not be allowed to become fixated on any particular food; items should be varied to provide a complete diet.

Periodic supplementation with vitamins and calcium may help prevent deficiencies due to undetected inadequacies in diet. Captive turtles in the author's collection are fond of calcium blocks made of plaster of paris with added vitamin and calcium powder. In addition to the benefits from the calcium and vitamins, the blocks also help keep a turtle's jaws worn down.

A final note of caution: some of the more aggressive species have been known to bite at cagemates during feeding, sometimes leading to loss of limbs (see for example the report on *K. scorpioides* in Pritchard et al., 1984).

WASTE MANAGEMENT

Most waste material can be eliminated or greatly reduced by feeding the turtles outside of their enclosure. To do this, simply fill a plastic container (cat litter trays work well, for example) with water, place the food into it, and then put in the turtle. After the turtle has consumed all the food it is interested in eating, replace the turtle in its enclosure and dispose of the dirty water. In addition to the elimination of food debris, this method also helps reduce fecal material in the aquarium, as many chelonians will defecate just prior to or immediately after feeding. An added benefit of exterior feeding is that it allows you to monitor the food intake of each turtle, and at the same time keep a check on the relative health of the chelonians. Note that, even if you feed the animals outside the main aquarium, you will still need to use filters to reduce the amount of waste material in the captive environment (see above).

PREVENTATIVE HEALTH CARE

Newly arrived individuals must be quarantined, even if they were captive-born and raised. A month of quarantine is recommended; longer is always better. Without quarantine, whole collections can be wiped out through the introduction of a novel disease or parasite to which the older chelonians have no resistance. New turtles should also be examined for the presence of internal and external parasites. Mud and musk

Yellow Mud Turtle, *Kinosternon flavescens*. Photo by Dr. Herbert R. Axelrod.

turtles are capable of harboring a wide range of parasites, including leeches, roundworms, tapeworms, and protozoans. Some turtles will also be covered with algae. Ernst and Barbour, in their 1972 book Turtles of the United States, give a list of parasites that have been identified as infecting various turtle species, including the North American mud and musk turtles. Also refer to the chapter on Reptile Rehabilitation for information about parasites. Treatment for any detected parasites will vary depending on the level of infection and the organism responsible. Veterinary aid should be sought if you are unfamiliar with parasite detection and elimination.

Once a turtle has been established in captivity, health care falls into three major categories:
—prevention of incidental infections
—treatment of injuries,
—dietary considerations

Incidental infections such as respiratory illnesses, scute infections, or parasite infestations can be controlled or eliminated by careful monitoring of the animals and their environment. This includes cleaning the aquarium at regular intervals, water changes, and quarantine for any new or ill turtles.

Injuries can occur because of improper cage design (sharp rocks, for example) or through aggressive interactions with other turtles. If one turtle consistently harasses other cagemates, provide a separate enclosure for that animal. Frequent examinations of the turtles for injuries, and prompt attention to any injuries discovered, will prevent minor cuts and abrasions from becoming infected. You can clean wounds with diluted iodine or betadine or a mixture of both. Topical Polysporin ointments also work well on minor injuries and have the advantage of being relatively water-insoluble. Refer to the reptile rehabilitation chapter for specific information on treating wounds and attending to the underlying causes of wounds.

The final major source of illness in turtles in captivity is an incomplete or inappropriate diet.

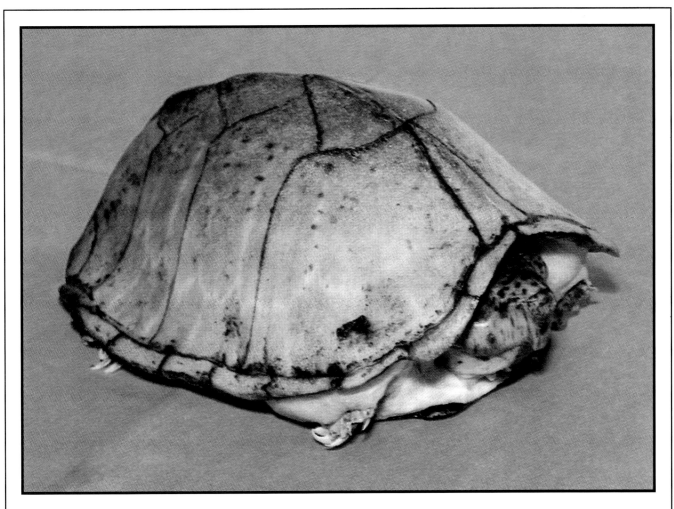

Razorback Musk Turtle, *Sternotherus carinatus*. Photo by W. P. Mara.

Do not allow a turtle to become fixated on one food item; instead, make sure you offer a variety of foods to the animal. For example, even turtles who are carnivorous will occasionally take some plant matter. It is also helpful to periodically supplement the animal's diet with vitamins and calcium, usually in the form of a powder sprinkled on food or a liquid injected into a favorite prey item.

Female turtles that are being bred or who are known to have mated require special care. They should receive a well-rounded diet, with increased supplementation of calcium. Also, carefully note changes in behavior. For example, if the enclosure is unsuitable for nest construction or incubation, the female may retain her eggs rather than lay them in an area with which she is not satisfied. Retained eggs can lead to health complications, especially if an egg ruptures or becomes over-calcified. Changes in behavior, such as loss of appetite or restlessness, in females known to be carrying eggs should serve as a warning signal to keepers.

COMMON PROBLEMS

Problems with kinosternid turtles can usually be grouped into two categories:

1. problems endemic to wild-caught turtles
2. problems related to incorrect husbandry.

As virtually all specimens encountered will be wild-caught individuals, the usual problems associated with free-living animals will be evident. Always check all turtles for parasites, both internal and external. Ticks are not often encountered, given the aquatic lifestyle of most of the species in the Kinosternidae family. However, leeches are occasionally found on freshly-caught individuals (see, for example, Ernst, 1986). Internal parasites can also cause problems in freshly caught individuals. Turtles can be infected with nematodes, trematodes, and protozoans. For a detailed list of species of parasitic species found on mud turtles in the United States, see Ernst and Barbour's Turtles of the United States (1972).

The stress and debilitating conditions suffered by chelonians during capture and transit can lead to a potentially fatal buildup in internal parasites, especially if the turtles have been grossly mishandled. All new arrivals should be examined and treated as appropriate, especially if high levels of parasites are detected. These problems can be alleviated or eliminated by obtaining captive-born individuals when possible.

Lack of knowledge on basic natural history for many of the kinosternid species from Mexico, Central and South America can lead to problems. Careful experimentation with husbandry may be necessary if information on dietary and habitat preferences is unavailable. Unfortunately, inadequacies in husbandry may take months or years to become apparent, and without careful observation may go unrecognized until too late.

RECOMMENDED READING

CLAUDIUS
—**Flores-Villela, OA; Zug, GR:**
Reproductive biology of the chopontil, *Claudius angustatus* (Testudines: Kinosternidae), in southern Veracruz, Mexico. *Chelonian Conservation and Biology*, 1995; 1(3): 181-186.
—**Platt, SG:**
The Narrow-bridged Mud Turtle (*Claudius angustatus*). *Reptile & Amphibian Magazine*, in press.

STAUROTYPUS:
—**Platt, SG:**
The Natural History of the Mexican Giant Musk Turtle *(Staurotypus triporcatus)* in Belize. *The Vivarium*, 1993; 5(2): 26-27, 35.
—**Sites, JW, Jr.; et al.:**
Derived X Chromosome in the Turtle Genus *Staurotypus. Science*, 1979; 206: 1410-1412.

KINOSTERNON
—**Iverson, JB:**
Notes on the Natural History of the Oaxaca Mud Turtle, *Kinosternon oaxacae. Journal of Herpetology*, 1986; 20(1): 119-123.
—**Iverson, JB:**
Life History and Demography of the Yellow Mud Turtle, *Kinosternon flavescens. Herpetologica*, 1991; 47(4): 373-395.
—**Iverson, JB;**
et al.: Growth and Reproduction in the Mud Turtle *Kinosternon hirtipes* in Chihuahua, Mexico. *Journal of Herpetology*, 1991; 25(1): 64-72.
—**Kofron, CP;**
Schreiber, AA: Ecology of Two Endangered Aquatic Turtles in Missouri: *Kinosternon flavescens* and *Emydoidea blandingii. Journal of Herpetology*, 1985; 19(1): 27-40.
—**Lamb, T; Lovich, J:**
Morphometric Validation of the Striped Mud Turtle (*Kinosternon baurii*) in the Carolinas and Virgina. *Copeia*, 1990; 1990(3): 613-618.

—**Long, DR:**
Yellow Mud Turtles. *Reptile & Amphibian Magazine*, 1993; 21(Mar/Apr): 22-26.
—**Monge-Najera, J; Moreva-Brenes, B:**
Notes on the Feeding Behavior of a Juvenile Mud Turtle *Kinosternon scorpioides. Herpetological Review*, 1987; 18(1): 7-8.
—**Pritchard, PCH; Trebbau, P:**
Kinosternon scorpioides scorpioides, In The Turtles of Venezuala, Society for the Study of Amphibians and Reptiles, 1984, pp. 239-248.
—**Webster, C:**
Substrate Preference and Activity in the Turtle, *Kinosternon flavescens flavescens. Journal of Herpetology*, 1986; 20(4): 477-482.
—**Welch, RF:**
Stalking the Elusive Eastern Mud Turtle. *Reptile & Amphibian Magazine*, 1994; 31(Nov/Dec): 88-95

STERNOTHERUS:
—**Bels, VL; Crama, YJ-M:**
Quantitative Analysis of the Courtship and Mating Behavior in the Loggerhead Musk Turtle *Sternotherus minor* (Reptilia: Kinosternidae) with Comments on Courtship Behavior in Turtles. *Copeia*, 1994; 1994(3): 676-684.
—**Cox, WA; et al.:**
A Model for Growth in the Musk Turtle, *Sternotherus minor*, in a North Florida Spring. *Copeia*, 1991; 1991(4): 954-968.
—**Ernst, CH:**
Ecology of the Turtle, *Sternotherus odoratus*, in Southeastern Pennsylvania. *Journal of Herpetology*, 1986; 20(3): 341-352.
—**Etchberger, CR; Ehrhart, LM:**
The Reproductive Biology of the Female Loggerhead Musk Turtle, *Sternotherus minor minor,* from the Southern Part of its Range in Central Florida. *Herpetologica*, 1987; 43(1): 66-73.
—**Jackson, JF:**
Evidence for Chemosensor-mediated Predator Avoidance in Musk Turtles. *Copeia*, 1990; 1990(2): 557-560.
—**Marion, KR; et al.:**
Prey of the Flattened Musk Turtle, *Sternotherus depressus. Journal of Herpetology*, 1991; 25(3): 385-387.
—**Mendonca, MT:**
Photothermal Effects on the Ovarian Cycle of the Musk Turtle, *Sternotherus odoratus. Herpetologica*, 1987; 43(1): 82-90.
—**Seidel, ME; et al.:**
Phylogenetic Relationships among Musk Turtles (Genus *Sternotherus*) and Genic Variation in Sternotherus odoratus. *Herpetologica*, 1981; 37(3): 161-165.

—**Zappalorti, RT:**
The Musk Turtle. *Reptile & Amphibian Magazine*, 1990; 3(Mar/Apr): 44-48.

VARIOUS/GENERAL:
—**Alderton, D:**
Turtles & Tortoises of the World. Facts on File, Inc., New York, NY, 1988, 191pp.

—**Bickham, JW; Carr, JL:**
Taxonomy and Phylogeny of the Higher Categories of Cryptodiran Turtles Based on a Cladistic Analysis of Chromosomal Data. *Copeia*, 1983; 1983(4): 918-932.

—**Bramble, DM; et al.:**
Kinosternid Shell Kinesis: Structure, Function and Evolution. *Copeia*, 1984; 1984(2): 456-475.Britson, CA;

—**Britson, CA; Gutzke, WHN:**
Antipredator Mechanisms of Hatchling Freshwater Turtles. *Copeia*, 1993; 1993(2): 435-440.

—**Carr, A:**
Handbook of Turtles: The Turtles of the United States, Canada, and Baja California. Cornell University Press, Ithaca, NY, 1952, 542pp.

—**Ernst, CH; Barbour, RW:**
Turtles of the United States. University Press of Kentucky, Lexington, KY, 1972, 347pp.

—**Ernst, CH; Barbour, RW:**
Turtles of the World. Smithsonian Institution Press, Washington D.C., 1989, 313pp.

—**Ernst, CH; et al.:**
Turtles of the United States and Canada. Smithsonian Institution Press, Washington, D.C., 1994, 578pp.

—**Ewert, MA; Nelson, CE:**
Sex Determination in Turtles: Diverse Patterns and Some Possible Adaptive Values. *Copeia*, 1991; 1991(1): 50-69.

—**Iverson, JB:**
Phylogenetic Hypotheses for the Evolution of Modern Kinosternine Turtles. *Herpetological Monographs*, 1991; 5: 1-27.

—**Iverson, JB:**
A Revised Checklist with Distribution Maps of the Turtles of the World. Privately Printed, Richmond, Indiana, 1992, 363pp.

—**Janzen, FJ; et al.:**
Observations on Basking Behavior of Hatchling Turtles in the Wild. *Journal of Herpetology*, 1992; 26(2): 217-219.

—**Mahmoud, IY:**
Courtship Behaviour and Sexual Maturity in Four Species of Kinosternid Turtles. *Copeia*, 1967; 1967: 314-319.

—**Moll, D:**
Population Sizes and Foraging Ecology in a Tropical Freshwater Stream Turtle Community. *Journal of Herpetology*, 1990; 24(1): 48-53.

—**Obst, FJ:**
Turtles, Tortoises and Terrapins. St. Martin's Press, New York, 1988, 231pp.

—**Pritchard, PCH:**
Encyclopedia of Turtles. TFH Publications, Inc., Neptune, N.J., 1979, 895pp.

—**Sites, JW, Jr.; et al.:**
Banded Karyotypes of Six Taxa of Kinosternid Turtles. *Copeia*, 1979; 1979(4): 692-698.

—**Slavens, FL; Slavens, K:**
Reptiles and Amphibians in Captivity: Breeding, Longevity and Inventory (Current January 1, 1994). Slaveware, Seattle, 1994, 534pp.

—**Stone, PA; et al.:**
Temporal Changes in Two Turtle Assemblages. *Journal of Herpetology*, 1993; 27(1): 13-23.

—**Tyning, TF:**
A Guide to Amphibians and Reptiles. Little, Brown and Company, Boston, 1990, 400pp.

—**Vogt, RC; Flores-Villela, O:**
Effects of Incubation Temperature on Sex Determination in a Community of Neotropical Freshwater Turtles in Southern Mexico. *Herpetologica*, 1992; 48(3): 265-270.

—**Vogt, RC; Guzman, SG:**
Food Partitioning in a Neotropical Freshwater Turtle Community. *Copeia*, 1988; 1988(1): 37-47.

—**Zimmermann, E:**
Breeding Terrarium Animals. TFH Publications, Inc., Neptune City, NJ, 1986, 384pp

HUSBANDRY OF LIZARDS,

GENERAL INFORMATION

John Coborn
P.O. Box 344
Nanango, Queensland 4615, Australia

TAXONOMY

Lizards form the suborder Sauria (sometimes referred to as Lacertilia) in the order Squamata (which includes lizards, amphisbaenians and snakes) which, in turn, is one of the four orders in the class Reptilia. The first lizards described were placed in the genus *Lacerta* (meaning lizard) and one of the first species to be catalogued was the European Sand Lizard, *Lacerta agilis.*

Until the middle of the eighteenth century, the classification of animals (and plants) posed enormous problems among the international scientific communities as there was no internationally recognized system for classifying the numerous species being discovered as the age of world exploration continued. Karl von Linne (1707-1779), a Swedish biologist was the first person to address the problem with any success and devised what is known as the binomial system of scientific nomenclature, publishing it in his work *Systema Naturae* (Systems of Nature). At that time (1758), Latin was the international language of science and so Linnaeus (a "Latinization" of von Linne's name by which he is better known) used Latin or Latinized words from other languages to name all of the animals known to him.

LIFESPAN

It is, of course, difficult to calculate the life expectancies of wild lizards. If we were to take an average life expectancy of any wild lizard it would, in most cases be a relatively short life, bearing in mind that the course of life in many individuals would be terminated by predators or disease.

Given optimum conditions in captivity, one could expect many lizards to live out their complete natural lifespans. However, as our husbandry techniques are still not perfect in many cases (still due to the ignorance of various species' complete natural requirements), it is reasonable to assume that at least some lizards do not reach the age that they might.

With regard to longevity we can say generally that small lizards (geckos, fence lizards, lacertids for example) live relatively short lives, rarely in excess of five years, when compared with large lizards (monitors, agamids, iguanids, for example), which frequently have lives in captivity for ten, twelve years and more. We do have a few statistics for a few captive species.

As an exception to the "small" rule above, a European Slow Worm, *Anguis fragilis*, at 54 years, appears to hold the lizard record for captive longevity. Compare this with a Wall Gecko, *Tarentola mauritanica*, which had a record (for this species) captive lifespan of just seven years (4-5 years would seem to be average for this species). The relatively large Tokay Gecko, *Gekko gecko* can be expected to live to a ripe old age of nine or ten.

A Komodo Dragon, *Varanus komodoensis*, lived for 16 years 7 months in a zoo. Other monitors are relatively long lived. A Savannah Monitor, *V. exanthematicus*, kept as a pet, survived for 17 years, a Nile Monitor, *V. niloticus*, for 15 years, a Water Monitor, *V. salvator*, 10 years, 8 months, and a Yellow Monitor, *V. flavescens*, for 10 years, 6 months.

The Green Iguana, *Iguana iguana*, one of the most popular exotic pet lizards, can be expected to live for 10-15 years under optimum conditions. Improving husbandry techniques should ensure that captive iguanas (and other lizards) become even older in the future.

Short-horned Lizard, *Phrynosoma douglassi*. Photo by R. D. Bartlett.

HABITAT PREFERENCES

Lizards have colonized most suitable land areas on earth and are really only absent from the polar regions, the upper altitudes of the higher mountains (but *Liolaemus multiformis* occurs as high as 5000 m (16250 ft) in the Andes!), and a few oceanic islands (however most islands have their own, some unique, lizard populations). The Eurasian Viviparous Lizard, *Lacerta vivipara* is the most northerly ranging lizard and, in Scandinavia, even occurs north of the Arctic Circle. The most northerly ranging North American lizard species include the Short-horned Lizard, *Phrynosoma douglassi* ; the Northern Alligator Lizard, *Elgaria coeruleus* ; the Five-lined Skink, *Eumeces fasciatus,* the Prairie Skink, *E. septentrionalis*, and the Western Skink, *E. skiltonianus*, all of which range into southern Canada. The most southerly species is probably *Liolaemus magellanicus* found on Tierra del Fuego at the tip of South America, while on Stewart Island at the Southernmost tip of New Zealand, we have three geckos, *Hoplodactylus granulatus* ; *H. maculatus* and *H. nebulosus*, as well as a skink, *Leiolopisma chloronoton.*

Numbers of lizard species increase towards the tropics. Also most larger lizard species live in the warmer areas. Most lizards spend a great deal of time under cover and, even when sun basking they ensure that they have an instant escape route should danger threaten. Some forest lizards such as Green Iguanas, Basilisks, Water Dragons and Sailfins, bask close to water and take to it for refuge should danger threaten. Many terrestrial lizards take to burrows, rock crevices, or hollow tree limbs when threatened. Some desert species virtually "swim" rapidly under the sand when frightened.

PHYSICAL CHARACTERISTICS

Lizards are typically elongated reptiles, mostly with well-developed limbs and a long tail but, as we will discuss later in the text there are exceptions. Lizard species range in length from as little as 2.5 cm (1in) (for example the Reef Gecko, *Sphaerodactylus parthenopion* and the Dwarf Ground Chameleon, *Brookesia minima*), to as much as 300 cm (10 ft) (in the Komodo Dragon, *Varanus komodoensis*).

The Skin: Lizards all have a covering of horny scales formed by folds in the skin. The shape of the scales varies greatly from species to species, and even individual species may have two or more types of scales on their bodies. The scales may be large and platelike, or small and granular, they may be juxtaposed (touching one another) or imbricate (overlapping). In many genera (*Cordylus, Moloch, Phrynosoma* for example) some of the scales are modified into sharp spines which may protect them from predators, while others (e.g. *Anguis, Gerrhonotus* (*Elgaria*), *Gerrhosaurus*) have osteoderms - hard bony plates beneath the scale layer for added protection. Scales may be smooth, or keeled - possessing one or more ridges; the former usually are glossy, the latter matt in appearance. The scaly layer is tough in most species and is able to stand up to a fair amount of wear and tear. It also helps reduce the loss of body water, and aids in the absorption of warmth from the sun. The shape, arrangement, and number of scales is often a diagnostic feature of species and subspecies. Those on the head of many species are large and platelike. In some forms (many *Agama* and *Iguana* species for example) a row of dorsal scales forms a spiny crest.

The Limbs: Most lizard species have four well developed limbs, each with five, sharp-clawed digits. In most cases the limbs are oriented laterally from the body, giving the lizard its characteristic swinging gait when it walks or runs. Many genera, and species show limb degeneration in various stages. Some burrowing lizards (e.g. *Anguis, Aniellia, Dibamus*), have no exterior traces of limbs. In others (such as *Ophisaurus*), the forelimbs are absent and the rear limbs reduced to tiny spikes. In the family Pygopodidae, the forelimbs are absent and the rear limbs reduced to scaly flaps. Many scincids have much reduced limbs, often with reduced numbers of digits. Almost all lizards with absent or reduced limbs still, however, possess both pectoral and pelvic limb girdles in their skeletons (as opposed to snakes which never have traces of pectoral limb girdles, though some of the more primitive species possess vestigeal pelvic girdles).

In a few families the feet show specialized adaptations. Many geckos, for example, have adhesive pads on their digits, allowing them to walk on smooth vertical surfaces. In chameleons, the digits are permanently opposed in groups of two and three, to allow a good, pincer-like grip on twigs. Some desert dwelling lizards (e.g. *Acanthodactylus*) have scaly fringes to their digits, allowing better traction in the sand, while some desert dwelling geckoes have webbed feet for similar reasons. In the "flying" geckos, *Ptychozoon*, the webbed feet act as auxiliary parachutes.

The Head: In the majority of lizard species the head is distinctly set off from the body by a narrower neck; exceptions include some of the bur-

Glass lizard, *Ophisaurus* sp. Photo by R. D. Bartlett.

rowing lizards and skinks, in which the head, neck and thorax are all more or less of similar diameter. Lizards generally have a large gape but, unlike snakes, the bones of the lower jaw are firmly united at the chin rather than being joined with elastic tissue, and the palatal bones are fixed, which means that lizards are unable to swallow such large prey as snakes. However, most lizards make up for this by having relatively stronger jaws, which allow them to crush, or tear prey before swallowing it. The teeth are usually relatively short and serrate.

The Tail: The tail is typically long and tapered in most lizard species. It is used as an organ of balance and as an aid to swimming in some aquatic forms. In many large species, especially iguanas and monitors, the tail may be used as a lashing means of defense. Many species practice autotomy, the shedding of all, or part of the tail in order to confuse predators. Lizards should thus never be picked up by the tail. While a lost tail may be regrown, it is almost never as long or as elegant as the original. Some geckos (turnip tails) use their tails as fat storage organs, while certain lizards have prehensile tails; the Solomon Islands Skink, *Corucia zebrata,* is a good example of the latter.

The Senses: Most lizards seem to have rea-

Prehensile-tailed Skink, *Corucia zebrata.* Photo by K. H. Switak.

Kuhl's Flying Gecko, *Ptychozoon kuhli*. Photo by K. H. Switak.

sonable eyesight. Initial recognition of moving prey in most species is optical. Unlike snakes, most lizards have upper and lower moveable eyelids, as well as a nictitating membrane. Exceptions include most geckoes and the pygopods (flap footed lizards). Hearing is also relatively good in the majority lizards, most species, unlike snakes, having external ear openings. The sense of smell is also good in most species. The tongue is used extensively as an organ of taste and smell, and is used, more or less, in conjunction with the vomeronasal organs (Jacobson's organs), sensitive pits in the palate adjacent to, but not adjoining the nostrils. The skin of lizards is richly supplied with nerve endings, giving them an excellent sense of touch to most parts of the body; they will react to the slightest touch on the skin during their periods of activity.

SOME DIAGNOSTIC FEATURES OF LIZARD FAMILIES

While this book is not meant to be a formal identification guide for taxa, it is considered that a few major diagnostic features of lizard families will be useful to the general reader. The characteristics given are typical of the families but, as ever, exceptions exist in many cases. The descriptions are followed by token examples of a few genera and their respective natural ranges.

FAMILY GEKKONIDAE (GECKOES)

Typically small, nocturnal, insectivorous lizards with more or less dorso-ventrally flattened body. The scales are usually small and granular, the skin generally soft and delicate. The digits are usually furnished with adhesive pads allowing geckos to scuttle over the smoothest of vertical surfaces. With the exception of members of the subfamily Eublepharinae (sometimes regarded as a separate family Eublepharidae), which have fairly normal upper and lower eyelids, all geckos have a fixed transparent spectacle protecting the eye, similar to that of snakes. The tongue is broad, protrusible, and only slightly notched at the tip.

With about 800 species in 85 genera, geckos form one of the largest lizard families. Four subfamilies of geckoes are generally recognised

1. Eublepharinae with genera including *Aeluroscabotes* (Southeast Asia), *Coleonyx* (SW USA to Central America) and *Eublepharus* (Southwestern Asia).
2. Sphaerodactylinae with genera including *Gonatodes* (Central and South America) and *Sphaerodactylus* (Central and South America).

3. Diplodactylinae with genera including *Diplodactylus* (Australia), *Hoplodactylus* (New Zealand), *Naultinus* (New Zealand), *Oedura* (Australia), *Phyllurus* (Australia) and *Rhacodactylus* (New Caledonia).

4. Gekkoninae with genera including *Afroedura* (Southern Africa), *Chondrodactylus* (Southern Africa), *Cyrtodactylus* (Europe and Asia), *Geckonia* (Northwest Africa), *Gekko* (Southeast Asia), *Hemidactylus* (Pantropical; including introductions), *Homopholis* (Southern Africa), *Lygodactylus* (Eastern Africa), *Phelsuma* (Day Geckos; Indian Ocean Islands), *Ptychozoon* (Southeast Asia), *Teratoscincus* (Central Asia) and *Uroplatus* (Madagascar). Species length range: from 2.5 cm (1 in) to 35 cm (14 in). The world's largest gecko is *Rhacodactylus leachianus* of New Caledonia.

FAMILY XANTUSIIDAE: NIGHT LIZARDS

Superficially similar to geckos, relatively small nocturnal lizards with small granular scales on the back, larger scales beneath. As in geckos the eyelids are fixed, but the tongue is not protrusible. There are four recognised genera and about twelve species. Species length range from 10 cm (4 in) to 15 cm (6 in). Best known genera are *Xanthusia* (SW USA and NW Mexico) and *Lepidophyma* (Central America).

FAMILY PYGOPODIDAE: FLAP-FOOTED LIZARDS

Although not similar in appearance to geckos, internal structures make pygopods close relatives. All are virtually limbless, with forelimbs totally absent, and the hindlimbs having degenerated to small scaly flaps. They are serpentine in appearance, with an extremely fragile tail up to three times the length of the head and body. There are no movable eyelids and the tongue is protrusible. There are about 30 species in eight genera all restricted to Australia and New Guinea. Species length range from 25 cm (10 in) to 70 cm (28 in). Genera include *Aprasia*, *Delma* and *Pygopus*.

FAMILY DIBAMIDAE: OLD WORLD BURROWING LIZARDS

Small, wormlike, burrowing lizards, the females limbless, the males having a pair of stump like vestigeal hind limbs. The tail is very short and the eyes and ears are covered with skin. There are 3 species in a single genus *Dibamus* (Southeast Asia and New Guinea). Species length range from 25 cm (10 in) to 30 cm (12 in).

Lokobe Flat-tailed Gecko, *Uroplatus henkeli*. Photo by R. D. Bartlett.

Spinytail iguana, *Ctenosaura* sp. Photo by M. P. and C. Piednoir.

FAMILY ANELYTROPSIDAE: MEXICAN BURROWING LIZARDS

Small burrowing lizard with a scaly, wormlike body and a large shovel-like rostral plate for burrowing. They are limbless, and the eyes and ears are covered with skin. The single species is *Anelytropsis papillosus* (Central Mexico). Length: to 25 cm (10 in).

FAMILY IGUANIDAE: IGUANAS

This family has recently been revised and it has been proposed that the original 60 genera and some 700 species should be divided up as follows:

1. Iguanidae: Large iguanas including *Brachylophus* (Fiji Islands) *Cyclura* (Central America and West Indies), *Ctenosaura* (Central and South America), *Iguana* (Central and South America), and *Sauromalus* (North America).
2. Corytophanidae: Basilisks and related species, including *Basiliscus* (Central and South America), *Corytophanes* (Central and South

Knight Anole, *Anolis equestris*. Photo by M. P. and C. Piednoir.

America) and *Laemanctus* (Central America).

3. Crotaphytidae: Collared and Leopard Lizards: *Crotaphytus* (USA and Mexico) and *Gambelia* (USA and Mexico).
4. Hoplocercidae: South American Spiny Tailed Iguanians including *Hoplocercus* and *Enyaloides*.
5. Opluridae: Malagasy Iguanians: *Chalarodon* and *Oplurus* .
6. Phrynosomatidae: Granite, Fence, and Horned Lizards including *Callisaurus* (USA and Mexico), *Holbrookia* (USA and Mexico), *Phrynosoma* (Northern and Central America), *Sceloporus* (Northern and Central America), *Uma* (USA and Mexico), and *Uta* (USA and Mexico).
7. Polychrotidae: Anoles and related species including *Anolis* (Southern USA, Central America, Northern South America and West Indies), *Enyalius* (South America), *Leiosaurus* (South America), *Polychrus* (Central and South America), and *Urostrophus* (South America).
8. Tropiduridae: Curlytails and their allies including *Leiocephalus* (West Indies), *Liolaemus* (South America), *Plica* (South America), and *Tropidurus* (South America and Galapagos Islands).

Due to the enormous morphological and behavioural variety among the members of the above families (formerly all in Iguanidae) lack of space makes it impossible to make more than a few comments on general characteristics. The group includes terrestrial, arboreal, semi-aquatic and even semi-marine (*Amblyrhynchus*) species. The bodies of arboreal species tend to be compressed laterally, in terrestrial forms dorso-ventrally. Dorsal spines are present in many species, as are expanding dewlaps used in territorial and sexual displays. Unlike members of the the Agamidae (below), which have their back teeth set on the summit of the jaw (acrodont) all members of the above eight families have all their teeth set in the sides of the jaws (pleurodont). Species length range from 10 cm (4 in) to 2 m (6ft 6 in).

FAMILY AGAMIDAE: AGAMIDS

A large family of old world lizards with many similar aspects to the iguanids and with an amazing morphological variety. There are terrestrial, arboreal and semi-aquatic forms, with or without dorsal crests and other appendages. Some species possess almost rodent-like incisor teeth at the front of the jaw, but the back teeth are acrodont. There are about 35 genera and over 3900 species. Genera include *Acanthosaura* (Southeast Asia), *Amphibolurus* (Australia), *Agama* (Africa and Asia), *Calotes* (South and Southeast Asia),

Chlamydosaurus (Australia), *Draco* (Southeast Asia), *Gonocephalus* (Southeast Asia), *Hydrosaurus* (Southeast Asia), *Hypsilurus* (Australia), *Moloch* (Australia), *Physignathus* (Southeast Asia, Australia), and *Pogona* (Australia). Species length range from 20 cm (4 in) to 120 cm (48 in).

FAMILY CHAMAELEONIDAE: CHAMELEONS

Generally regarded as a sister family to the agamids, however, chamaeleons possess a number of unique modifications. The body is usually laterally compressed. The scales are granular and capable of extensive and rapid color change. The upper and lower eyelid is fused together to form a pyramid shaped mound with the eye peering out of a small aperture in the centre; each eye is capable of independant movement. The toes are fused together and permanently opposed in groups of two and three. The tail is prehensile. There are no external ear openings. The tongue is rapidly extensible to a distance of at least the body length (for catching insects with the sticky tip). There are about 80 species and four genera are usually recognised: *Bradypodium* (Southern Africa), *Brookesia* (Madagascar), *Chamaeleo* (Southern Europe, Africa, Middle East, Madagascar), and *Rhampholeon* (Southern Africa). Species length range from 2.5 cm (1 in) to 60 cm (24 in).

FAMILY SCINCIDAE: SKINKS

A large family of lizards with about 50 genera and over 600 species found on all continents except (of course) Antarctica. There are fully limbed, partially limbed, and limbless forms. Most species have elongated bodies and short stocky limbs. The body is more or less round in cross section and the neck is typically fairly indistinct from the head and body. The scales are usually smooth, overlapping and glossy. Most skinks are terrestrial or fossorial, but there are a few tree dwelling forms including the popular Solomon Islands Skink, *Corucia zebrata*. Other genera include *Chalcides* (Southern Europe, North Africa, Middle East), *Ctenotus* (Australia, New Guinea), *Dasia* (Southeast Asia), *Egernia* (Australia), *Eumeces* (North and Central America), *Hemisphaeriodon* (Australia), *Mabuya* (North and South America, Africa, Asia), *Riopa* (Africa, Asia), *Scincella* (Southeast Asia, North and Central America), *Scincus* (North Africa, Middle East), and *Tiliqua* (Australia, New Guinea). Species length range from 7.5 cm (3 in) to 60 cm (24 in).

FAMILY CORDYLIDAE: GIRDLED AND PLATED LIZARDS

Two subfamilies:
1. Cordylinae, which includes the sungazers

Frilled Dragon, *Chlamydosaurus kingi*. Photo by K. H. Switak.

(zonures) and flat lizards; the former are covered with protective spiny scales; the latter have spines on the tail only, but have flat bodies to allow them to squeeze into tight rock crevices. Genera include *Cordylus* (Eastern and Southern Africa), *Platysaurus* (Southern Africa), and *Pseudocordylus* (Southern Africa)
2. Gerrhosaurinae, the plated lizards, with large platelike groups of scales along the body supported by osteoderms. Genera include *Cordylosaurus* (Southern Africa), *Gerrhosaurus* (Eastern and Southern Africa), *Tetradactylus* (Southern Africa), and *Zonosaurus* (Madagascar). Species length range from 20 cm (4 in) to 60 cm (24 in).

FAMILY LACERTIDAE: TYPICAL OLD WORLD LIZARDS

The original "lizards". They are typically "lizard-shaped" with four, well-developed limbs, a robust body, and a long tail. The head scales are large and fused to the skull, while the body scales

Southeastern Five-lined Skink, *Eumeces inexpectatus*. Photo by Mark Smith.

Jewelled Lizard, *Lacerta lepida*. Photo by R. D. Bartlett.

are mainly small and granular. There are over 200 species in about 22 genera. Genera include *Acanthodactylus* (Southwestern Europe, North Africa, Middle East), *Adolfus* (Central Africa), *Algyroides* (Southern Europe), *Bedriagaia* (Central Africa), *Cabrita* (India, Sri Lanka), *Gallotia* (Canary Islands), *Lacerta* (Europe, Western Asia, Africa), *Podarcis* (Mediterranean Region), *Psammodromus* (Southwestern Europe, Northwestern Africa) and *Tropidosaura* (Southern Africa. Species length range from 12.5 cm (5 in) to 60 cm (24 in).

FAMILY TEIIDAE: TEGUS AND THEIR ALLIES

Typical members of the Teiidae show many similarities to lacertids. However, teiids include arboreal, terrestrial, and almost limbless fossorial forms. As in lacertids, the head scales are large, the body scales small or granular. There are over 200 species in about 40 genera including *Ameiva* (Southern Mexico into tropical South America), *Arthrosaura* (Northern South America), *Cnemidophorus* (USA to Argentina), *Crocodilurus* (Northern South America), *Dracaena* (Tropical South America), *Euspondylus* (Northwestern South America), and *Tupinambis* (South

Ameiva, *Ameiva* sp. Photo by R. D. Bartlett.

America). Species length range from 10 cm (4 in) to 100 cm (39 in).

FAMILY FEYLINIDAE: LIMBLESS SKINKS

A group of poorly known limbless, scaly, worm-like burrowing lizards. There is only a single genus, *Feylinia*, and four species, all native to tropical Africa. Length to 35 cm.

FAMILY ANGUIDAE: SLOW WORMS, GLASS SNAKES AND ALLIGATOR LIZARDS

Mostly elongated lizards with overlapping scales supported by osteoderms. There are fully limbed, partially limbed, and limbless species. There are about 70 species in eight genera including *Anguis* (Europe, Western Asia), *Gerrhonotus* (North and Central America), and *Ophisaurus* (Southeastern USA, Southeastern Europe, Middle East, Northwest Africa, Southeast Asia). Species length range from 15 cm (6 in) to 100 cm (39 in).

FAMILY ANNIELLIDAE: CALIFORNIA LEGLESS LIZARDS

Limbless burrowing lizards with no external ear openings. The single genus, *Anniella*, and two species are native to California and Baja California. Length to 25 cm (10 in).

FAMILY XENOSAURIDAE: CROCODILE AND STRANGE LIZARDS

Medium-sized lizards with well developed limbs and a moderately long tail. Large external ear openings. The scales are supported by osteoderms. Four species in two genera: *Shinisaurus* Southern China), and *Xenosaurus* (Central and Southern Mexico). Species length range from 20 cm (8 in) to 40 cm (16 in).

FAMILY VARANIDAE: MONITORS

Typically large lizards with well developed limbs and a long, often laterally flattened tail. The body scales are generally small. The head is relatively long and the snout is usually pointed. The tongue is long and forked likc that of a snake. The family contains just a single genus, *Varanus*, with about forty species distributed in Africa, Southern and Southeast Asia, and Australia). Includes the world's largest lizard the Komodo Dragon, *V. komodoensis*. Species length range from 25 cm (10 in) to 300 cm (10 ft).

FAMILY HELODERMATIDAE: BEADED LIZARDS

Stout bodied lizards with short, powerful limbs. The tail is relatively short and thick. The scales are granular and supported by small osteoderms. The single genus, *Heloderma*, and only two spe-

Emerald Monitor, *Varanus prasinus*.
Photo by M. P. and C. Piednoir.

cies, are the only venomous lizards. The lower teeth are grooved to conduct venom from a series of labial glands. Native to southwestern USA and adjacent Mexico. Length 35-45 cm (14-18 in).

FAMILY LANTHANOTIDAE: EARLESS MONITOR

A small semi-aquatic monitor-relative with an elongated body, short, but well-developed limbs and a relatively long tapered tail which is tound in section. There is no external ear opening; the snout is pointed and the tongue forked. There is a transparent window in the lower eyelid. The single genus, *Lanthanotus*, and species occurs in western Borneo (Sarawak, Malaysia and Kalimantan, Indonesia). Length up to 43 cm (17 in).

GROWTH AND DEVELOPMENT

With the numerous species of lizards and their size ranges, it is clear that there can be no hard and fast rules with regard to their rate of growth in the wild. However most lizards, at birth in viviparous species, or at hatching in egglaying species, are of a relatively small size and particularly subject to predation. It is an important strategy to increase size by growth at the maximum possible rate. That is why breeding seasons usually occur at the most favorable times of the year, when the climate is amenable and food is abundant. Occasional unsuitable seasons will result in fluctuations in wild populations. In captivity, where we seek to provide optimum conditions, growth rate is usually maximum. In general, smaller lizard species reach sexual maturity and maximum size in shorter periods than do their larger counterparts. For example the smallest monitor lizard, *Varanus brevicauda*, with a maximum total adult length of about 25 cm (10 in), under favorable conditions can reach maximum size at twelve months of age, whereas *V. komodoensis* with a maximum total adult length of about 3 m (10 ft) takes ten or more years to reach maximum size and probably never completely stops growing, though, as in all lizards, the rate of growth decreases with age.

SEXING

The determination of the sexes of lizards is an important aspect of breeding as, with the exception of a very few parthenogenetic species, a

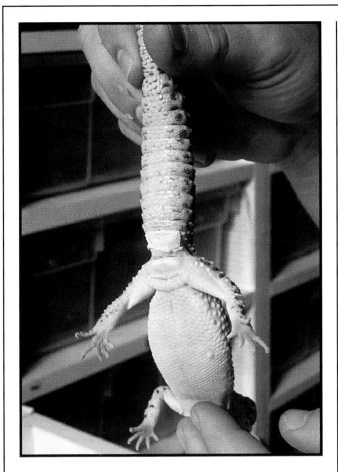

Leopard Gecko, *Eublepharis macularius*. Male specimen. Photo by Isabelle Francais.

male must fertilize a female before offspring can be produced. Parthenogeneticy, a condition in which the female is self fertile and does not require to copulate with a male, occurs in a few species, including several species of North American whiptails (*Cnemidophorus*).

Sexual dimorphism is distinctive in some groups and individuals, less so in others. There may be differences in adult size (males often larger than females but the reverse applies in some species) but sufficient comparative material is required if this method is to be useful. In some species the males take on more brilliant colors than the females, and perform aggressive territorial and sexual displays, especially in the mating season. The presence of femoral and/or anal pores in the males of many species is a good guide; females having no pores or very few. In some species with similar numbers of pores, the male's are usually larger than those of the female. These pores pro-

duce a waxy substance probably containing chemicals used to attract females and for territorial marking. One of the best visual methods of determining sex in many species is to examine the base of the tail. In males, the inverted hemipenes (sex organs) are housed in pouches within the tail base and make a conspicuous bulge, which is absent in females.

In many cases the visual differences are so vague that other measures of sex determination have to be taken. Sex probing, which was all the rage a few years ago has now lost favor for lizards (as opposed to snakes) because of the possibility of injuring the lizards, especially the small, delicate species, but may still be useful with large species such as varanids. Probing consists of inserting a suitably sized, lubricated probe into one side the cloaca and gently pushing it in the direction of the tail. The probe cannot be pudhed very far in the case of females while, in males, it should enter the inverted hemipenis and can be pushed a relatively greater distance before resistance is felt. Probes, made of stainless steel or nylon, are available in sets of various sizes from biological suppliers.

Recently, more technical methods are being used by some veterinarians to sex lizards. These include hormonal examination of blood or feces samples, or in some cases by the use of endoscopy. Unfortunately, both blood sampling and endoscopy involve possible traumatic invasion of the tissues or body. It is suggested that hormonal examination of the feces, which is stress free, should be developed to a fine art and used more extensively. Of course, it is necessary to keep a lizard on its own until a feces sample can be collected.

Day gecko, *Phelsuma* sp. Male specimen. Photo by Isabelle Francais.

SELECTION AND ACQUISITION

There are several ways in which you may acquire your lizards but most hobbyists start by purchasing their first specimens from a pet shop. Other ways include getting them from another hobbyist who has surplus specimens, or by collecting your own from the wild.

The latter course must be considered with great caution. In most countries the native reptiles are protected by various forms of government legislation and in some cases collecting is a very serious offence.

During the last few years reptile retailing has become a fairly large part of the pet industry. Apart from that, petshops are themselves becoming ever more professional in their activities, and you can expect fair and reliable service from most outlets. However, there are still a few less conscientious dealers around, and you should look carefully before buying any specimens. If you don't consider the dealer's displays to be hygienically and professionally presented, then you should go elsewhere.

It is highly recommended that the beginner to lizard keeping should start with a single pair of easy to keep lizards and gain experience with these before becoming more ambitious. Examine each specimen carefully before making a decision whether or not to purchase. It will be necessary to handle the specimens at this time and, if you are not adept at this stage it will be wise to ask the dealer to show you how or, even better, to take an experienced hobbyist with you. That is one reason why it is quite important to become a member of a herpetological club or society. Senior club members will usually be all too glad to help newcomers out in any ways they can, and and these include providing handling tuition and assisting with purchases of stock.

Examine the general profile of the lizard and ensure thare are no genetic malformations such as a spinal kink or a twisted tail. Although lizards come in a vast variety of shapes and sizes it it usually fairly easy to tell if a particular specimen is healthy. Most healthy lizards will show some kind of interest on being handled. Lethargic animals that make no attempt to struggle and lay limply in the hand are most probably sick. The specimen should be reasonably plump, with no sunken areas along the backbone, along the flanks or, especially, at the base of the tail. The tail base is a good

Sand Lizard, *Lacerta agilis*. Photo by R. D. Bartlett.

Green Iguana, *Iguana iguana*. Photo by M. P. and C. Piednoir.

indicator of a lizard's health. Unhealthy lizards tend not to feed and lose weight. The first place to show signs of weight loss is at the broad tail base. In an emaciated specimen the tail base will have sunken furrows in the skin where the flesh beneath has wasted away. Examine all parts of the skin surface. The scales should be sleek and unblemished and there should be no sign of external parasites such as ticks or mites. Animals with wounds, tumors, or abscesses should not be considered. The snout should be clean and wound free (many nervous lizards injure their snouts in attempts to escape and the wounds often are infected with pathogens). There should be no obvious discharge from the nostrils. The eyes should be clean and bright. Examine the limbs and ensure the joints are operating smoothly and are not swollen Check the toes for missing claws or swellings. The area around the vent should be clean and free of caked fecal material which is a sign of diarrhea.

Once you have ensured that there are no obvious visual signs of disease, you can go ahead and make your purchases. Newly acquired lizards should be transported home and placed in their new accommodations (which you should have already prepared in advance) as quickly as possible. If you already have some lizards it is wise to quarantine your new acquisitions (see preventive health care).

Small lizards up to about 15 cm (6 in) long are often transported in small cardboard or plastic boxes loosely packed with shredded paper to provide cushioning and security. Larger lizards are usually placed individually in cloth bags of suitable sizes. In excessively cold weather it is advisable to pack the bags or boxes in an insulated outer container to retain warmth (styrofoam boxes are ideal). For obvious reasons, never leave containers of livestock in the hot sun in a vehicle, nor for protracted periods in cold weather.

Once installed in their new home the lizards should be left undisturbed for 24 hours so that they can become accustomed to their new surroundings. Provide them with the necessary heating, lighting and water requirements, but do not feed them until the following day.

In the case of excessively nervous specimens it is best to cover the terrarium glass for a few days so that the reptiles do not panic each time they observe movement outside the cage.

BEHAVIOR

The word behavior, in a biological sense, can be described as the way an animal reacts to stimuli from its environment. These include influences of the climate, gravity and of other animals. In these contexts we will here discuss some examples of the behavioural aspects of locomotion, feeding, thermoregulation, hibernation, aestivation, defense and social reaction. Reproductive behaviour is discussed in the section on reproduction.

LOCOMOTION

Locomotory behaviour is generally influenced by the nature of the habitat in which the animal lives. A typical lizard has four well-developed limbs, each furnished with five sharp-clawed toes. Unlike the limbs of mammals, which tend to hold most of the body weight directly from below, those of most lizards are oriented outwards so that the body of the reptile is virtually slung between the front and rear limbs. This poses a relatively greater strain on the limbs during locomotory activity and explains why lizards often run or walk in short bursts, pausing frequently to lower the belly to the ground in order to rest. Most lizards also make undulatory movements of the body and tail when moving, so that momentum is added to the limbs as they move back and forth.

The respective sizes of limbs vary greatly among taxa and are influenced by the lifestyles of the various species. Some species lack external limbs completely, but possess vestigial internal limb girdles showing that the limbs have been lost through evolution. Examples of these include the European Slow Worm, *Anguis fragilis*, the Eastern (USA) Glass Lizard, *Ophisaurus ventralis*, and the California Legless Lizard, *Anniella pulchra*. Limblessness has probably evolved through living in habitats that involve moving among dense ground vegetation, among loose soil or debris, or completely below the substrate. A number of lizards show partial loss of limbs, suggesting that they are still in a state of evolution leading to limblessness. The skink family (Scincidae) probably shows the most interesting variations of limb sizes; there are spe-

Eastern Glass Lizard, *Ophisaurus ventralis*. Photo by Aaron Norman.

cies with no limbs, species with either front or rear limbs only, species with tiny limbs lacking one, more or all digits and, of course, species with more conventional lizard limbs. The family of Australian flap-footed lizards (Pygopodidae) is interesting in that the species have hind limbs only that have degenerated to tiny, digitless flaplike appendages. Limbless or partially-limbless lizards move with undulatory body movements, pushing, or pulling themselves along by applying body pressure to vegetation, rocks or other imperfections in the substrate. Most partially-limbless lizards move with their limbs held close to the body, but may still use their diminished limbs to some extent as the occasion arises.

Many terrestrial lizards such as many monitors are furnished with powerful but, relatively short limbs, designed for running, digging into the substrate in search of food, or in excavating burrows. Quick moving arboreal lizards such as certain iguanas and agamas have long, slender limbs, useful for running and jumping around among the tree canopies; most of these also have a long tail which is used as a balancing device. The arboreal Solomon Islands Skink, *Corucia zebrata*, has relatively short limbs, but moves fairly slowly and has a prehensile tail to help its stability. The slowest lizards, the chamaeleons (Chamaeleonidae), have

long slender limbs with zygodactylous feet (some digits facing forward, some back); and the the toes are fused together in twos and threes to increase their gripping potential on twigs and branches. While geckos (Gekkonidae) are considered to be evolutionarily primitive lizards, most of them have remarkably advanced locomotory attributes, the best known being the adhesive pads beneath the toes which allow the reptiles to move with ease over the smoothest of surfaces and even upside-down on ceilings etc.

Other special locomotory adaptations in certain lizard taxa include the partially webbed toes and laterally flattened tail in the Galapagos Marine Iguana, *Amblyrhynchus cristatus*, which improve its swimming ability; the flaps of skin on the toes of Central and South American basilisks (*Basiliscus* species), and the Sail-finned Lizards (*Hydrosaurus* species) of Southeast Asia, which enable them to scuttle some distance over the water surfaces and also help in swimming; and the scaly-fringed edges to the toes of certain desert dwelling lizards (such as the North African *Acanthodactylus* and the North American *Uma* species) which enable them to move rapidly over shifting sands.

Perhaps the most remarkable locomotory adaptation is that shown by the so-called flying dragons (*Draco* species) of Southeast Asia. A fanlike flap of skin laid along either side of the body between the limbs can be opened up by the action of five or six pairs of long, hinged ribs to form a gliding surface which allows the lizards to "fly" up to 30 meters (100 feet) from one tree to the next. The "flying" geckos (*Ptychozoon* species) possess similar but smaller flaps of skin which assist in camouflage as well as provide limited gliding capabilities.

FEEDING BEHAVIOR

Feeding behavior is influenced by the habitat and the food which is available. It must be remembered that species have evolved in certain habitats over millions of years and that every lizard has formed an ecological relationship with its available diet. Most lizards are carnivorous (used in its broadest sense), the size of the prey animal being dictated by the size of the lizard that preys on it. Thus small lizards such as geckos, feed on tiny insects and other invertebrates, medium sized lizards devour larger invertebrates and some small vertebrates,

Philippine Sailfin Lizard, *Hydrosaurus pustulatus*. **Photo by R. D. Bartlett.**

while the largest lizards may even attempt to overpower fairly big mammals.

The Komodo Dragon, *Varanus komodoensis*, the largest of all lizards illustrates the latter case and there are well documented reports of adult specimens of these huge reptiles overpowering pigs, deer, and even water buffalo. They lie in wait along game trails and catch prey using the ambush method of grabbing the animal by a leg and immobilising it by tearing the tendons. A number of the lizards can soon bring the prey down and feed upon it by tearing off strips of flesh.

Juvenile Komodo Dragons, and most other monitor species, feed by foraging, using the extremely sensitive tongue, coupled with the Jacobson's organs to find burrowing prey, eggs,

and carrion. Although reptile populations generally seem to be on the decline in most parts of the world, in Australia several species of monitor are actually maintaining, even increasing, their numbers because the escalating amount of road traffic means a greater number of road kills. Although monitors themselves also often become road victims, the amount of available road-kill carrion means that many monitors never need to go hungry, and are thus able to breed to the extent that the population is maintained. It will be interesting to see how long this phenomenon can go on before the situation alters to the detriment of the monitors! Many large lizards will swallow whole any prey that is not too large, but larger prey is torn apart with the strong jaws and limbs.

Many small insectivorous lizards, like some unruly human children, obtain their prey by the "spot and grab" method. In most cases the, feeding stimulus in these lizards is triggered by the vision of prey movement. As soon as the lizard has decided that the item is of suitable size and variety it rushes at the prey and grabs it before it has time to take flight. Some lizards are extremely agile in their prey catching abilities; in southern Italy I once saw a Green Lizard, *Lacerta viridis*, leap clean out of an orange tree and into the air to catch a moth, before crashing back down into the foliage! Certain lizards, such as many geckos, stalk their invertebrate prey in the manner of a cat until within suitable striking distance, before grabbing it with a flourish of speed.

Some lizards are fairly specialized in their diets. The North American horned toads, (*Phrynosoma* species), feed largely on ants, which they lap up avidly with their tongues. The Australian Thorny Devil, *Moloch horridus*, has similar feeding habits, feeding exclusively upon ants. The South American Caiman Lizard, *Dracaena guianensis*, feeds almost exclusively on aquatic snails, cracking the shells with its powerful jaws and discarding them before eating the soft inner parts. The specialized feeding habits of some lizard species makes them difficult to maintain in captivity unless a continued supply of the special diet is available.

A small number of lizard species are mainly herbivorous, an even smaller number are exclusively so. Two of the latter include the Marine Iguana, *Amblyrhynchus cristatus*, which feeds exclusively on seaweed, and the North American chuckwallas (*Sauromalus* species) which feed on the flowers leaves and fruits of desert plants.

Mainly herbivorous species include the well-known Green Iguana, *Iguana iguana*, the various West Indian Ground Iguanas (*Cyclura* species), the Solomon Islands Skink, *Corucia zebrata,* and the spiny tailed agamids (*Uromastyx* species) of North Africa and the Middle East. Most of these mainly herbivorous species are known to take more or less animal based food from time to time.

Partially herbivorous species include the large blue-tongued skinks (*Tiliqua* species) of Australia and New Guinea, and some of the larger lacertid lizards of Southern Europe and North Africa which will occasionally eat ripe fruit. Some geckos, es-

pecially day geckos (*Phelsuma* species) will opportunistically lap up nectar from flowers, and juices from ripe fruits in addition to their normal insectivorous diet.

BEHAVIOURAL THERMOREGULATION

Reptiles were once described as "cold-blooded" or "poikilothermic" meaning that their body temperatures were always lower and more variable than those of the mammals and birds which were said to be "warm-blooded" or "homeothermic". In recent times, however, zoologists have increasingly been using the terms "ectothermic", which describes the derivation of body heat from outside the body, and "endothermic", describing the production and maintenance of body heat by internal metabolic processes. Ectothermy and endothermy are, in effect, more correct than the terms quoted above.

Being ectothermic, lizards have to rely on external warmth; in nature that which is usually provided directly from the sun's rays, or indirectly from objects that have been warmed by the sun's rays. As the sun rises on a summer's day in the temperate northern or southern hemispheres the lizards

Emerald Lizard, *Lacerta viridis*. Photo by Michael Gilroy.

Ornate Mastigure, *Uromastyx ornata*. Photo by Paul Freed.

emerge and place themselves in a position where they can gain maximum benefit from the sun's rays, often flattening and widening the body to expose the maximum skin surface to the sun. Early in the morning the lizard will probably bask on foliar vegetation rather than on a log, rock, or ground substrate which will have not yet warmed up from the cool of the night, and would reabsorb some of the valuable warmth from the lizard's body. Later, as the more solid surfaces absorb some heat, the lizard may change its basking spot so that it can absorb warmth from above and below. It is important for the lizard's body core to reach optimum levels as soon as possible so that it can operate efficiently. The brain in particular needs warmth to operate and control the rest of the body. The hypothalamus is part of the brain that acts as a kind of thermostat, and controls the lizard's thermoregulatory behaviour. Once the optimum body temperature has been reached the lizard is at its most active and can efficiently forage for food and indulge in territorial and sexual behaviour. As soon as the body temperature begins to rise above optimum, the lizard has to move into the shade to bring it back to optimum. By shuttling backwards and forwards from sun to shade (sometimes referred to as "heloithermal shuttling"), the lizard can effectively maintain a preferred temperature almost as efficiently as an endotherm. A lizard becomes increasingly inactive as body temperatures drop

below the optimum and, as sunset approaches, it will have to seek out its refuge for the night before it becomes too inactive.

Different species of lizards have different preferred body temperatures. Those from high latitude temperate areas, or from high altitude tropical and subtropical areas can operate efficiently at lower body temperatures than those from tropical or subtropical areas. Lizards from subtropical desert regions have the highest preferred body temperatures and can operate with a body temperature as high as 42 °C (107° F) while lizards from high latitude temperate regions can operate efficiently with a body temperature as low as 22° C (71° F). In some cases the body temperature can be partially controlled by means other than heliothermal shuttling. Lizards emerging in the morning often are dark colored, and gradually lighten in color as the body warms up. It is a well known fact that dark colors absorb heat and light colors reflect it. A good example of this color use is that exhibited by the Desert Iguana, *Dipsosaurus dorsalis*. On emergence in the morning, its brown to gray body markings almost cover the dorsal surface. As the reptile warms up the dark markings become lighter and smaller until, on reaching optimum body temperature, the lizard often appears to be almost gleaming white in the bright sunlight. When the ground temperature becomes too hot for comfort, many desert lizards move into bushes to cool off. Where vegetation is sparse, some desert lizards stretch their limbs and lift their bodies high above the warm surface; to get a bit of extra relief, some even alternately raise one or two limbs into the air. Once the temperature becomes unbearably hot, they must retreat to their burrows.

Some secretive lizards thermoregulate by moving under solid objects that have been warmed through by the sun. Many geckos, for example, spend their days beneath loose bark on trees, moving from sun warmed parts to cooler parts as the situation demands. Other lizards behave similarly beneath ground litter. Burrowing species will come close to the surface when they need to warm themselves, and burrow deeper into the soil when they need to cool off.

Overheating can be more dangerous to a lizard than suboptimal temperatures. All species have what is known as a critical high body temperature above which they will not survive for long. This temperature may be relatively high in desert dwelling species, but lower in temperate species and even in many tropical species. Though the Desert Iguana, for example can operate at a temperature as high as 46° C (115° F), another degree above this may become critical, and the reptile will die if it cannot cool itself. Most lizards from cool temperate regions cannot tolerate temperatures in excess of 30 °C (86 °F). Because temperatures in the tropics remain relatively constant, especially in lowland equatorial areas, lizards from these habitats have less problem with regard to thermoregulation and can often operate efficiently day and night without need to resort to it. As equatorial temperatures rarely reach the height of summertime desert temperatures tropical lizards usually have less heat tolerance than desert species; the critical high temperature for most species is about 35° C (95 °F).

HIBERNATION

Lizards living in temperate and many subtropical regions, hibernate during the winter months. The lessening of photoperiod and reducing temperatures as winter approaches causes the lizards to become increasingly inactive. During the spring, summer and early fall, the lizard has been feeding avidly in order to boost its body reserves ready for the demanding period of hibernation. Cool weather will cause the

Desert Iguana, *Dipsosaurus dorsalis*. Photo by W. P. Mara.

lizards to burrow below ground, into leaf litter, or enter crevices, burrows of other animals or any suitable place where the frost cannot reach. During hibernation metabolism reaches almost zero and little energy or oxygen is required. The minimum temperatures tolerated by hibernating temperate species is in the range of 4-6° C (approx. 39-43 °F); for subtropical species 10-15 °C (approx. 50-59 °F). The period of hibernation ranges from four to seven months for temperate species, two to four months for subtropical species (often depending on the latitude of the habitat and its influences on seasonal climate patterns). A reverse of the seasonal weather changes in the spring will cause the reptiles to emerge from hibernation and warm themselves in the sun before beginning to feed and prepare themselves for the breeding season ahead (see Breeding). Most lizards from temperate and subtropical habitats seem to require a period of hibernation in order to reproduce successfully in the following season. Lizards from tropical areas do not hibernate as such, though may estivate during times of drought. They burrow down into moist soil and go into a state of semi-torpor, while waiting for better times. The onset of a wet season often is a trigger for tropical species to breed.

Brown Basilisk, *Basiliscus vittatus*. Photo by R. S. Simmons.

DEFENSE

Predators of lizards are many and varied and include carnivorous mammals, birds, other reptiles (especially snakes and larger lizards) and even amphibians. The major defense mechanism of most active diurnal lizards is flight, most of them being so speedy as to easily out-distance most predators. Certain lizards such as Green Iguanas (*Iguana*), Water Dragons (*Physignathus*), and Basilisks (*Basiliscus*). often live near water to which they will take if scared. Slower moving lizards such as some large Australasian pink and blue-tongued skinks (*Hemisphaeriodon* and *Tiliqua* for example), instead of taking flight, will open the mouth threateningly, showing the brightly colored tongue and

mouth lining while hissing and lunging. The Bearded Dragons (*Pogona* species) show similar behaviour, exposing the bright yellow color of the mouth interior. The Beaded Lizards (*Heloderma* species) also threaten by gaping and hissing, and will not hesitate to use their venomous bite if further provoked. Though not generally fatal to humans, the bite of these lizards is said to be extremely painful and debilitating. Some large geckoes, such as the Tokay, *Gekko gecko*, will open the mouth and make a loud noise if threatened and, if this doesn't put off an intruder it will bite with a vice-like grip.

One of the most dramatic defensive measures taken by a lizard is that of the Frilled Lizard, *Chlamydosaurus kingii*, of Australia. This 60-90 cm (2-3 ft) long lizard has a large scaly frill around its neck which, under normal circumstances is folded back like a fan and is relatively inconspicuous. If threatened by a predator, the lizard quickly erects the frill (using a framework of bony cartilage) opens its mouth wide and hisses furiously. The brightly colored frill, when erect, is about four times the diameter of the head and offers an impressive display to the would-be aggressor. If the display does not work (as is often the case with human "predators"), the lizard turns and scuttles off upright on its hind limbs with a remarkable turn of speed. Some Horned Toads (*Phrynosoma* species) "shock" their predators by squirting streams of blood from the corners of the eyes; others, when danger threatens, pretend to be dead!

Many lizards rely on cryptic coloration for camouflage. Tree dwelling species are often green to match the foliage among which they live, while rock-dwelling species are often shades of gray or brown, like the surfaces on which they move or rest. A few taxa, particularly chameleons, are able to rapidly change their skin colors to match their backgrounds.

One interesting means of defense many lizards have which is almost unique among the vertebrates is the ability to shed part or all of the tail. Known as autotomy (literally: self-mutilation), the tail breaks across a fracture plain through one of the tail vertebrae and not between the vertebrae as was once thought. If a predator seizes the tail, it is cast off. The shed tail wriggles violently for some time after it has been detached and occupies the predator while the lizard makes it escape. After losing its tail, the lizard will grow a new one, but this is never as elegant as the original and contains no vertebrae. In cases where the original tail only partially breaks, a new tail may grow out of the wound giving the lizards a double (bifurcated) tail. Several lizard species, including many geckoes have a short, thick tail, which resembles the head, and thus confuses predators. Members of the agamid genus *Uromastyx* use their stout spiny tails to block the entrance to their burrows when resting. Some members of the Australian gecko genus *Diplodactylus* can eject a sticky, viscous fluid from pores in the tail which gums up the mouth and eyes of would be predators.

SOCIAL BEHAVIOR

Social interaction among lizards is largely concerned with territoriality and reproduction. Reproductive behaviour is discussed in the section on breeding. Many diurnal, sunloving lizards, especially the males are extremely territorial and will display aggressively if they feel their territory is being threatened. Many *Agama* species live in almost hierarchal, social colonies, with the dominant male taking the highest point in a tree or among a group of rocks. The dominant male takes on the brightest of hues while protecting his territory and will further advertise his importance with much head bobbing. *Anolis* and *Iguana* species, among others, behave similarly while distending their, sometimes colorful, throat fans (dewlaps). Other lizards use a combination of body inflation, mouth opening, color changing, tail waving, push-ups and so on to maintain their claim of territory ownership. Serious fighting rarely occurs as the non-dominant animal will usually move away before things get too hot for it!

HANDLING, TAMING AND TRAINING

Most lizard species are not suitable for handling and petting on a regular basis. Small lizards in particular tend to stress on being handled, although some of the larger iguanas and monitors seem to take handling in their stride once they are accustomed to it.

Most lizards are therefore to be admired, rather than cuddled, but there will always be times when you need to handle them for one reason or another. Such times are routine health examinations, administration of treatments, inspection before

Frilled Dragon, *Chlamydosaurus kingi*. Photo by Paul Freed.

initial purchase, or when it becomes necessary to transfer them from one cage to another. Methods of handling vary, depending on the size, and sometimes on the species of lizards. It takes a while to become adept in lizard handling, but once you acquire the skill you will be able to do it almost instinctively. Do not allow small children to handle small lizards, they (the kids) tend to squeeze them much too tightly and could seriously injure or even kill them. No lizard should ever be held by the tail, apart from the fact that many species are likely to shed their tail if you do this, the weight of the body could injure the tails of those that don't.

Tiny lizards and juveniles up to say 5 cm (2 in) in length are very fragile and must be handled with the greatest of care. A small net, of the type used for catching tropical fish fry may be useful. Catch the lizard in the net and turn the net so that the lizard is trapped among the material. The reptile can then be inspected, without physically handling it, by moving a little material away at a time.

Small, fast moving lizards up to 20 cm (8 in) in length should be first restrained by quickly, but gently, cupping the whole hand over the lizard. Then manipulate the digits, so that the thumb and forefinger grip the the lizard firmly but gently around the thoracic area, allowing the tail to hang free. Try to keep the weight of the reptile in your palm. Fragile species such as geckos are best captured in a soft cloth.

Medium sized lizards up to 45 cm (18 in) in length should be gripped firmly around the body with the thumb and forefinger just behind the head to prevent the lizard turning and biting (some mean lizards, even of this size, can give you a nasty bite if you are not careful). Some people may prefer to wear leather gloves when handling feisty lizards in this size range.

Large lizards above 45 cm (18 in) all have to be treated with the utmost respect. With the exception of those large specimens that you are sure are tame you must restrain them so that they cannot injure you, or others with their teeth, their claws, or their lashing tail. I once got into a whole lot of trouble when, as a reptile curator in a public zoo, I accidentally allowed a 120 cm (4 ft) "tame" Water Monitor, *Varanus salvator,* to lash out with its tail and strike the face of a little girl during a zoo education class I was taking. The very brave little girl ended up with an angry red weal across her cheek which, fortunately, turned out to be not as serious as it looked. But I ended up with a severe dressing down from my director, and had to make an embarrassing apology to angry teachers and parents. Another time, I got a real nasty, deep bite on my hand from a 75 cm (2 ft 6 in) Desert Monitor, *V. griseus,* which I had not restrained properly. It is experiences like these that make herpetologists progressively careful when handling reptiles. Never become complacent!

It is best to wear tough leather gloves when handling a large aggressive lizard. The reptile should be gripped firmly around the neck with one hand, using some of the fingers to restrain the forelimbs. With the other hand, grip the lizard around the waist, and tuck the rear limbs and tail under your elbow. With exceptionally large, feisty monitor lizards it may take two people to restrain them. Never throw caution to the wind when dealing with such powerful animals, some large males can suddenly turn aggressive during the breeding season.

The only two species of venomous lizards, the Beaded Lizard, *Heloderma horridum,* and the Gila Monster, *H. suspectum,* are not recommended as household pets. If you must keep them, however, they require extra special caution when being handled. Indeed they should not be handled at all unless strictly necessary. Although both species tend to become docile in captivity, the risk of a bite should never be underestimated. Though the venom from either species is rarely fatal to humans, a bite is said to be extremely painful and temporarily debilitating and thus to be avoided. If one of these lizards must be handled, it should first be restrained around the neck with one (gloved) hand so that it is unable to turn its head and bite. Some workers prefer to use a "T" stick to pin the head down first. The other hand can be used to hold the rear end of the reptile. When releasing it, always let go of the rear end first, then release the neck and withdraw the hand as quickly as possible.

**Beaded Lizard, *Heloderma horridum.*
Photo by K. H. Switak.**

TAMING AND TRAINING

As mentioned above, most small lizards are not suitable for taming. They often remain extremely nervous throughout their lives, and will stress if interfered with too often. They are best left in peace in their cage, and admired only.

Some of the larger lizards, including Green Iguanas, *Iguana iguana,* and most of the monitors (Varanidae), fortunately, are usually raised from juveniles and are tamed by regular handling. It is quite easy to tame them when they are little and, once tame, they will usually continue to remain docile even when they reach full size. At first, juvenile specimens will struggle and may attempt to bite, each time you pick them up. You should start the taming process by touching them; slowly approaching the animal, in its cage, with your hand. If you do this several times a day, over several days, the lizard will realise that you mean no harm to it and will not take flight. Next, begin to scratch the lizard on its back, or on top of its head with your fingers. Again, it may take a few days before the reptile, gets used to this. Once it accepts your hand touching it without panicking you can start offering little snippets of food. Iguanas can be given something attractive like dandelion flowers, monitors maybe a large grasshopper, or a piece of lean, raw meat.

Once you have the lizard's confidence, you can begin trying to pick it up. Place your hands under its belly and lift it. You may have to restrain it by gripping but eventually it should sit on your hand without trying to flee. You should do your initial training in an escape proof room just in case a fast moving lizard should make a break for it. Anyone whose Green Iguana has legged it up a neighbour's *Sequoiadendron* will tell you how difficult they are to retrieve! Once your lizard is tame you must handle it regularly. When it gets too large to sit on your hand you can place it on your arm or shoulder, or on your lap.

HOUSING, HEATING AND LIGHTING

There are many options available for housing lizards. Housing may be referred to as a cage, a terrarium, or a vivarium and these three words will be used interchangably in this text. The main criteria to be considered when deciding on a type of cage are that it must be escape proof, must be of sufficient size for the inmates to live and behave naturally, must provide the appropriate environmental conditions for the species being kept, and must be easy to clean and service. Other considerations may include such items as cost, amount of space available and so on. With regard to cost

Green Iguana, *Iguana iguana*. Photo by Isabelle Francais

there are lizards and vivaria in most price ranges; there is something for everyone. Obviously, if you do not have much room to spare, you would go for smaller lizards and correspondingly smaller cages rather than larger ones.

Glass and Plastic Tanks: Many lizard species can be successfully maintained in glass fish tanks; in fact, for many geckoes, small skinks, lacertids, fence lizards and so on, glass tanks are probably the most convenient forms of housing. Your aquarists' suppliers will usually have a fish tanks in a range of sizes and qualities. Most of these will be simple rectangular glass tanks, constructed with five panels cemented together with silicon adhesive. The versatility of silicon adhesive means that it is also quite simple to construct your own tank to a particular or unusual size or shape. Most glass tanks have a glass lid which is simply laid on the strengthening strips attached across the top of the tank. Such a lid is suitable for small lizards that require a humid environment but is less suitable for larger lizards (which will be able to escape by pushing the lid up), or for species that require lots of ventilation. In such cases it is best to buy a specially made terrarium lid or make one that can be secured to the glass strengthening strips with a couple of swiveling catches. There is a number of terrarium lids on the market, with screening made to fit most standard size tanks. Other kinds of lids include those made in a box shape, which allows heating and lighting apparatus to be concealed above the tank, but separated from the inmates by screening to prevent burns.

Plastic tanks also have their uses. They come in convenient sizes and are useful as spare cages, as rearing cages for neonates and so on. They are not really suitable for display cages as the surfaces soon dull after regular cleaning, making it difficult to view the contents. One very good feature of some of these tanks which are specially designed for small animals, is that they have a secure lid.

Fiberglass: Fiberglass is another material that is becoming increasingly used by herpetoculturists. Several excellent models are usually available commercially. The glass fiber itself is opaque, which offers a feeling of security to the lizard inmates (they cannot see movement approaching from all directions as is the case with glass tanks), but they have a removable (usually sliding) glass viewing panel, often set at an angle in the front of the cage.

Timber Cages: Many hobbyists prefer to use custom built timber cages with a glass (sliding or with hinged frames) door or doors in one or more sides. One great advantage of timber cages is that they can be built to greater dimensions than are normally standard in glass or plastic tanks. Any timber used must be thoroughly primed and treated with several coats of non toxic waterproof (polyurethane or epoxy) paint or varnish to lengthen its life. Untreated timber will eventually warp or rot, even with minimal dampness. Cages can be made of hardboard, blockboard, or particleboard as long as it has been thoroughly waterproofed, but the most rugged material is undoubtedly exterior quality plywood. The sides, top and base can be made of 2 cm (3/4 in) thick sheets, cut to size and glued and tacked together. The back of the cage can be made of thinner material (say 6 mm - 1/4 in)to help cut down on overall weight and cost.

The viewing/access door or doors are mounted on the front of the cage. Some hobbyists like to have an additional small service door in one of the cage ends to reduce the possibility of escapes when feeding or watering etc. The doors can consist of sheets of glass fitted into runners for smaller cages, but for larger cages framed (with timber or aluminium) doors will be required. I have found second hand aluminium framed windows (sliding or hinged) to be very useful and versatile. Demolition yards often have a range of sizes but you will usually have to build, or adapt, the cage to suit the size of the window, rather than vice versa.

Brick or Block Terraria: For large lizards such as various iguanas, monitors, sailfinned lizards or tegus, purpose built, brick or concrete block cages, with framed glass viewing windows, are undoubtedly the best option providing you have the space and the finance. The advantages of such cages (which are quite common in zoos and public reptile exhibits) are that you can build in some quite spectacular internal landscaping (natural looking rock faces, caves, crevices etc.) and you can have a substantial, drainable pool which will be enjoyed by large semi-aquatic species. Another advantage is that you can build additional drainage into the substrate areas, allowing regular hosing down. You will of course need to have a permanent and solid base on which to construct such a heavy structure and you may have to consult experienced builders, plumbers or engineers before going ahead with such a grand project.

Stock Cages and Breeding Batteries: Herpetoculturists breeding large numbers of lizards commercially will require simple methods of housing breeding stock, for rearing neonates, and for juvenile specimens that are awaiting sale. Most breeders have a special room, building or shed set aside for batteries of breeding cages, and they have come up with various ingenious types of caging. One common method, is to use numbers of plastic food storage boxes all the same size and to construct shelving so that the boxes can be slid, drawer-like between two shelves, the top shelf acting as a lid to the cage. The boxes must, of course, fit pretty snugly if escapes are to be avoided. Ventilation holes are drilled into the sides of the boxes. Such batteries are suitable for geckoes and small burrowing species that do not require supplementary lighting. Lizard species requiring broad spectrum lighting are generally held in rows of cages with screened lids through which light is directed (see lighting, below). When large numbers of cages are maintained in a reptile room, individual cage heating is not usually practicable. The best method is to heat the whole room, with the ambient temperature controlled thermostatically.

Substrate Materials: For simple stock, quarantine or isolation cages absorbent paper is the best material to use as bedding. Soiled paper is easily destroyed by burning and is simple to replace. Newspaper, though not particularly esthetic, is quite acceptable in non display cages. If you want to be little more fussy, use paper towels. Some hobbyists use colored (green or brown is more natural - not pink, or patterned with Disney characters!) cotton handtowels, which can be washed and replaced as necessary. Pieces of old carpet can be used similarly. If you want to go to the expense there is a few commercially manufactured terrarium mats available, some of which resemble turf.

Though it may seem old fashioned to some, I still prefer gravel as a substrate in most lizard display cages - to me it just seems to be closer to natural, and more esthetic, than most other materials. It needs to be taken out and replaced at regular intervals, but can be disinfected and washed (soak in ten percent household bleach solution for an hour then swill out thoroughly with a hose). Tree bark or orchid compost is also used on a regular basis by many enthusiasts. Peat, or fine sand is not generally recommended as it gets dragged about by the lizards and makes quite a mess, though course sand can be used for desert settings. Natural, planted earth substrates are only recommended for large terraria with small species.

Hide Boxes: Many lizards are less stressed when they have some kind if retreat in which they can hide when not basking or feeding. A hide box need not be substantial, cardboard food cartons of various sizes, while not esthetic, are quite acceptible in non display cages and can be simply discarded and replaced when soiled.

Display Cage Decoration: Most enthusiasts like to have at least one cage in which their lizards are displayed in a semi-natural environment. While it may be difficult, or impossible to provide a natural set-up for a large iguana or monitor (plants would be eaten or trampled), it is quite feasible to do so with species such as geckos, small lacertids, small agamids, skinks, and so on. Every effort should be made to construct a facsimile of the natural habitat of the species being kept, and this is a good reason for not mixing species from different habitats. Petshops supply colorful "backing sheets" showing various scenic photographs of habitats. Choose one that is appropriate for your setup. Some artistic enthusiasts may even like to paint a suitable picture of their own. Arranged at the back of a tank, these sheets add a third dimension to the display, providing you arrange the interior of the tank to complement the whole picture.

Desert species can be supplied with a coarse, sandy substrate a few rocks and a couple of desert plants (cacti or succulents would seem a good choice). Arboreal, tropical rainforest species can be supplied with a tall terrarium with several secure branches on which they can climb. Potted plants (what are generally referred to as "houseplants" are usually the hardiest) with their pots hidden behind rocks or sheets of bark, will add to the effect as well as help maintain humidity.

Semi-aquatic species require an aqua-terrarium, a cage in which there is a large area of water and a similar area of land. In the glass tank this is simple to achieve, by siliconing a sheet of glass across the centre of the tank and making the joins watertight. One side is filled with gravel to become the "land" while the other side is filled with water. A couple of sloping rocks or slates placed against the edge of the partition will allow lizards to enter or leave the water easily.

Rocks and Logs: Natural logs and branches are frequently used for terrarium decoration, and are essential for arboreal lizards. Any lumber used should be from hardwood or fruit trees, not from pines, cedars or other needle bearers, the sap of which could be toxic to some lizards. It is best to select branches that have been dead for some time, rather than cut them from a living tree. Local woodland will often reveal a selection of fallen branches. Branches collected from the sea shore or along a river bank are even better, often having an interesting shape, smoothed and bleached by the action of sun, sand and water. All branches should be scrubbed clean and dried before use and they should be affixed securely in the terrarium to prevent them falling and possibly injuring the residents.

Rocks can sometimes be purchased from pet shops or garden centers, but in some areas you can collect your own. Look for interesting shapes and colors. Like logs, they should be thoroughly cleaned before use. If using piles of rocks, make sure they are completely secure. They can be cemented together to form hiding caves or crevices.

Plants: There is no doubt that living plants provide the ultimate esthetic touch to the natural display terrarium though, for reasons that are obvious, they are not practical to use with large or herbivorous lizards. In such cases, leave the plants out or provide plastic plants, of which ever more lifelike forms are appearing on the market.

It is best to leave living plants in their pots rather than try to plant them in the terrarium substrate, unless you are going in for the completely natural paludarium type setup. The pots can be buried in gravel, or concealed behind rocks or bark. Being in pots it is easy to interchange them as necessary. Wear and tear of plants in the terrrium will mean changing them at intervals. Keep a spare set of plants on the windowsill or in the greenhouse, ready to replace those suffering from the rigors of terrarium life! The plants taken out can be given a period of recovery before being used again.

HEATING AND LIGHTING

Being ectotherms, lizards are very sensitive to changes in temperature. All species have a preferred body temperature, which they will attempt to maintain during periods of activity. They do this by moving from warmer to colder areas and vice versa. It is therefore important to offer a temperature gradient in the terrarium by directing the main source of heat to one end of the enclosure. Artificial means of heating usually have to be applied in indoor terraria. This is not only because many species come from a warmer climate than that which prevails where they are being kept, but also because natural sunlight entering through terrarium glass will soon heat the interior of the cage up to lethal temperatures. It is important for all lizards to be able to reach their preferred optimum body temperature for a few hours each day during the active season. Inferior temperature will cause digestive and other health problems

Temperature requirements vary among the species and you should obtain details of the climate of the natural habitat of your particular species. Your supplier will advise you here, and you can also get much valuable climatic information about most countries from a good world atlas (you will find one in most local public libraries). In most natural habitats there is a reduction in temperature at night. This varies from just a few degrees in lowland equatorial areas, to as much as twenty degrees or even more in desert, montane, and temperate areas. A compromise temperature reduction in the terrarium is usually sufficient for most species. This is simply accomplished by switching off the heaters at night, and on again in the morning. The average night temperatures in most dwellings do not fall significantly at night, even in the winter. In cases where reptiles are kept in unheated rooms or sheds, especially during the colder parts of the year, it will be necessary to provide some form of night heater with lower temperature than the day heater. This can be accomplished with the use of a red or blue colored (to reduce the amount of light emitted) incandescent bulb of low wattage. The following is a brief discussion of the heating options available.

Incandescent Light Bulbs: These ordinary domestic bulbs were once the standard type of heating and lighting apparatus used in the terrarium until it was discovered that the quality of light produced was not adequate for various species of basking lizards (see below). These bulbs do still have their uses, however. They emit a fair amount of heat and supply useful additional background lighting. They are relatively inexpensive, and come in a range of sizes (wattages). Using a thermometer (you should have a thermometer monitoring the temperature in every cage), you can experiment with various wattages until you come up with the right temperature for individual cages (you should do this before any lizards are installed). If controlled by a thermostat they have the disadvantage of the light going on and off unnaturally throughout the day. In such cases it is best to instal the bulb inside a metal canister or clay flowerpot and the heat will be transferred through the

container and radiate into the airspace and to use a separate source of lighting.

Ceramic Bulbs and Plates: These are small heaters that can be simply plugged into an ordinary bulb socket. They are available in various sizes and can emit directed heat (via a reflector for a bulb, or by the shape of the plate) without producing any light.

Heat Lamps: Various types of heat lamps are available. These include the infrared lamps used in hatcheries to rear chicks as well as several types specially marketed for reptiles. Infra red lamps can be dangerous if the source of rays is too close to the reptiles; severe burns have been reported in many species that have basked too close to the lamps. It is best to suspend the lamp outside the cage and direct the beam through screening onto a basking site at one end of the cage. With the aid of a thermometer, ensure that the temperature on the surface of the basking site does not exceed 40° C (104° F)

Aquarium Heaters: An aquarium heater is useful for supplying background heat in humid terraria. Such heaters are available in various sizes and usually have a thermostat build in for temperature control. In an aqua-terrarium the heater will warm the water to the set temperature and the slow evaporation of the water will also warm the airspace. If used with large, boisterous lizards, the glass heater should be protected within a plastic tube affixcd below the water level to prevent accidental breakage. If there is no large area of water in your terrarium, you can still use an aquarium heater set in a concealed jar of water. The jar should have a lid with a hole cut to take the heater cable, and more holes to let out the humidity. You must inspect such a heater every day and top up the water as necessary.

Cable Heaters, Pads, Boards and Tapes: Cable heaters are normally used by horticulturists to provide bottom heat in propagation chambers. They have limited use in warming the substrate in terraria, but are less suitable for burrowing species, which are likely to unearth the cable time and again. Pads (which are flexible) are normally placed beneath terraria, while boards can be used against the walls. In some cases a single heat board can be used to heat two adjacent cages. Heat tapes have limited uses when attached along the sides of terraria. Most of these appliances are used to provide low background temperature and are additional to sources of heat provided for basking.

Sizzle Stones and Hot Rocks: Recent innovations for herpetoculturists include various heating appliances going under such names as "Sizzle Stones" and "Hot Rocks". These are natural or artificial rocks hollowed out to take a heating element supplied by a cable from the mains. They are simply laid on the vivarium substrate and liz-

487

Oaxacan Spinytail Iguana, *Ctenosaura quinquecarinata.* **Photo by Paul Freed.**

ards can warm themselves at will. Such heaters should be used with care as they tend to overheat and the lizards could be burned. If you must use these items try and obtain one that is thermostatically controlled.

Safety Measures: Take great care to avoid overheating the terrarium airspace, almost all lizards will expire if exposed to a temperature of 35° C (95° F) or more for a few hours. Hotspots to 40° C (104° F) are acceptable, but there must be other areas in the vivarium where the air temperature is 25° C (77° F) or less. It is best to use thermostats on all heating equipment which will cut out the heaters should the maximum required temperature be overridden. Personal safety measures are also important with regard to electric shock. Only use standard electrical equipment and do not improvise electrically unless you know exactly what you are doing. In most cases it is best to employ the services of an expert electrician for major or complicated installations.

LIGHTING

It was not until relatively recently that the importance of photoperiod and light quality for terrarium animals was realized. For heliophilic (sun basking) lizards, the quality of light seems to be extremely important to general health, though exact and individual specific requirements still require much research. Most herpetoculturists are now of the opinion that diurnal lizards kept under full spectrum lighting (see below) fare better than those kept under ordinary incandescent bulbs or white fluorescent tubes. Manufacturers of lighting equipment have done much research into the production of fluorescent lighting with a spectral power distribution (SPD) similar to that of natural daylight (initially this research was done for the benefit of the horticultural plant propagation industry). While the light intensity produced by any lamp would never substitute that of natural daylight, especially in full summer sun, it seems that the presence of a full spectrum leads to healthier captive lizards. While the ultra violet (UV) end of the spectrum seems to be very important (among other things, probably helping in the synthesis of vitamin D3 in the skin; this phenomenon and its relationship with calcium/phosphorus metabolism, is presently a subject of much research and speculation), overdoses of UV can be dangerous, so full spectrum lamps emitting small but significant amounts of UV over several hours a day, are preferable to the so-called black lights (high intensity UV) even if these are used only for short periods at a time.

A suitable type of lighting for the average small lizard cage would include an incandescent bulb or spot light for extra light intensity, (and supply part of the heating at the same time) plus a full spectrum daylight type tube, of which there are several brands available. Your pet shop will provide you with details of available lamps. Should you wish to go into terrarium lighting in more detail, most of the commercial companies producing full spectrum lighting will be pleased to supply you with specifications of various types of lamps.

With regard to photoperiod, it is important to supply seasonal variations, depending on the natural habitat of the species in question. Days will be longer in the summer and shorter in the winter. The increases and reductions in photoperiod as far as is known need not be exact, and most species will respond favorably to compromise changes. As an example, many temperate lizards will respond well to the following regime: Summer (April to September): 14 hours daylight and 10 hours darkness each day. Fall (October): gradually reduce to winter regime during the month. Winter (November to February): 10 hours daylight and 14 hours darkness each day. Spring (March): gradually increase to summer regime during the month. With this system, a slightly longer "summer" than "winter" will ensure the reptiles feed up well for the winter rest period and the following breeding season. It is important also to manipulate the temperature seasonally, together with the photoperiod.

THE LIZARD ROOM

A few enthusiasts devote a spare room in their house, or use a garden-shed, garage, or greenhouse, and give their large lizards free run of it. Such a system is particularly suitable for keeping a small colony of large iguanas (*Iguana*, *Cyclura*, *Ctenosaura* for example). A room with a sunny aspect is best. Heating can be supplied via a centrally heated radiator and a few strategically placed heat lamps (screened) placed over basking areas. Fluorescent lighting may be used to varying degrees depending on the amount of natural light that reaches the room interior.

If possible a room with a concrete floor and a drain should be used. This will facilitate cleaning and hosing down when necessary. If a timber floor is used, you will have to find some way of sealing and waterproofing it to protect the floorboards. A large drainable pool can be provided, plus a number of tree limbs and rocks for decoration and for providing surfaces on which the lizards can climb and bask. You may be able to include a few robust shrubs in large pots or tubs for added effect. All heating appliances must be screened so that the lizards cannot come into direct contact with them. Also be sure to screen off any potential escape routes,

Rhinoceros Iguana, *Cyclura cornuta*. Photo by R. D. Bartlett.

such as fire places, pipe ducts and so on. Screening on the outside of external windows will allow you to open them for fresh air on warm days. With some careful planning you can fit a large area of window or glass sliding door to a south facing wall. This will let in sunlight and, if the windows are screened with strong mesh on the outside, your lizards can enjoy the benefits of natural sunlight on suitable days.

KEEPING LIZARDS OUTDOORS

Lizards native to, or from one similar to the climate in which they are being kept can be housed outdoors all year round providing a few simple rules are obeyed. In temperate areas, lizards from sub-tropical habitats, and even some from tropical habitats can be kept in outdoor enclosures during the warmer months. There are several advantages in keeping lizards in outdoor enclosures, including the fact that they will benefit from the natural sunlight and seasonal fluctuations. They may be able to catch a variety of their own live-food, and herbivorous species can browse on natural plants growing in the enclosure.

A standard type outdoor vivarium for lizards (sometimes called a reptile "pit") is an excavated area surrounded by a brick or concrete wall. The enclosure should be sited in a situation where it receives sun for most of the day but also is sheltered from strong winds and driving rains. In the northern hemisphere a south facing site backed by the wall of a building or a thick stand of trees is ideal. The height of the wall will depend on the size of the lizards you are keeping, and their jumping abilities. In most cases, the wall should be twice or more the height of the total length of the longest lizards you intend to keep. An inward facing, overhanging ledge at the top of the wall will further help prevent escapes.

As an example for say a group of Chuckwallas (*Sauromalus*), Desert Iguanas (*Dipsosaurus*) and Collared Lizards (*Crotaphytus*), dig a trench about 60 cm (2 ft) deep and 90 cm (3 ft) wide around the areas to be enclosed (I would suggest an area of not less than two square meters (2.39 square yards) for each lizard you intend to be keep, more if possible); so if you have two pairs of each of the above mentioned species you will require a total enclosed area of not less than 24 square meters (28.7 square yards). The excavated soil can be used to form a mound in the centre of the enclosure. The outer side of the trench should be vertical, the inner side sloped up, to include the mound at an angle of about 45 degrees. The enclosure

Chuckwalla, *Sauromalus obesus*. Photo by Isabelle Francais.

should be rounded or curved at the perimeter with no sharp corners. Place a 10 cm (4 in) thick layer of concrete in the bottom of the trench and allow it to set thoroughly before building the wall at the perimeter. The wall should be built to a height of 90 cm (3 ft) above ground level. This will mean that the actual height of the wall, including that in the trench below ground level is 140 cm (about 4 ft 8 in). The inside of the wall should be rendered to a smooth finish so that lizards cannot get a foothold on it. Ensure that no part of the top of the wall is closer than 120 cm (4 ft) to the central mound.

The mound should be landscaped with rocks, logs, a small shallow pool, planted areas including an area of weeds, and a few areas of bare sand in a sunny position for egglaying sites. Ensure that the branches of plants do not grow close to the wall allowing lizards to escape; they (the plants not the lizards) should be pruned regularly. If you intend to keep lizards in the enclosure throughout the year in temperate areas you must provide adequate hibernaculae, by leaving shallow pits beneath some of the rocks. Arrange the rocks so that rainwater cannot flood into the refuge pits.

Black-collared Lizard, *Crotaphytus insularis*. Photo by R. D. Bartlett.

FEEDING AND WATER REQUIREMENTS

In the past, the feeding of inadequate diets, mainly through ignorance on the part of the hobbyist, frequently led to the rapid demise and death of many captive lizards. During the last few years concerned veterinarians and biologists with an interest in reptiles have been making increasing studies into the nutrition of reptiles and, as a result, it seems that most species can now be successfully maintained nutritionally, provided a few important rules are adhered to. Perhaps the most important rule, derived from a very old but true proverb, is that variety is the spice a life. A lizard maintained on a staple diet of say, mealworms, will not thrive, but one maintained on a minimum of five different kinds of invertebrate foods will flourish. This is because all animals need a balanced diet with the correct ratios of macronutrients, vitamins and minerals to allow their bodies to function efficiently. A dietary deficiency will result in imperfect metabolism, followed by debility and often death, unless the diet is corrected.

Most lizards are carnivorous and these can be conveniently divided into mini carnivores (small insectivorous lizards that feed mainly on insects and other small invertebrates) and maxi carnivores (larger lizards that prey on large invertebrates and vertebrates).

A few lizards are herbivorous and feed mainly on plant material, while some are more or less omnivorous feeding on a mixture of plant and animal material.

FEEDING MINI CARNIVORES

If you intend to keep small insectivorous lizards you must be sure that you will have an ongoing supply of live food with which to feed them. One of the biggest problems of raising neonate tiny lizard, (take the hatchling ground chameleon, *Brookesia minima,* which is little more than 1.2 cm (0.5 in) in total length) is that they require very tiny food insects, and a lot of them. Let us look at some of the commoner types of live insect foods available for our lizards.

Captured Live Foods: Some controversy exists as to the use of food invertebrates captured from the wild because of the possibility of contamination from insecticides, herbicides and other chemicals which could have toxic effects on our animals, plus the

Longnose Snake, *Rhinocheilus lecontei 'clarus',* eating an Eastern Fence Swift, *Sceloporus undulatus.* Photo by W. P. Mara.

Bighead Anole, *Anolis capito*. Photo by W. P. Mara.

possibility of the transmission of internal parasites. However, in all the time I have fed such livefood to many species over the years, I have never been able to ascertain any conclusive proof that such food is debilitating, provided it is collected sensibly. For the benefit of the added variety you can offer your lizards, the advantages outweigh any risks you may take. If you avoid collecting near treated agricultural or horticultural areas, areas close to roads, or to factories, you should have few problems.

The smallest kinds of livefoods offered to tiny lizards on a regular basis are springtails and other tiny denizens of the ground litter. A method of catching large numbers of these little creatures is to use a Berlese funnel. This consists of any type of fairly large funnel (plastic is fine) with the spout passing through a hole in the lid of a jar. A circular piece of fairly fine mesh is placed near the mouth of the funnel and a few handfuls of ground/ leaf litter, collected from a moist, shady area, are placed on top of the mesh. The whole contraption is then placed in the sun, the heat of which drives the little invertebrates down to the bottom of the litter from whence they fall through the mesh into the collecting jar. In colder or duller weather, you can substitute the sun by suspending a shaded 60 watt bulb near to the surface of the the litter. The

small inertebrates can simply be sprinkled into the cages with the tiny lizards, which will eat them voraciously.

Aphids are another kind of very small livefood that is easy to collect in certain areas during the warmer months. These little sapsucking insects (sometimes called, greenfly or blackfly depending in the species) are the bane of the gardener. They congregate on the succulent growing tips of many plants and can be collected by simply cutting off the growing tip complete with its resident population. You can either place the whole piece of plant in with your lizards or you can remove the aphids by tapping the plant sharply on the edge of the terrarium so that the aphids fall inside, or by gently teasing them off with a fine artist's brush.

Numbers of small beetles and other insects often congregate in the calyxes of flowers. These are best collected with an aspirator (commonly called a pooter), a glass or plastic jar with two tubes through the stopper. One tube is flexible and is placed near the insects, while the other tube is sucked sharply with the mouth. The insects will be pulled into the jar via the tube. A piece of gauze placed over the sucking tube will stop you getting an unwanted entree to your evening meal!

All sorts of flies of various sizes provide a

Holding/breeding enclosure for Domestic Crickets, *Acheta domesticus*. Photo by Isabelle Francais.

plethora of food possibilities for your lizards. Fruit flies, *Drosophila* species, are an essential standby item for all herpetoculturists raising tiny herptiles. These flies are cultured extensively in laboratories for studies into genetics (because they breed so fast through many generations) and it should be easy to purchase stocks of them complete with their food medium and instructions on how to propagate them, from specialist suppliers. There is even a wingless variety which is very useful as these flies are less likely to escape into the home. Fruitflies can also be collected quite easily during the warmer parts of the year in many areas, you only need some overripe fruit, even banana skins will do. Place these in a box in some remote corner of the garden and within a few days they will be literally infested with flies. Take a small meshed net and tap the box sharply with your toe. This will cause a cloud of the little flies to take to the air and you can easily catch them in the net.

Houseflies, bluebottles, greenbottles and similar, all make excellent food for many insectivorous lizards. Most of these kinds of fly are easy to catch

Holding/breeding enclosure for mealworms. Photo by Isabelle Francais.

in a flytrap. You can purchase a fly trap but it is also quite easy to mke your own. One of the simplest can be made with a flat board (6 mm - 1/4 in ply is ideal) about 30 cm (12 in square), some 5 cm x 5 cm (2 in x 2 in) lumber, a funnel (the top third of a quart plastic bottle makes a serviceable funnel), some wire, and some muslin netting (old net curtain material is fine). Make a 2.5 cm (1 in) diameter hole in the centre of the board and nail a piece of lumber to two sides of the board, so that it leaves a 5 cm (2 in) space under the board when you lay it down. Make a roughly cubic frame with the wire so that it just fits around the edges of the board. Sew some netting material around the framework to form a sort of cage, leaving a "sleeve" in one side for access. The sleeve is loosely knotted until you need to pass your hand inside it. Place the funnel, wide end down, over the hole in the board and affix the cage over this. Now find a piece of fish or meat and place it somewhere on some flat ground or on a slab (well away from the house) and place the trap over it. The flies will be attracted to the flesh as it begins to rot and will make for the nearest source of light when they have finished feeding. This will be through the hole in the board and through the funnel, where they will be trapped inside the netting cage. You can remove flies from the cage by unknotting the sleeve and passing a jar through the sleeve.

Some pet shops or bait shops may sell maggots, or fly larvae. Purchase those that have not been treated with dye. Maggots themselves should not be fed in great numbers as they have tough, rubbery, indigestible skins. However, one or two a week should do no harm. The maggots are better kept until they pupate, and then allowed to hatch into adult flies. Place a few pupae in some clean, slightly moist bran in a small plastic container with a 1 cm (1/2 in) hole in the lid. The container can be placed in the terrarium and the lizards will catch the hatching flies as they leave through the hole in the lid.

Earthworms may be eaten by some larger lizards. If you have an abundance of earthworms in your garden you can simply dig a few up as needed. One method of obtaining larger numbers of earthworms is to place a layer of compost (any organic matter including dead leaves, kitchen scraps, grass clippings and so on will do) about 15 cm (6 in) thick on a piece of flat ground. Wet it thoroughly with a hose then cover it with a piece of sacking. Spray the sacking with water daily in dry weather so that the compost beneath stays moist. Earthworms will congregate and breed in the compost, and can be collected often in large numbers. The process is also good for the garden soil and you can move the earthworm station to another spot if the supply is exhausted. Earthworms should be kept in a bucket of moist, sterile potting mix for 24 hours before being fed to the lizards so that their intestinal contents are purged of any putrid material.

Many insect species, quaintly known as "meadow plankton", can be collected (but only in the summer in areas with cold winters) by passing a fine meshed net through tall grass and foliage. Nylon gauze netting seems to be the strongest and will last longer than other types; a metal hoop is pushed through the hem of the net and attached to a handle (just like a butterfly net). If you pick the right places to use your net you will come up with a variety of moths, grasshoppers, caterpillars, beetles, spiders and so on. Carry a selection of small plastic containers into which you can size-grade your insects at regular intervals. Many lizards will go bananas when you tip a smorgasbord of mixed insects into their cage.

Another method of collecting small invertebrates is to look under logs, rocks, garbage and so on. Here you are sure to find a variety of suitable food items, including pill bugs, beetles, spiders, millipedes and earthworms. To avoid handling the insects you can scoop them into a container with a spoon or similar object.

Termites will be eaten by most small insectivorous lizards. Ants are eaten by certain specialist feeders such as Horned Toads (*Phrynosoma*) and Thorny Devils (*Moloch*), but most lizards will avoid them due to their hard chitinous exoskeletons and their acidic taste. If you are lucky (or perhaps unlucky, depending on how you may look at them) enough to live in an area inhabited by termites you will have an excellent, permanent source of small livefood. Termites can be collected by breaking open their causeway tunnels and and brushing them (with a soft brush - many termites are incredibly fragile and squash easily) into a container. Another method is to find the nest, which is like a large ball of honeycomb and to break a piece out of it with screwdriver or similar instrument. The whole piece, complete with its population of termites can be put into the terrarium and the lizards will eat the insects as they emerge.

Cultivated Live Foods: Many enthusiasts who live in high rise apatments or similar often have few opportunities to go out and collect live food. In temperate areas, also, most wild invertebrate fauna becomes very sparse during the winter months. Fortunately an ever increasing variety of live foods are being offered by the pet trade for mini-carnivores. It is your choice whether you purchase small batches of food insects on a regular basis, as you need them, or decide to start your own breeding colonies. The most commonly avail-

Termites on a rotting piece of wood. Photo by Isabelle Francais.

able invertebrate live foods are not particularly difficult to breed.

★ Mealworms, the larvae of certain kinds of grain beetle (*Tenebrio molitor* is the most usual species), are perhaps the best known live food and one of the oldest used in the pet trade. Unfortunately, on their own, mealworms are not considered to be nutritionally complete and, although they are a good staple, they should be used in conjunction with other foods. Mealworms can be kept in plastic shoe boxes, lunch boxes or similar. Drill a number of small (2 mm - 1/8 in) holes in the lid and along the upper sides for ventilation purposes. Put a 5 cm (2 in) layer of cereal in the box (a mixture of bran, rolled oats, and muesli is ideal) and place your purchased mealworms in this. They will soon burrow into the cereal and start feeding on it. Cover the culture with a cut-to-size piece of cloth (cotton or hessian for example) and place a cabbage leaf, pieces of carrot, apple or similar on top of this to provide moisture (the vegetable should be changed frequently before it spoils). Make sure the lid is secure to prevent beetles escaping.

Adult and 'fuzzy' mice in a holding/breeding enclosure. Photo by Isabelle Francais.

Mountain Horned Lizard, *Phrynosoma orbiculare*. Photo by Mella Panzella.

only one or two small insectivorous lizards it is hardly worth starting a cricket culture of your own, as you can buy a small quantity each time you need them. However, if you have a lot of hungry little lacertilian mouths to feed it will pay you to breed your own crickets. A large old fish tank with a screen lid makes an excellent container for breeding crickets; alternatively a reasonably sized plastic box, or even a plastic trash-can can be used. Always cut out a large ventilation hole in the lid and glue screening over it, to prevent escapes. Balls of crumpled newspaper and pieces of papier mache eggboxes make good bedding and hiding material for the crickets. They should be fed on a good mixture of cereal, finely chopped greenfood, lightly moistened dog, cat or chicken pellets, and so on. A commercially manufactured cricket diet is now available; it contains all of the necessary dietary constituents which are passed on, in turn, to the lizards. It is best to place the food in a dish to maintain hygiene. Another dish with a layer of moistened potting compost or vermiculite mixed with an equal part of sand will provide an egg laying vessel. A small bottle of water with a loosely packed wadding "wick" will provide a drink for the insects (do not provide an open water vessel as the insects will drown).

Maintain your cricket culture at a temperature range of 25-30° C (77-86°F) for best results. Eggs hatch in about three weeks in optimum conditions and the tiny 3-6 mm (1/8 - 1/4 in) long (depending on the species) hatchling nymphs are ideal food for juvenile and small lizards. A carefully planned and managed cricket colony will provide you with an almost limitless supply of good, wholesome livefood for your lizards.

★ Wax moths and their larvae are an excellent nutritious source of food for many of out smaller

Kept in a temperature of 26-31°C (79-88°F) the larvae will grow rapidly and pupate, soon hatching into adult beetles ready to mate and lay eggs. You should start a new culture each month, using beetles from the previous culture, for four months. Once you have four cultures going, you can discard the oldest one (use all the remaining insects up for feeding) each month and start a new one. Using this method you should never be short of mealworms.

★ Crickets have become increasingly popular as food for mini-carnivores over the past few years. They are indeed being bred in vast quantities for the pet trade by so-called "cricket farmers". Most of the crickets supplied are domestic or field crickets of the genera *Acheta* and *Gryllus*. If you keep insectivorous lizards. Two species of wax moths are commonly propagated as live food, the Greater Wax Moth, *Galleria mellonella* and the Lesser Wax Moth, *Achroea grisella*.

The Greater Wax Moth has a wingspan of about 3.5 cm (1.4 in) the forewings are dark grey, the hindwings silvery. The fertilized female moth lays up to 1000 eggs on the honeycomb in a beehive (which makes the moths a major pest in the honey industry). The larvae hatch in about a week and, feeding on the honeycomb, go through three instars before pupating. The larvae range from 6mm - 2.5 cm (1/4 - 1 in) in length, ideal for feeding to small to medium sized lizards. The adult moths which emerge from the pupae are also excellent food items.

The moths can be propagated in ventilated metal canisters packed loosely with waste honeycomb (which you may be able to obtain from a bee keeper) or a substitute made from a mixture prepared as follows: 115 grams/4 oz of honey, 115 grams/4 oz of glycerine, 450 grams/1 lb of bran, 450 grams/1 lb of poultry meal and 60 grams/2 oz of yeast. The ingredients should be mixed together thoroughly and any unused should be refrigerated until required. A piece of honeycomb complete with moth eggs or larvae is placed on the mixture. Start up a new culture every two months until you have about six cultures operating and, from then on, the oldest culture is discarded each time you start up a new one. The larvae can be taken out at various sizes and fed to your lizards. Always allow enough larvae to pupate for future cultures.

The adult Lesser Wax Moth has a wing span of just 15 mm (about half an inch) and the wings are plain silvery gray. They may be bred in a similar way to the Greater Wax Moths. Larvae and adults of this species are ideal for feeding to tiny hatchling lizards of small species.

* Silkworm Moths and their larvae have been cultivated in China and other eastern countries for centuries to obtain the fine silk from the cocoons spun by the larvae just before they pupate. Both the larvae in their variously sized instars and the adult moths will be accepted by a range of insectivorous lizards. They have a higher protein and calcium content than mealworms and are thus more nutritious. Silkworm larvae feed on the leaves of mulberry trees (*Morus* species). Silkworm eggs may be obtained from biological supply houses and some petshops. Silkworms can be propagated in large screened cages (a wooden frame covered with insect screening is ideal). You must be sure to have a supply of fresh mulberry leaves available during the spring and summer breeding season. Place a number of mulberry twigs complete with leaves, in a jar of water, and block the mouth of the jar with cotton wadding to prevent loss of insects by drowning. Place the eggs near to the mulberry and when the larvae hatch they will start feeding on the leaves. You will have to replace the mulberry twigs each time they become deplete. Place an-

Great Plains Skink, *Eumeces obsolefus*. Photo by R. D. Bartlett.

other jar of new twigs next to the original and the silkworms will transfer themselves in the search for food. Discard the twigs in the first jar when the silkworms have transferred (you may have to "help" some of the insects). Use paper towels or similar on the cage floor and clean out the copious droppings regularly.

Use the insects as food well before they start spinning their cocoons as they will lose some of their nutritive value at this time. When full sized, the plump larvae are about 5 cm (2 in) long. Allow some of them to spin cocoons and pupate, so that you will have adult moths to start the next generation.

Another method of cultivating silkworms is to keep them actually on the mulberry tree itself. Whole leafy branches can be covered with muslin "sleeves" and the silkworms placed inside for protection against birds etc.

THE FRIDGE AS A FEEDING AID

Many fast moving insects such as flies, crickets and so on, can be subdued by placing them in a fridge for 15 minutes or so. Put a jar of the insects in the fridge until they are subdued then you can easily shake them out into lizard cages with little risk of them escaping. Mealworms can be stored in the fridge for a month or so and will stop feeding and growing. This is useful for stopping surplus mealworms from pupating and saving them for use later. Silkworm eggs can be stored in a refrigerator over winter when mulberry leaves are not available.

FEEDING MAXI CARNIVORES

Monitor lizards, tegus, large water dragons, and some large iguanas fall into the category of lizard maxi carnivores. Juvenile specimens of many of these lizards will start in a diet of some of the items discussed for mini carnivores above, but as they grow they will require increasingly large food items.

The staple diet for many of these large lizards in captivity often is mice, rats or young chickens. Each of these items are generally available through petshops or specialist suppliers; they can be obtained live or deep-frozen. These various food animals offer a good balance of flesh, bone and fur or feather. The availability of deep frozen food animals at reasonable prices really makes it unnecessary for average lizard hobbyists to breed their own. Most larger carnivorous lizards will swallow food animals whole. Frozen animals must, of course, be thoroughly thawed out and brought to room temperature before use.

Lean raw meat such as beef or chicken will be taken by some lizards, but meat on its own is not a complete diet and it should be offered only in supplementary quantities. Lizards fed exclusively on raw meat diets are liable to suffer demineralization of the bones and other deficiencies (see vitamin/mineral supplements - below). Eggs will be eaten by many lizards, especially monitors, tegus and beaded lizards. Large monitors will dispatch hens' eggs whole, shell and all, while tegus and beaded lizards seen to prefer their eggs mixed in with some lean hamburger mince or similar. Canned dog or cat food will also be eaten eagerly by many lizards, but should only be offered in moderation as the protein content tends to be rather high for reptiles. Whole freshwater fish (guppies, minnows etc.) and aquatic snails should be offered to such species as Caiman Lizards (*Dracaena* species), Crocodile Lizards (*Shinisaurus*) and some monitors.

FEEDING HERBIVOROUS LIZARDS

Few lizards are totally herbivorous and many of those species that are primarily plant eaters may occasionally take animal matter opportunistically or accidentally. At one time, herbivorous lizards were a problem to keep healthy in captivity, but nutritional studies, mainly on the Green Iguana, have alleviated the problem to a certain extent. The most popular pet lizards which are primarily herbivorous include the Green Iguana, *Iguana iguana* ; the Chuckwalla, *Sauromalus obesus* ; the Desert Iguana *Dipsosaurus dorsalis* ; the Solomon Islands Skink, *Corucia zebrata* ; and several of the spiny tailed agamids (*Uromastyx* species).

The Green Iguana can be regarded as a model for herbivorous lizard nutrition. At one time it was thought that Green Iguanas were mainly insectivorous in their juvenile stages, becoming more herbivorous as they matured. Research has shown, however, that Green Iguanas are primarily herbivorous throughout their lives, but will take the occasional livefood or carrion opportunistically. Herbivorous lizards generally have highly efficient digestive systems which allow efficient microbial fermentation of plant fiber.

The biggest portion (about 60%) of a herbivorous lizard's diet should consist of a variety of green food, such as lettuce (especially the darker green outer leaves), spinach, kale (in small quantities), mustard leaves, cress, endives, parsley, alfalfa sprouts, bean sprouts, sprouted wheat or corn, dandelion leaves and flowers, hibiscus leaves and so on. About 20% of the diet should consist of vegetables including peas, beans, squash, zucchini, broccoli, grated carrot and so on. **Frozen** mixed vegetables can be included as part of this percentage. Fruit should consist of no more than 15% of the diet and can include banana (with skin), melon, apple, pear, grapes and various berries. Only 5% of the diet should con-

Argus Monitor, *Varanus panoptes*. **Photo by Isabelle Francais.**

Green Iguana, *Iguana iguana*.
Photo by Anthony L. Del Prete

sist of high protein items such as crickets, meal-worms, dog or cat food, chicken meat etc.

High protein items, however, should make up about 15% of the diet of growing juvenile and sub-adult lizards. Once the lizards have almost reached adult size the protein portion should be reduced gradually. Recent research has shown that a large proportiion of veterinary problems in adult Green Iguanas, including calcification of the tissues and joints, visceral gout, and so on are directly related to an overabundance of high protein foods in the diet.

Some companies have produced balanced iguana diets in pellet form that contain all of the nutrients required and, theoretically at least, your iguanas should thrive on it. While it may be a good idea to give such pellets to your lizards, I would still advocate giving them a regular ration of greens to go with it.

FEEDING STRATEGIES

In general small insectivorous lizards and all her-bivores should be fed daily, larger carnivores can be fed a substantial meal two or three times per week. All green and vegetable food should be washed thor-oughly and chopped to suitable size befire being served in a dish. Uneaten food of all kinds should be removed before it begins to spoil.

VITAMIN AND MINERAL SUPPLEMENTS

These should be used with caution as a too much of a certain item can be as bad as too little. However most veterinarians recommend a regular vitamin/mineral supplement to the diet of most captive liz-ards as it will ensure that any shortfall in the general diet is alleviated. Many regular foodstuffs are short in calcium or vitamin D3, or have an inadequate calcium/phosphorus ratio; supplements can fix this problem if used properly. If possible always use com-mercial products that are recommended for reptiles, and use them to the manufacturer's instructions. Powdered supplements are the most widely used as these can simply be sprinkled over the foodstuffs whether it be insects of greens. Growing lizards should be given a pinch of vitamin/mineral supple-ment sprinkled on their food at each meal. Adults can be given a pinch about once per week. The nu-tritional quality of cultivated livefoods such as meal-worms and crickets can be dramatically improved by mixing a little vitamin/mineral sipplement in with their food.

WATER REQUIREMENTS

A dish of fresh water should always be available in the lizard cage. Even desert species that rarely drink should be given a small dish of water. Many small tropical species normally drink droplets from foli-age after rain, or from morning dew. Though they should have a dish of water available at all times, it is wise to daily mist-spray foliage in terraria for lizards from humid areas so that they can drink the drop-lets if required. Semi-aquatic lizards and many moni-tors, iguanas and so on like to bathe regularly. There is evidence to suggest that such bathing helps to keep the skin healthy and aids shedding.

WASTE MANAGEMENT

Most forms of terrarium keeping pose few prob-lems with regard to waste management, though if you intend to start a large breeding setup you will have to make arrangements for disposal of bigger amounts of waste material. The home hobbyist with just one or two terraria can dispose of organic waste material (bedding, feces) either by placing it on the garden compost heap or digging it directly into the garden. Waste water can also be used on the garden. By varying your points of disposal each time you will never have any problems of pollution or smell.

If you don't have a garden, you can dispose of waste water and fecal matter via the w.c. (sewage system). To avoid possible food contamination, never use the kitchen sink for terrarium waste disposal. Those enthusiasts with bigger amounts of waste material should contact their local authority with a view to having it taken away by the garbage disposal service. Always keep soiled material in closed trash containers until it can be safely disposed of.

REPRODUCTION AND CAPTIVE BREEDING

Many wildlife lovers are concerned about the de-struction of the native habitats of animal (and plant) species in various parts of the world, especially in the poorer, so-called "undeveloped" countries. "Un-developed" is indeed a poor choice of word for such an application, as it infers that, once "developed", there will be an overall improvement. Unfortunately the environment and natural habitats seem still to be the last items considered with regard to develop-ment, which mainly addresses the improvement of the economy. Unfortunately, the easiest way to tem-porarily improve the economy in many of these countries is to overexploit the natural resources by logging, mining, and promoting a tourist in-dustry, all activities which impact seriously on the natural environment.

Many animal species have evolved in certain eco-logical niches and are unable to adapt to sudden dramatic changes in their makeup. Once certain niches are destroyed, then the indigenous animals, including many lizard species will be lost forever. The moral judgement of collecting wild species for the pet markets of "developed" countries such as those in North America and Western Europe will have to be reconsidered if certain species are

Roughskin Anole, *Anlois trachyderma*. Photo by R. D. Bartlett.

to be saved. It is ironic that species endangered in the wild may only be saved from total extinction if they are maintained as captive breeding stocks. This is by no means a good solution, but surely better than the loss of a species forever. With this in mind, it is essential that we develop captive breeding groups of as many species as possible. Even those species that are apparently not endangered at the present time (Green Iguanas for example) there is every reason to speculate that the situation will deteriorate in the future.

The increase of interest in exotic pets has led to the development of a fairly lucrative industry. Though we continue to import wild captured specimens from countries that are destroying their natural habitats at an alarming rate (Brazil, Malagasy Republic, Malaysia, Indonesia, Solomon Islands to name just a few), in most cases the wildlife seems to have become one of the by-products of logging, and supply will cease when all of the forests have been felled. It will then only be possible to acquire certain species if they have been bred in captivity.

A few forward-thinking herpetologists have taken to breeding species on a commercial basis, but we need more of these forward-thinking people and, indeed, every hobbyist has a moral obligation to try and breed his lizards, or at least to make them available for breeding. The author recently had a conversation with a hobbyist whose ambi-

tion was to own a single pet of each monitor species, but was not keen to take up breeding. This is more the philosophy of a philatelist than a herpetologist!

The following text discusses the reproduction and captive breeding of lizards in general. A knowledge of the wild habitat and habits of species is important if breeding is to be successful.

General Reproductive Behaviour: In wild habitats courtship and mating is seasonal in most species. The seasons are an important influence on reproductive behaviour. In temperate regions with warm summers and cold winters, native lizards usually hibernate from mid- to late-fall, to early spring. In the spring the gradual increase of photoperiod (length of daylight) and temperature cause progressive bouts of activity, followed by release of hormones which promote reproductive behaviour. Lizards from sub-tropical regions may not hibernate completely, but are still affected by the seasonal changes in a similar way, after a period of reduced activity during the cooler months. Lizards from equatorial regions may breed at any time of the year, but are more likely to do so at the approach of the wet season. In countries with unreliable wet seasons, such as Australia, lizards have an almost uncanny sense of predicting when the rains are due to start and will begin sexual activity well before they arrive. The strategy of breeding at the beginning of the wet seasons ensures that eggs have sufficient moisture to develop and that the hatchlings have an abundant food supply in the early period of growth.

All lizards practice courtship to a greater or lesser degree before actual mating occurs. It is always the male who initiates the courtship. In many species there is rivalry between males at mating time; this rivalry is an added sexual stimulus to the dominant males who drive their rivals away. Aggressive behaviour among rivals includes head bobbing, body posturing, limb stretching, tail writhing, and expansion of the dewlap in those species that have them (*Iguana* and *Anolis*, for example). In some cases, minor wrestling matches may occur, but these are usually a trial of strength rather than a serious fight, the weaker male making his escape before any serious injuries occur (but in the confines of a cage, the situation has to watched carefully). In many geckos, a fair amount of vocalizing may accompany the proceedings. A dominant male approaches a female and may display in a similar manner to the threat display. If not receptive, the female will retreat, or sometimes fight, in which case the male gives up and searches for another female. If receptive the female typically crouches low and remains still. The male may nudge her body with his snout, taste her with his tongue, or scratch her with his claws. Eventually he gets on her back and, in many species, seizes her by the neck in his jaws. The male uses his tail, and/or one of his hind limbs to raise the female's tail so that their cloacas come into apposition. With a few pelvic thrusts he inserts one of his hemipenes into the receptive female's open cloaca.

Copulation may take a few minutes to several hours; sometimes copulation takes place several times, with the male using each hemipenis alternately, or one exclusively; there seems to be no particular pattern. Sperm is transferred from the male testis, via a channel in the hemipenis, into the female cloaca, where it is ready to fertilize the ova as they descend from the female oviduct. In some species (e.g. certain chameleons and skinks) the female is able to store sperm in the cloaca for protracted periods enabling consecutive clutches to be fertilized without further matings.

The Gravid Female: Once fertilised eggs are developing in the female, she is said to be gravid. The time this takes varies greatly from species to species and may also be affected by climatic conditions. At higher temperatures the time from fertilization to oviposition will be somewhat shorter than at lower temperatures. The embryo begins to

Common Flat-tailed Gecko, *Uroplatus fimbriatus*. **Photo by Isabelle Francais.**

Eggs of the Bearded Dragon, *Pogona barbata*, incubating in vermiculite. Photo by Isabelle Francais.

develop in the egg prior to oviposition in most species and, in ovo-viviparous species, the embryo develops full term within the maternal body. This means that the period of gravidity in ovo-viviparous species is relatively longer than in oviparous species In such species the shell is poorly formed and consists of a soft, moist membrane which is easily broken by the neonate lizards at birth, making the event more or less a live birth. In a few species, including a Brazilian Skink, *Mabuya heathi*, developing young possess a placental connection with the mother, similar to that which occurs in mammals. At birth the fully developed neonates are virtually unattached to any placental material.

Oviparous species usually become increasingly restless as egglaying time approaches. Many species stop feeding temporarily at the later stages of gravidity, though they will usually still drink profusely. At this time they begin to search out suitable egglaying sites. Lizards may lay their eggs in damp situations under logs or rocks, or in specially constructed burrows. Some monitors construct burrows in termite mounds so that the incubationg eggs can benefit from the more or less constant warm temperature and high humidity. Temperate species usually select nesting sites that are exposed to maximum sunlight, so ensuring maximum temperatures for development. This seems less important to species from subtropical areas, where the summer breeding season is long and hot, or those from tropical areas where the temperature is relatively high and constant throughout the year.

There is little or no parental care in most lizard species. Once the eggs have been laid, and carefully concealed, the mother will leave them entirely to their own devices. Some monitor lizards have been observed to stay in the vicinity of the nest for a few days, and even drive away intruders. A few species brood or guard their eggs. Examples of this are the Glass Lizards (*Ophisaurus* species) and Alligator Lizards (*Elgaria* species). The female Great Plains Skink, *Eumeces obsoletus*, is said to guard her eggs until they hatch and to assist in the hatching by pulling away the egg material.

The Lizard Egg: Most lizard eggs have a soft but tough, white, parchment-like shell. Exceptions include most gecko species, the eggs of which are soft on being laid but develop a hard shell when exposed to the air. In most lizard species the eggs are typically elongate, but some species (especially geckos) lay almost spherical eggs. The soft shelled eggs are capable of absorbing moisture during incubation and can actually increase in weight; eggs often have dimples when laid, but these disappear as moisture is absorbed. The period of incubation varies depending on the size of the species and the temperature, for examplc the eggs of the tiny *Varanus brevicauda* may hatch in 75 days, whereas those of the Asian Water Monitor, *V. salvator*, may take as long as 250 days.

CAPTIVE BREEDING

The most obvious requirement for breeding in captivity is possession of a sexually mature male and a female of the species to be bred (we will ignore unisexual species here - see below). There are no simple rules to cover the breeding of all species but the breeding seasons usually are dictated by the climate in which they live. Temperate species, for example, usually breed in the spring after a period of hibernation while many tropical and subtropical species may breed at any time the situation is suitable. This may be at the beginning of a wet season when there is plenty of moisture for eggs to develop and a good supply of food foe the neonates when they hatch.

Males and females of many species are kept separately until a breeding response is required. Success with many species is often greater when a number of males are introduced to a number of females at breeding time. Two or more males per female also, often gives the dominant male additional incentive to mate. In some cases two males can be introduced to two females and, when they are in full display, the pairs can be separated. This may fool each male into believing he have driven off the other and both will proceed to mate with their respective females! Most species will respond to an increase in temperature and photoperiod after a winter "rest period". This can be full hibernation in temperate species, or just a few weeks at slightly reduced temperature and photoperiod for subtropical and tropical species. The latter may also be influenced by an increase in humidity at a strategic time.

It is best to leave male and female together for a few says, even if copulation has occurred. There may be two or three repeat copulations and, the more there is, the more likely is the female to be fertilized. When sexual activity ceases, or if the female seems to be becoming stressed from the persistant advances of the male, it is best to take him away to a separate cage again. The gravid female should be left in peace as much as possible. In the later stages there will be an obvious swelling in her abdomen as the eggs develop. She may refuse to feed for a week or two before laying time, but should always have a supply of fresh clean water. Pro-

vide her with some kind of egg laying site. This will vary from species to species, but many smaller lizards will use a plastic box lightly packed with moist sphagnum moss. Others will use a box of moist sand in which to bury their eggs. Whatever facilities you provide your lizards in which to lay their eggs, there will always be some who are not satisfied and, after hours of searching in vain for a suitable site they may end up just scattering the eggs across the substrate or even in the water bowl.

Artificial Incubation: You should keep a close eye on your female lizards as laying time approaches. As the conditions in the average terrarium are unsuitable for egg incubation, it is important that they are removed for artificial incubation. At one time it was traditional to always keep the eggs the same way up throughout the incubation period. Some hobbyists now maintain that it does no harm to turn them occasionally. However having usually had reasonable results with the old method and not having tried the new one, the present author prefers to stick to traditional method. The "top" of the egg is marked with a non-toxic marker so that you always know which is "the right way up".

Stump-toed Gecko, *Gehyra mutilata*. Juvenile specimen. Photo by W. P. Mara.

504

The eggs must be placed in a hatching container which contains a layer of incubation medium. Moistened sand, peat, potting mixture, paper towels, cotton wadding and so on have all been used successfully as incubation media and still will be, but the general consensus today seems to be that granular vermiculite is the best. Vermiculite is an inert, absorbent, material generally used for insulation and for improving potting mixtures for plants. Its suitability as an incubation medium is enhanced by its cleanliness and its capacity for holding more than its own weight of water for relatively long periods. For normal incubation, the vermiculite should be mixed with an equal amount, by weight, of clean water. If possible, place the eggs in neat rows as it makes them easier to inspect. They should be buried in the incubation medium to about three quarters their depth (in other words a quarter of the egg surface is left exposed).

Though special incubators are available on the market a simple, adequate incubator can be made with an aquarium tank or a watertight styrofoam box and a thermostatically controlled aquarium heater. Place the heater in the tank and cover it with water. A couple of bricks or similar, breaking the water surface, will serve as a stand for the incubation boxes. Place a ventilated lid on the incubation box. Set the thermostat so that the temperature in the incubation box is maintained in the range of 28-31° C (83-88 °F) which is about right for most species. You will need a thermometer in the box and may have to use trial and error to get the temperature right. It will be easier to monitor the temperature if you use a thermistor cable in the incubation medium attached to a digital thermometer outside the incubator. Set a sheet of glass over the incubation boxes at an angle, so that condensed water runs away from the boxes and does not fall into them.

You should inspect the eggs at regular intervals, and regularly monitor the temperature and humidity. A lid over the incubator will help keep humidity high, but it should be ventilated. Eighty percent relative humidity in the incubator should be adequate to keep the incubation material moist, but if it should dry out on the surface, it can be occasionally moistened with a fine mist spray. Developing eggs should have a taut, healthy appearance. Occasionally a mold may develop on the egg surface, discoloring it. This can be gently brushed off with a fine brush though the mold itself does not seem to do any harm. Infertile eggs, or eggs in which the embryos have died for one reason or another will usually collapse and discolor. However do not be in too much of a rush to dispose of them; I have often seen lizards hatch from the most awful looking eggs.

At hatching time the neonate lizards will make their way to the surface of the incubation medium. They should be removed to suitable rearing cages as soon as possible. Sometimes the lizards seem to take an awfully long time to hatch. Having slit the eggshell with their egg

Blackbelly Racerunner, *Cnemidophorus deppei*. Photo by R. D. Bartlett.

Caiman Lizard, *Dracaena guianensis*. **Photo by K. H. Switak.**

tooth (a sharp projection on the snout which is lost shortly after hatching) they may stick out their head and lay there for hours as if summoning up courage to make the final break. Though it is a great temptation to "help" hatching lizards, they should generally be left to their own devices. Occasionally a lizard taking a long time to hatch may become stuck to the eggshell due to the drying out of the egg fluids. The neonate can be released by gently brushing away the hardened albumin with a fine brush and some lukewarm water.

UNISEXUAL LIZARDS

A few species of lizards are parthenogenetic (virgin birth). Parthenogeneric populations consist solely of females which are capable of producing offspring without being first fertilized by a male. Well known unisexual lizards include some lacertids from the Caucasus region of Asia, and some teiids from north and Central America, particularly those in the genus *Cnemidophorus* (Whiptails and Racerunners). Parthenogenetic species lay unfertilized eggs that produce only female young that are genetically identical to their parent. They are believed to originate as a result of hybridization between two, closely related species. While most hybrids are sterile, there is some mechanism in parthenogenetic species which makes them capable of continuing to reproduce asexually.

PREVENTIVE HEALTH CARE

At least ninety percent of all diseases in captive lizards could have been prevented if they had been supplied with optimum conditions from the outset. Newly captured wild specimens seem to be the most vulnerable to disease. The trauma of being captured, confined and transported, often in exposed, overcrowded, unhygienic conditions leads to stress and a reduction in resistance to disease (stress-related immunosuppression), which activates latent pathogens already in the body, and allows newly encountered pathogens to invade easily.

Remember that the source collector of wild reptiles is not usually an expert in their welfare, nor in most cases would this aspect even be considered, especially in countries where herptile collecting has become more or less a by product of the new lumber industry. The collector's sole aim usually is to get as many specimens as possible and sell them as quickly as possible. Unfortunately this is sometimes not very quickly as far as the animals are concerned; they may be stored for days on end in dirty, overcrowded baskets, boxes or bags, often mixed with other species from different habitats, until the collector can get to his point of sale. The lizards then have to be exported to their country of destination; a further journey, and more time. Many imported specimens arriving in petshops are already too far gone to be saved even if veterinary treatment is available at this stage. Others may look all right, but could be suffering from a disease in its early stages; the symptoms are not yet showing.

QUARANTINE

As we have already discussed it is important to inspect new purchases carefully to insure, as far as possible, they are not sick. But it doesn't end there. If you already own reptiles and you are perhaps buying more to make up breeding groups, or perhaps starting with an additional species or two, you must be very careful. Outbreaks of infectious diseases in hobbyists' collections start out almost always as a result of introducing new stock to the original animals.

All new livestock, wherever it has been obtained, and however good it may look, must be isolated for a period of quarantine. The quarantine cage must have all of the necessary life-support systems for optimum living, but keep decorations to a minimum and, keep it in a separate room to your main collection for a period of at least three weeks (the original word quarantine, in fact, meant "forty days"). Keep the quarantine animals in clean conditions, and have special utensils etc. for them. On no account should you transfer items from quarantine cages to your main cages unless they have been thoroughly sterilized. The same goes for yourself, make sure you wash your hands after dealing with quarantine animals.

During the period of quarantine, keep a close eye on the new specimens. If, after the period of quarantine they still show no signs of disease, you can be reasonably certain that they are not sick. If any symptoms of disease should arise during the quarantine period, the animals should be treated by a veterinarian and completely cured, before they are introduced to your existing stock.

ISOLATION OF SICK LIZARDS

If a lizard in your normal collection becomes sick, it must be immediately isolated in conditions as described for quarantine. The quicker you do this, the less likelihood of an epidemic breaking out among your stock. Consult your veterinarian after the animal has been isolated.

OPTIMAL LIVING CONDITIONS

We must aim for nothing less than optimum living conditions for our lizards. This means careful considerations of the terrarium climate, and topography, plus the provisions of a proper diet. Most lizards show an "escape reflex" on being captured. This is a result of them being unable to go where they want to, as they would be able to in the wild. Frustrated attemps to escape lead to increasing stress and the possibility of injury (especially to the snout). Some lizards show greater stress than others; for example the Green Iguana, *Iguana iguana,* often settles well within a few days of captivity, while the similar looking Green Water Dragon, *Physignathus cocincinus,* rarely loses its "panic syndrome" completely. Lizard husbandry should be adapted to the emotions of the particular lizards rather then expect the lizards to adapt to yourself; especially in the case of quickly stressed species. The latter should be placed in terraria with adequate hiding places and perhaps it is best to cover the terrarium glass over for the first few days to stop an animal panicking each time it sees movement. Lizards that stress easily should never be handled and petted to the same degree as those that tame readily.

One of the most important aspects of disease prevention is cleanliness of the accommodations. If you have a number of cages, you should service them individually, always washing your hands and sterilizing utensils before moving from one cage to the next.

Clean out cages as necessary; if they are dirty with feces and food leftovers, they need cleaning, but in any case at least twice per week. Additionally, it is recommended that cages and furnishings are completely stripped and disinfected at least once per month. This will include removing substrate material and washing or replacing it; scrubbing all branches, rocks, hideboxes etc.; as well as the cage interior. The lizards should be taken out and placed in a spare cage while you are doing this (a plastic tank with a secure lid is ideal as it can easily be disinfected between uses). One of the safest disinfectants to use in lizard cages is household bleach. Use a ten percent solution in tepid water. Wipe out the interior of the cage with the solution and soak furnishings in it. Rinse off with clean water and dry before reinstalling and returning the lizards to their cage.

Water Dragon, *Physignathus cocincinus*. Photo by M. P. and C. Piednoir.

IGUANIDS (IGUANIDAE)

Jennifer Swofford
851 Kimball Rd.
Highland Park, IL 60035

Jennifer Swofford has a Bachelor of Science degree from Carnegie Mellon University and is currently studying herpetology.

Green Iguana, *Iguana iguana*. **Photo by Adam Britton.**

BASIC TAXONOMY, LIFESPAN, AND HABITAT PREFERENCES

The process of taxonomic classification can be an ongoing one, and such is the case with iguanian lizards. For many years, the Iguanidae family had been recognized as an enormous, diverse group of lizards—the most prominent group in the New World. At least eight subfamilies had been recognized, with a total of at least 50 genera and 900 species comprising the large family. (Zug, 1993.) These lizards seemed to have little in common, with characteristics ranging from being ground dwellers to arboreal, carnivores to herbivores, desert animals to tropical ones. They all, however, possess pleurodont dentition (teeth on the inside of the jaw bone) and are native to the Americas, with the exception of few species on and around the islands of Fiji and Madagascar.

In recent years, the classification of these lizards has been reconsidered, and to a large extent the subfamilies which once existed were reclassified as distinct families. (Frost and Etheridge, 1989.) However, the new taxa have not yet been accepted by all herpetologists. Since the reclassification, some publications still rely on the old hierarchy. (Zug, 1993.) The new set of eight families, and the genera that will be included in this discussion are shown in Table 1.

Lizards in the Iguanidae family are referred to as "true iguanas" or "iguanines." The entire group of lizards to be discussed in this chapter are referred to as "iguanian lizards" or "iguanids" (Bartlett, 1995). As a whole, the iguanian lizards are a very diverse group; however, the lineages do reveal distinct commonalities.

This chapter will ultimately cover most of the popular iguanian lizards, and will focus on the families rather than the individual species in many cases. Although some of the lizards covered here are hardly ever seen in captivity (such as *Brachylophus* and *Amblyrhynctus* species) they are included because they have still proven interesting to the herpetoculturist. Hopefully, captive breeding projects will someday ensure that all iguanids will be plentiful both in the wild and in captivity.

With regard to lifespan, smaller species generally live the shortest length of time, and larger species live the longest. Smaller species in families Polychrotidae, Phrynosomatidae, Crotaphytidae, Tropiduridae, Corytophanidae and Hoplocercidae usually live only one to four years. Larger species of the same families can be expected to live up to ten years. The large Iguanidae lizards should live at least twenty years in captivity when cared for properly. Lifespan tends to be lower in the wild due to the threat from predators, parasites, and other harmful elements. Lifespan can also be greatly affected by diet.

Except for Iguanidae, each family tends to have distinct habitat preferences. Hoplocercidae, Crotaphytidae, Opluridae, and Phrynosomatidae prefer dry, desert-like conditions, and are primarily ground dwellers. Also ground dwellers, Tropiduridae prefers more of a forest setting. Polychrotidae and Corytophanidae prefer tropical regions, and are primarily arboreal.

The true iguanas, however, are not tied together due to their habitat preferences. While *Brachylophus* and *Iguana* species are arboreal, the rest of the true iguanas are primarily ground-dwellers. The arboreal species are found in the tropics. *Dipsosaurus* and *Sauromalus* are desert iguanids. *Amblyrhynctus* lives along rocky shorelines to keep in close proximity to its food, which lies underwater. The remaining true iguanas prefer dry rocky or forest environments. See Table 2 for a summary of the lizards covered here and their habitat preferences.

Table 2: Common Iguanian Lizards

Family	Genus	Species	Common name	Habitat	Diet	Length (max)	Origin
Iguanidae	*Iguana*	*I. iguana*	Green iguana	tropical, arboreal	herbivorous	2 m	Mexico-South America
Iguanidae	*Iguana*	*I. delicatissima*	Lesser Antillean iguana	tropical, arboreal	herbivorous	2 m	Antilles
Iguanidae	*Dipsosaurus*	*D. dorsalis*	Desert iguana	desert, ground-dweller	herbivorous, insectivorous	35 cm	Southwestern U. S.
Iguanidae	*Sauromalus*	*S. obesus*	Chuckwalla	desert, ground-dweller	herbivorous	45 cm	Southwestern U. S., Northwest Mexico
Iguanidae	*Cyclura*	*C. cornuta*	Rhinocerous iguana	dry rocky, ground-dweller	herbivorous, omnivorous	1.2 m	Caribbean islands
Iguanidae	*Cyclura*	*C. nubila nubila*	Cuban iguana	dry rocky, ground-dweller	herbivorous, omnivorous	75 cm	Cuba, Caribbean islands

510

Iguanidae	*Cyclura*	*C. nubila lewisi*	Cayman Island blue rock iguana	dry rocky, ground-dweller	herbivorous, omnivorous	50 cm	Grand Cayman Island
Iguanidae	*Ctenosaura*	*C. similis*	Spiny-tailed iguana	dry forest, ground-dweller	herbivorous, omnivorous	1 m	Mexico, Central America
Iguanidae	*Ctenosaura*	*C. palearis*	Paleate spiny-tailed iguana	arid to moist tropical, ground-arboreal	herbivorous, omnivorous	1.25 m	Central America
Iguanidae	*Amblyrhynchus*	*A. cristatus*	Marine iguana	rocky shoreline, ground-dweller	herbivorous	1.75 m	Galapagos Islands
Iguanidae	*Brachylophus*	*B. fasciatus*	Banded iguana	tropical, arboreal	herbivorous	90 cm	Fiji, Tonga Islands
Iguanidae	*Conolophus*	*C. subcristatus*	Galapagos land iguana	dry rocky, ground-dweller	herbivorous	1 m	Galapagos Islands

**Black Iguana, *Ctenosaura similis*.
Photo by Stephen R. Swofford.**

Hoplocercidae	*Hoplocercus*	*H. spinosus*	Prickle-tail iguana	dry savannah, ground-dweller	insectivorous	15 cm	Southern Brazil
Polychrotidae	*Anolis*	*A. carolinensis*	Green anole	tropical, arboreal	insectivorous	22 cm	Southeast U. S
Polychrotidae	*Anolis*	*A. equestris*	Knight anole	tropical, arboreal	omnivorous	55 cm	Cuba
Tropiduridae	*Leiocephalus*	*L. carinatus*	Curly-tailed lizard	forest, ground-dweller	insectivorous	25 cm	Antilles
Tropiduridae	*Liolaemus*	*L. tenuis*	Jewel swift	forest, ground-dweller	insectivorous	25 cm	South America
Tropiduridae	*Tropidurus*	several	Lava lizard	desert, ground-dweller	insectivorous, carnivorous	35 cm	Galapagos, South America
Corytophanidae	*Basiliscus*	*B. basiliscus*	Common basilisk	tropical, arboreal	insectivorous, carnivorous	80 cm	Southern Mexico to Northern South America
Corytophanidae	*Basiliscus*	*B. plumifrons*	Green basilisk	tropical, arboreal	insectivorous, carnivorous	80 cm	Southern Mexico to Northern South America
Corytophanidae	*Laemanctus*	*L. longipes*	Cone headed iguana	tropical, arboreal	insectivorous, carnivorous	70 cm	Central America
Corytophanidae	*Corytophanes*	*C. cristatus*	Helmeted iguana	tropical, arboreal	insectivorous	35 cm	Southern Mexico to Northeastern. Colombia
Crotaphytidae	*Crotaphytus*	*C. collaris*	Collared lizard	desert, ground-dweller	insectivorous	40 cm	Southwestern U. S.
Crotaphytidae	*Crotaphytus*	*C. reticulatus*	Reticulate collared lizard	desert, ground-dweller	insectivorous	40 cm	Southwestern U. S
Crotaphytidae	*Gambelia*	*G. wislizeni*	Leopard lizard	desert, ground-dweller	insectivorous	38 cm	Southwestern U. S., Northern Mexico

511

Phrynosomatidae	Phrynosoma	P. cornutum	Horned lizard	desert, ground-dweller	insectivorous	15 cm	Southern U. S., Northern Mexico
Phrynosomatidae	Sceloporus	S. malachitus	Emerald swift	mountain forest, ground-dweller	insectivorous	20 cm	U. S. to South America
Phrynosomatidae	Sceloporus	S. poinsetti	Crevice spiny lizard	dry rocky, ground-dweller	insectivorous	30 cm	U. S. to South America
Phrynosomatidae	Holbrookia	H. maculata	Lesser earless lizard	dry steppes, ground-dweller	insectivorous	19 cm	Southwestern U. S. to Mexico
Phrynosomatidae	Uta	U. stansburiana	Side blotched lizard	desert, ground-dweller	insectivorous	14 cm	Southwestern U. S., Northwestern Mexico
Opluridae	Oplurus	several	Madagascan swifts	dry rocky, ground-dweller	insectivorous	20 cm	Madagascar

Emerald Swift, *Sceloporus malachiticus*. Photo by Stephen R. Swofford.

PHYSICAL CHARACTERISTICS

All iguanians possess the traditional lizard body: all have four legs and a tail. The tail is usually one to three times the length of the body. Most iguanids have the ability to regenerate their tails when portions are broken off. None have the ability to regenerate legs. Most have sharp claws, but some have lamellae which are used for climbing smooth surfaces. Some iguanids have femoral pores on the undersides of their rear legs. Iguanians exhibit both smooth and keeled scales. Obviously, many different morphologies occur in iguanian lizards. The only manageable way to describe the physical characteristics of the popular iguanids included in this chapter is to take each one in turn. A summation of the appearance of each lizard follows.

Member	Characteristics
Iguana species	Large, laterally compressed body, with nuchal crest and dorsal crest. Large gular pouch. Large, conspicuous subtympanic plate defines *I. iguana*. Large bodied. Color mostly green; tail and sometimes body have darker bands. To 2 m. Tail up to three times snout to vent length (SVL).
Dipsosaurus species	Medium-sized, dorso-ventrally flattened body. Slight dorsal crest, rounded head. White to cream-colored scales, with darker broken spots on body, banded tail with keeled scales. To 35 cm. Tail at least SVL
Sauromalus species	Medium-sized, dorso-ventrally flattened body. Slight dorsal crest. Color brown to tan, with mottled markings. Large bodied. Extremely plump lizard. To 45 cm. Tail at least SVL.

Rhinoceros Iguana, *Cyclura cornuta*. Photo by K. H. Switak.

Ctenosaura species	Large, weakly laterally compressed body. Slight dorsal and nuchal crests. Large gular pouch. Color mostly brown/gray, with weak mottled bands. Large bodied. Tail covered with drastically keeled scales. To 1 m. Tail up to twice SVL
Cyclura species	Large, weakly laterally compressed body. Very similar to *Ctenosaura*, but uniform in coloration and no keeled tail scales. Snout slightly flattened and elongated. Large-bodied. *C. cornuta* has horns on snout. To 1.2 m. Tail up to twice SVL
Amblyrhynchus species	Large, laterally compressed body. High nuchal and dorsal crest. Color gray to green, with mottled markings. Rounded head. Large-bodied. To 1.75 m. Tail at least twice SVL.
Brachylophus species	Medium-sized, laterally compressed body. Dorsal crest. Bright green in coloration; males have bands of different shades. To 90 cm. Tail up to 3 times SVL.
Conolophus species	Large, laterally compressed body. Extremely similar to *Amblyrhynchus*, but yellow-brown in coloration. To 1 m.
Hoplocercus species	Small, dorso-ventrally flattened body. Brown, with lighter bands. Tail has highly keeled scales. Males exhibit femoral pores (unlike other Hoplocercidae). Brown, with lighter bands. To 15 cm. Tail about SVL
Anolis species	*A. carolinensis*: small, dorso-ventrally flattened body. *A. equestris*: medium-sized, laterally compressed body, with slight dorsal crest. Coloration varies from species to species. *A. carolinensis* and *A. equestris* have basically solid-green bodies. A. carolinensis has the ability to change color to brown/gray with moods, and has large gular pouch. Most have pointed noses. Other anolis species are mainly small, with various spotted markings. *A. carolinensis* to 22 cm. A. equestris to 55 cm. Tail twice SVL.
Leiocephalus species	Small, dorso-ventrally flattened body. Slight dorsal crest. Coloring is brown, with lighter mottled markings. Belly and throat are white. No femoral pores. To 25 cm. Tail up to twice SVL.
Liolaemus species	Small, dorso-ventrally flattened body. Some species have keeled scales. *L. tenuis* has smooth-scaled, bright-green body with turquoise tail. White belly and throat. No femoral pores. Coloration varies from species to species. To 25 cm. Tail at least SVL.
Tropidurus species	Medium-sized, dorso-ventrally flattened body. Slight dorsal crest. Color brown with lighter and darker mottled markings. No femoral pores. To 35 cm.
Basiliscus species	Medium-sized, laterally compressed body. High helmet and dorsal crest. *B. plumifrons* has striking green coloration with orange-yellow eyes. B. basiliscus is brown, with mottled markings in brown to cream tones. To 80 cm. Tail twice SVL.
Laemanctus species	Medium-sized, laterally compressed body. Has blunt helmet and slight dorsal crest. Green to brown, with darker bands. Thin, long legs. To 70 cm. Tail three times SVL.
Corytophanes species	Medium-sized, laterally compressed body. Slight dorsal crest. Mostly brown coloration, with mottled darker bands. Thin, long limbs, large helmet. To 35 cm. Tail twice SVL.
Crotaphytus species	Medium-sized, dorso-ventrally flattened body. Large head. Color is brown to green, with white to yellow bands or mottled bands. Plump lizard. To 40 cm. Tail twice SVL.

**Collared Lizard, *Crotaphytus collaris*.
Photo by R. T. Zappalorti.**

Phrynosoma species	Smaller, drastically dorso-ventrally flattened body. Slight dorsal crest. Dramatic horned scales around the head, and smaller horns covering the body. Head is rounded. Color is tan to brown, with mottled markings. To 15 cm. Tail less than SVL.
Sceloporous species	Small, dorso-ventrally flattened body. Keeled scales. Color varies from green to brown; belly is often bright blue. To 20 cm. Tail up to twice SVL.
Holbrookia species	Small, dorso-ventrally flattened body. No external ear openings. Color is brown to tan, with bands and spots. To 19 cm. Tail up to twice SVL.
Uta species	Small, dorso-ventrally flattened body. Similar to *Sceloporous* species. To 14 cm. Tail up to twice SVL.
Oplurus species	Small, dorso-ventrally flattened body. Similar to *Tropidurus* species, except no dorsal crest. To 20 cm. Tail at least SVL.

GROWTH AND DEVELOPMENT

All iguanian lizards begin life the same way: fertilization is internal in all species. Most iguanids are oviparous, and the females lay leathery eggs terrestrially within a few weeks of fertilization. A few species are ovoviviparous however (notably many *Sceloporous* species), and their eggs hatch internally. For egg-layers, the incubation period varies greatly from species to species. Even within species, incubation temperature plays an important role in determining the time until hatching. See the reproduction section for details regarding incubation times and temperatures. Also refer to chapter on Egg Physiology and Biology for more information about incubation.

After hatching, the lizards are on their own. They are left completely to their own devices in terms of foraging for food, thermoregulation, and escaping predation. Hatchlings grow quickly. In larger species, such as *I. iguana*, hatchlings can increase their body mass one-hundred fold in the first three years (DeVosjoli, 1992.). Important factors in growth rate include: availability of food, quality of food, and temperature.

During the time it takes for an iguanid to reach sexual maturity, the animal experiences dramatic growth. As a general rule, iguanids can become "full grown" by the time they reach sexual maturity. It takes up to one year for shorter-lived species to achieve sexual maturity, and up to three years for longer-lived species. However, it is unclear whether iguanids have the potential to grow for the duration of their lives (Zug, 1993.). *Iguana iguana*, as well as the other large iguanines, certainly continue to grow for years after they reach sexual maturity, but the much smaller species such as *Sceloporous* and *Liolaemus* seem to "top out" before they are one year old. In either case, during the active, growing years, adequate diet, high temperatures, and stress-free conditions (see Common Problems section) are essential for normal growth. If an iguanid is not provided with the things it needs during its formative years, its growth will be stunted for life.

SEXING

Methods of gender determination vary across species. Most species exhibit sexual dimorphism of some kind. In iguanids, these characteristics usually include coloration, presence or absence of bands, body size, size of femoral pores, and behavior or special coloration during the mating season. Sometimes it is difficult to determine sex based on these characteristics because many of these characteristics are relative. In some species, some characteristics do not develop until the animal reaches sexual maturity or even later. With some species, however, the gender can be easily determined on sight.

Characteristic	Interpretation
Casques and Crests	Corytophanidae and many Iguanidae species have casques atop their heads or have crests that start at the neck and extend down their backs. Males of each species invariably develop higher casques or crests. In addition, *Anolis carolinensis* possesses a gular pouch (dewlap) which in males is much larger and usually bright pink.
Femoral Pores	All iguanian lizards except Hoplocercidae and Tropiduridae have at least one row of femoral pores on the underside of the rear legs. (Only *Hoplocercus* of Tropiduridae has femoral pores.) The pores of males are always better developed than those of females. The male pore is always much larger, and within a male's pore, there is always more secretory matter present.
Color and Pattern	In most cases, color and patterns offer very few clues as to the sex of the animal. Some animals, however, such as *Sceloporous malachitus*, exhibit extreme dimorphism. The following list briefly describes some differences between males and females of various species: *Sceloporous malachitus* - Males have a bright-green body, a turquoise tail, and their bellies are bright blue. The females are basically dark brown with intermittent green scales, and have a colorless underside. *Sceloporous poinsetti.*- Males have more blue on their undersides than do their female counterparts. *Crotaphytus* - Males tend to be more brightly colored than their duller females. *Holbrookia*- Males exhibit dark bands on their sides; females do not. *Sauromalus obesus* - It has been suggested that females have dark bands across the body whereas the male exhibits only scattered markings, but this does not seem to be consistent with all specimens. *Iguana* - Males are generally more brightly colored, some offering an orange hue during the mating season. The coloring of females tends to wash out as they age. *Amblyrhynctus* -Males develop a reddish coloration during the mating season.

Southwestern Earless Lizard, *Cophosaurus texana.* **Photo by K. H. Switak.**

Size	Size is another relative characteristic that can be helpful in gender determination. Males of *Anolis* species are larger than females. *Sauromalus obesus* males have thicker necks than females. Many males in the Iguanidae family develop larger jowls and occipital humps (fatty protrusions behind the eyes) than females. These areas are used for fat storage during the mating season, at which time males eat much less than usual.
Hemipenal Bulge	Male iguanian lizards develop a hemipenal bulge as they mature. This is a bulge by the vent that indicates the presence of hemipenes. Females do not develop a bulge.
Hemipenes	It is possible to judge the sex by physically determining whether or not the animal has hemipenes. These methods should not be used by the inexperienced. When performed incorrectly, the animal can easily be physically harmed. One common method is to place the thumb about 3/4" from the vent (toward the tail) and firmly ease the thumb towards the vent, manually everting the hemipenes. (DeVosjoli, 1992.) The other most common method is to use a thin rod to probe the animal. The rod is slipped into the vent towards the tail. The rod will insert farther into the male than the female as it slides into the inverted hemipenes.
Behavior	Behavior can also help reveal mature males. Males of all iguanian species tend to be extremely territorial once they are sexually mature. Males do not usually welcome the presence of other males, except perhaps juveniles. Some males chase and attack intruders once their territory has been breached. Males also head bob, or do "push ups" with their entire upper bodies. This can be either a territorial or mating display. Females can exhibit this behavior as well, but males tend to do so much more often. In situations where only one male is present, sometimes these mating displays and territoriality are not observed. (Bricker, 1995.)

SELECTION AND ACQUISITION

Captive breeding has earned a very important role in herpetoculture. Diminishing wild populations have prompted the need for captive breeding and propagation. In addition, animals that are bred in captivity are less likely than wild-caught animals to succumb to a host of problems that can be compounded by stressful conditions. Moreover, an enormous number of imported animals die during transport. All of these factors increase the need for captive-breeding programs and the need to obtain captive-bred animals whenever possible.

Both captive-bred and wild-caught animals are available from pet stores, breeders, and other wholesalers. It is the decision of the herpeto-culturist to locate the best place (pet store or mail order) from which to make a purchase. However, it is a good idea to refrain from buying animals from establishments that are not reputable. Doing so only supports their efforts and keeps them in business. The advantage to mail-order purchases is that the cost is usually much lower than that of pet stores. However, purchasing from a pet store allows the buyer to examine the animal before it is taken home. (Of course, any reputable mail order company should honor at least a week-long guarantee that the animal is not ill or injured.) Look for the following characteristics when examining an animal for purchase:

—The iguanid should be alert to other animals inside the cage, movement ouside the cage, and to food placed in the cage.

—Whenever possible, the iguanid should be ob-

Green Basilisk, *Basiliscus plumifrons*. Photo by David Dube.

served eating to ensure that it indeed has an appetite.

—There should be no visible lumps or wounds on the animal.

—The iguanid's mouth should be closed, and the eyes should be open.

—The lizard should be active, and it should be observed walking or running.

—There should be no debris attached to the vent.

—The animal should not be too thin: there should not be excessive flaps running down the sides of the lizard and the base of the tail should be plump.

—There should be no signs of metabolic bone disease.

If the lizard seems healthy based on the previous checklist, then it is probably a good candidate for purchase. Despite the urge to purchase the smallest iguanid present, it is sometimes a good idea to buy the slightly larger one simply because it is either older or a better eater, both traits which help ensure survival.

BEHAVIOR

Iguanian lizards lead relatively simple lives. They spend most of their waking hours basking in the sun and the rest is spent searching for food. Generally speaking, the lizard's first morning chore is to seek out a sunny spot and warm up. Then, the lizard forages for food. After the animal is sufficiently stuffed, it returns to a sunny spot where it will begin the process of digestion. Reptiles spend much of their energy simply digesting their food. As the day progresses, the lizards thermoregulate by moving into and out of the sun. This is especially important with desert lizards because if they sit in the sun for too long, they will overheat and die. As a general rule, iguanids try to keep their body temperature between 28°C and 32°C for the duration of the day.

In captivity, much of the same behavior can be observed. When the lizard's lights turn on in the morning, it will emerge from its sleeping spot and warm up under its heat lamp. After it is sufficiently warm, it will begin its hunt for food. Naturally, lizards in captivity do not need to devote as much of their time on the hunt because their food is provided for them. This leaves the captive lizard much more time to bask and basically lounge around. Captive iguanids usually eat several times and do little more than sit in one place for most of the day. Because a temperature gradient is being offered, the lizard will be able to choose a location that offers the exact temperature it needs to thrive.

As iguanids mature, they become increasingly interested in more than just basking, eating, and sleeping. As males become sexually mature, they develop an interest in seeking out mates and scaring off rivals. Many iguanids perform a head-bobbing ritual which is used as a territorial or mating display. Males may head bob as an indication that they are interested in mating with a female present. It could also be a message to other males present to get away from "his" female. In many cases, it becomes impossible to house more than one mature male iguanid in the same enclosure due to violent territorial acts.

In addition to head bobbing, large iguanines such as *I. iguana* use their tails to whip at potential threats, especially humans. Some specimens are quite adept at this defense mechanism. These large lizards must be tamed through frequent gentle handling if welts from tail whipping are to be avoided.

Another interesting defensive behavior is exhibited in *Phrynosoma* species. These amazing horned lizards are able to squirt blood from their eyes to deter predators. *Sceloporous occidentalis* exhibits a similar mechanism (Obst, 1988).

Another behavioral trait which should be noted here is sneezing. Iguanids possess salt glands in their nasal cavities which are used for salt excretion. The salt is actually sneezed out, leaving nice white spots all over everything in the iguanid's path. This is normal behavior, and no dietary adjustments need to be made (Frye, 1993).

HANDLING

Most iguanians have sharp claws, which suggests that they are inclined to dig into the objects that they climb. This must be taken into consideration when handling these lizards. First, iguanids do not want to be held by people; rather, they want to hold on to people. For purely social purposes (rather than medication or examination purposes) the lizard is usually picked up and then placed on an object such as a hand, arm, shoulder, chair, etc. Most iguanids do not respond well to being

Green Iguana, *Iguana iguana*. Photo by Isabelle Francais.

held by the body with their legs dangling. Usually, they squirm and try to grab onto something in such situations.

Larger iguanids (such as the true iguanas, *Basiliscus*, *Corytophanes*, and *Laemanctus* species) and medium-sized lizards (such as *Anolis equestris*, *Crotaphytus*, and *Gambelia* species) should be picked up with one hand supporting the upper body, and one hand supporting the ventral region. For example, from behind and above the lizard, your right hand could reach underneath the front legs and hold the body gently with the fingers while the wrist supports one of the front legs. You can use one or two extended fingers to support the other front leg. Your left hand would then reach down underneath the hind legs and gently hold the body, while the wrist supports the base of the tail. For the medium-sized species, it may be necessary only to use the right hand, because the wrist and arm can support the rest of the body. The lizard should then be ready to be transported to its next destination. When picking up a large lizard it is especially important to unhook the claws from whatever material they might be attached to. A lizard of any size should never be grabbed on the back from above and tugged straight upward.

Doing so will only prompt the lizard to dig into the substrate with its claws and squirm.

You can pick up smaller animals in a similar manner, except that they tend to be more flighty. It is often necessary to put the left hand in front of the lizard to "halt" it and then use the right hand to grab the body. You can place your thumb under the front legs, and cup the remaining fingers over the animal's neck and back. The farther forward the hand is placed, the more control you will have over the lizard. Many small lizards can then be placed on an arm or shoulder without incident. Alternately, friendlier lizards respond well to a flattened palm in their path; they will actually walk right up onto it if it is nudged underneath their heads.

For examination or medication, you can pick up smaller iguanids as described above. During examination, usually the thumb is placed under the jaw, and the fingers extend from above the head to the neck. By gently squeezing, the lizard cannot move its head and squirm. Medium-sized lizards can be handled this way as well, but because the body is larger and stronger, a second hand is usually needed to stabilize the lower body. Large iguanids are usually pinned down for examination

Serrated Casquehead Iguana, *Laemanctus serratus*. Photo by R. G. Sprackland.

Fiji Island Iguana, *Brachylophus fasciatus*. Photo by Mark Miller.

of the dorsal region. One hand can be placed over the head and neck, also holding down the front legs, while the other can hold down the rear legs and lower body. If a ventral examination is necessary, the upper body can be firmly held with one hand while the lower body is firmly held with the other hand. The thumb and forefinger can be used to hold the head in place. For extremely large specimens, a very strong individual or two individuals may be required.

HOUSING, HEATING, AND LIGHTING

The main objective when designing an enclosure is to provide the lizard with a space that can be kept clean and warm enough for its survival. Also important are the furnishings in the enclosure, the size of the enclosure, and the use of full spectrum lighting. The cage design for all iguanian lizards can be roughly the same, except for size.

ENCLOSURE SIZE

The size of the enclosure should depend on the type and number of lizards housed inside. Arboreal lizards should have ample climbing space, so the cage should be at least as tall as the lizard is long. Ground-dwellers should be able to run around freely on the floor of the cage, so for the smallest species, a cage the size of a ten gallon aquarium is minimal. As a general rule, iguanids

should be supplied with the largest possible cage that can be afforded. The large iguanines are probably best off in a house-roaming environment.

CONSTRUCTION MATERIALS

The cage itself can be an aquarium or it can be constructed of wood, particle board, plexiglass, wire, etc. The key elements are that there must be enough room and there must be appropriate ventilation. If an all-glass or plexiglass cage is used, the top should be screen so there is ample airflow. If the cage is made of wood, it should be sealed with a varnish or waterproof paint to prevent the cage from rotting. It is especially important that the floor material be waterproof so that bacteria or fungus does not grow in the water and excrement that would otherwise soak into the floor. In addition, the floor of the cage should be covered in a substrate which is easily cleaned. The next several paragraphs describe advantages and disadvantages of different substrates.

Newspaper and Paper Bags. Many people successfully keep their reptiles on newspaper or paper bags. When soiled, the paper can be pulled right out and replaced.

Astroturf or Carpet. Astroturf or some other kind of carpet is a bit more aesthetically pleasing than paper, but is slightly more difficult to keep clean. If multiple pieces of carpet are purchased, the soiled carpet can be replaced with the clean carpet. The soiled carpet can then be rinsed and cleaned with a 1:10 bleach-water solution. Always thoroughly rinse and dry any items that have been cleaned with bleach (or any detergent) before you allow the reptile to come into contact with the item.

Wood Chips. Some reptile owners like the look of wood chips. If you choose to use wood chips as the substrate, do not use cedar or pine chips because the oils from these woods can be toxic to iguanids and other reptiles. Also, if you use wood chips, you must remove them as soon as they are soiled so that bacteria does not accumulate. In addition, make sure the iguanid does not ingest the wood. If you feed your iguanid in its cage, use a bowl so that wood cannot get mixed in with the food items. If the animal is an insectivore, you can pinch off cricket legs so that the crickets cannot hop out of the bowl. You can also construct a separate feeding cage which does not contain wood chips.

Rabbit Food. Another popular substrate is rabbit food. These pellets are not harmful to ingest (as long as they are clean) and some people find them more aesthetically pleasing than carpet or paper. As with wood chips, you must remove soiled rabbit pellets immediately to prevent bacterial growth.

Corn-Cob Bedding. This is another substrate that is available in pet stores. Like wood shavings, it must not be ingested.

Sand and Gravel. These substrates are less desirable, as sand is almost always ingested, and both are difficult to keep clean.

CAGE TOYS

After the substrate is chosen, the next logical decision is what cage toys to include. Arboreal lizards need sturdy branches on which to climb. Many arboreal lizards like to climb up branches and ultimately lounge on a shelf near the top of the cage. You should supply one or two sturdy branches for each arboreal lizard in the cage. The branches should be about the same diameter as the lizard. Ground-dwellers like to dart around on rocks and wood. Many also like to hide, so make sure to provide a hiding place. Many ground dwellers like to climb up branches once in a while, so you should also consider supplying diagonal branches in the cage.

HEAT SOURCE

The best way to heat an iguanid's cage is by using incandescent spotlights. If a screen top is being used, the lights can be screwed into standard shop light fixtures and set right atop the cage. The area directly below the spotlight is the lizard's basking spot. It is a good idea to place a branch (in the case of arboreal lizards) or a rock (in the case of ground dwellers) below the spotlight. The basking spot is the hottest part of the cage, and the temperature decreases the farther one gets from it. It is a good idea to put the basking spot at one end of the cage so that an effective temperature gradient can be maintained. At one end of the cage, the basking spot will provide the lizard with temperatures between 29°C and 37°C. Desert species require a hotter environment, and the basking spot should easily reach 37°C. Tropical species do not require such a hot basking spot; 30-32°C should be sufficient. The other end of the cage might reach down to 26°C. This way, the iguanid can warm up or cool down as it chooses.

Do not use hot rocks for iguanids. This is because in their natural habitats, iguanids seek out sunny spots to warm themselves, which are not necessarily warm rocks. Hot rocks are also not effective at warming the air temperature of the cage. A lizard would need to actually sit on the rock all day to maintain the proper temperature. In addition, sitting on a hot rock is one of the major causes of burn in lizards.

LIGHT SOURCE

When an iguanid's skin is exposed to UV-B, a chemical called 7-dehydrocholesterol is ultimately transformed into vitamin D3 (Ball, 1995). Vitamin D3 is an essential component in calcium absorption. It is currently speculated that iguanids are unable to extract vitamin D3 from the food they ingest, which makes exposure to UV-B radiation not just important (Bernard et al., 1991), but possibly a matter of survival. Because of this, in addition to an incandescent lamp for heating, you must use a fluorescent, full-spectrum light to provide the iguanid with UV-B radiation. (Incandescent "full spectrum" bulbs do not emit UV-B radiation—Gehrmann, 1992.) If you do not use a fluorescent, full-spectrum light, you must house the animal in an outdoor or screened window enclosure. UV-B is present in natural sunlight, but it is filtered out through glass and plastic.

There are several fluorescent, full-spectrum bulbs on the market which emit small amounts of UV-B. As UV-B rays can cause cataracts and skin cancer in humans, manufacturers are wary of selling high-intensity UV-B bulbs (Ball, 1995). The use of a full-spectrum bulb for 12 hours a day, however, significantly increases the synthesis of vitamin D3 in the iguanid's skin, and in effect, increases calcium absorption. Full-spectrum bulbs are only effective from six months to one year, however, and should be replaced periodically. In addition, it should be noted that exposure to natural sunlight is much more beneficial, and iguanids should be taken outside whenever possible.

You can hook up both the heat lamp and the full-spectrum lamp to a timer that will automatically turn them on in the morning and off at night. As a general rule, the lights should be on for 12-14 hours per day. If the lizard is in a room with many windows, chances are that it will wake with the sun, so the timer can be set to turn on at sunrise. The timer can then turn off 12-14 hours later. (Many people set their timers to turn off when it gets dark outside.) A stable photoperiod such as this will help the lizard feel comfortable in its captive environment. It is also very important that lights in the room do not stay on all night, because this can stress the lizard.

HUMIDITY

Tropical iguanid species have evolved to live in climates with high humidity. Humidity greatly helps the shedding process. In addition, it appar-

FEEDING AND WATER REQUIREMENTS

Naturally, all reptiles require water for survival. In most cases, a bowl full of water in the terrarium is suffcient. The bowl should be cleaned daily, as any waste or debris which may enter the water can, in such high temperatures, promote bacterial and fungal growth. Iguanids will drink from bowls, unlike some reptiles such as chameleons (*Chamaeleo* spp.) that only drink from water droplets on leaves. Sometimes it may be necessary to show the water to the iguanid by placing the bowl in front of the lizard and by splashing the water with a finger. Iguanids also tend to notice that there is water in the bowl when they step into it.

Many iguanids like to bathe in their water. Whenever possible, a water bowl large enough

Cayman Islands Rhinoceros Iguana, *Cyclura nubila*. Photo by A. J. Whitney.

ently makes the lizards feel more comfortable. Some genera such as *Basiliscus* will not reproduce when the humidity is low (DeVosjoli, 1992).

You can keep the humidity in the cage higher than ambient humidity by placing a large water bowl in the cage. If a basking light shines down close to it or an undertank heater is placed underneath it, water evaporates continuously. Alternately, you can spray the cage frequently to keep it moist.

If the humidity is kept high, it is essential that the cage be cleaned frequently and that there be plenty of ventilation. High humidity promotes bacterial growth, and it is common for lizards to develop skin infections when their cages are not kept clean of these bacteria. In many cases, the cons outweigh the pros when dealing with high-humidity enclosures.

for the entire lizard to fit into should be used. In addition, water bowls are used to help keep the humidity high in lizard terrariums. Refer to the previous discussion of housing, heating, and lighting for further details.

The true iguanas are similar to one another in that they are all primarily herbivorous. A host of microorganisms live in the hindgut of true iguanas; these microorganisms aid in the digestion of cellulose (the main component of plant cell walls) and fiber. Iguanines also possess an elongated and partitioned colon, which evidently aids in the digestion of plant matter (Iverson, 1982). As indicated in Table I, some of these lizards also have omnivorous tendencies. Those lizards will take in both arthropods and small animals in addition to plant matter. The remaining lizards are insectivores. Larger

Fuzzy mice on a newspaper substrate. Photo by Isabelle Francais.

insectivores will also accept small animals, but arthropods remain their main dish.

For both insectivores and herbivores, variety in the diet can help ensure that the animal is receiving the proper nutrients. Both types of iguanas will still require periodic vitamin and mineral supplementation, however, and those keeping herbivores still need to pay close attention to the foods offered. Variety is very important.

"Pinky" mice and rats (newborn specimens) are the most popular food items for those with carnivorous tendencies. Small, inexpensive lizards are also available to add variety to the diet. Crickets and mealworms are the most common insects used for the insectivore diet. They are available in large numbers, they are easy to breed, and they do not fly away. Other food items such as waxworms, butterworms and fruitflies are also used.

The use of insects as the primary food source poses a number of problems:
—inadequate ratio of calcium to phosphorus in food items
—inadequate calcium absorption from foot items because of the lack of proper cage lighting
—difficult digestion of insect chitin
—high fat content (which inhibits calcium absorption) of worms

First, iguanian lizards need to consume about twice as much calcium as phosphorus for effective bone growth and maintenance as well as for muscle contraction. However, the most commonly used arthropods have Ca:P ratios well below the 2:1 standard. The calcium-phosphorus ratio in crickets is 0.13:1; in mealworms, it is 0.06:1; in wax worms, it is 0.08:1. (Rep-Cal Research Labs, 1992). Therefore, you must use supplemental calcium powder to boost the amount of calcium in the diet. Furthermore, it is best to use a calcium supplement that contains no phosphorus.

Food items should also be fed a high quality diet. Calcium-rich greens such as collard and dandelion are good choices. Not only are those plants high in calcium, but they also have a large amount of water which diminishes the need to supply additional water to the insects. (Inappropriate vegetables and problems with calcium oxalate are discussed later in this section.) Other foods such as fish flakes or commercial "cricket food" are also options, but if you use those food items, you must also supply additional water to the insects.

Gut-loading is an alternative to keeping cultured food items on a regular, balanced diet. With gut loading, the insect is basically stuffed with high quality food right before the insect is fed to the lizard. The insect must first be deprived of food for a day or two to ensure that it is very hungry, and then it is allowed to feast on something nutritious. Before the food is processed through the insect's body, it is fed to the lizard. In effect, the lizard eats what the insect eats.

Whether or not you gut-load the insects, they should be fed high-quality foods prior to being themselves fed to iguanids. The insects should also be coated with a calcium supplement and a multivitamin supplement before feeding time. Taking these measures should help ensure that the lizards ingest the nutrients they need.

The second problem deals with calcium absorption. Even if you use calcium supplementaion to achieve a Ca:P ratio of 2:1, iguanids can still suffer from calcium deficiency. This is due to a lack of exposure to UV-B radiation. You must use fluorescent, full-spectrum lighting to ensure that calcium absorption takes place.

The third problem with these insects is their chitin content. The exoskeletons of arthropods are high in chitin, which can be difficult for an iguana to digest. If you use mealworms as food items, serve the mealworms right after they molt so their exoskeletons are still soft when eaten. Also, use younger crickets rather than older ones, because the younger insects have less exoskeleton relative to body mass.

The fourth problem is the fat content of the worms used. Worms should not be offered as the primary food source. Fat inhibits calcium absorption, which is already a problem with iguanids in captivity. Instead, offer crickets or some other insect as the primary food. Offer mealworms, waxworms, and butterworms only as supplements.

Iguanids in the Corytophanidae family grow sufficiently large that they can also eat pinky mice, small lizards and frogs. These additional diet items decrease the need for vitamin and mineral supplementation, but you should still occasionally use supplements.

Herbivorous iguanids encounter most of the dietary problems in captivity that insectivores do. Here, there are essentially two problems:
—vegetables with low nutritional content
—calcium absorption

First, vegetables with low nutritional content are invariably chosen as food items. The iguanine body is highly specialized for digestion of plant matter, yet the digestive system remains inefficient because it can only extract 30-70% of the nutrtients present in the ingested food (Iverson, 1982.) Therefore, only high-quality food items should be chosen. Table II gives a short list of calcium to phosphorus ratios of some fruits and vegetables. The items on the list are relatively high in nutrients, and all are fairly good choices as part of a varied diet. In addition, you should use calcium and vitamin supplements 2-3 times per week to avoid nutritional deficiencies.

Second, there remains the problem of calcium absorption. You must always provide natural or artificial full-spectrum lighting for iguanines. One of the most common lizards kept as pets, *Iguana iguana*, is notorious for developing metabolic bone disease (see Common Problems section) due to calcium deficiency. However, owners must also be aware of the dangers of oversupplementation with calcium. See the chapter on nutrition for more information.

It should also be mentioned that even vegetables which appear to be nutritious may in fact cause problems in herbivores when fed in excess. Members of the cabbage family (cabbage, chinese cabbage, kale, broccoli, cauliflower, turnips, rutabaga, brussels sprouts) can be goitrogenic when eaten in excess. Many members of the Brassica plant family (spinach, beet greens, swiss chard, rhubarb, beets, celery stalk) contain large amounts of oxalic acid (calcium oxalate), which binds with calcium and makes it unavailable. This can cause calcium deficiency. (Wissman and Parsons, 1994.) Therefore, it is crucial that you offer a wide variety of vegetables and fruits to herbivores to ensure that they do not suffer from nutritional problems. You can offer the listed food items to a lizard, but they should not be the staple items of the herbivore diet.

It cannot be stressed enough that herbivorous lizards need to be offered high-quality food items, supplemented with calcium and multivitamin supplements, and that the lizards must have exposure to UV-B radiation. Green iguanas die every day in captivity (based on statistics from the U.S. Fish & Wildlife Service) and the most frequently diagnosed illness is metabolic bone disease (Wissman and Parsons,

Green Iguana, *Iguana iguana*, eating a raw carrot. Photo by Isabelle Francais.

1994). If and when the remaining iguanine species attain the same popularity in captivity as the green iguana, the mortality from poor nutrition will likely be passed along to them.

TABLE II: CALCIUM TO PHOSPHORUS RATIOS FOR SOME FRUITS AND VEGETABLES

Collard greens	7.79:1
Papaya	4.50:1
Coriander	4.0:1
Parsley	3.25:1
Dandelion greens	2.89:1
Kale	2.61:1
Figs	2.1:1
Watercress	2.0:1
Endive	1.86:1
Raspberries	1.80:1
Mustard greens	1.79:1
Okra	1.11:1
Strawberries	0.75:1
Broccoli	0.72:1

(Pennington, 1989.)

WASTE MANAGEMENT

Most iguanians defecate once a day, or at least every two to three days. There is no separate defecation and urination; rather, it all comes out at

Eggs of the Water Dragon, *Physignathus cocincinus*, incubating in vermiculite. Photo by Isabelle Francais.

once. In the case of the smaller insectivorous species, there are generally two parts to the excrement: a brown stool, and a white blob which is comprised of urates. This form of excrement is relatively self-contained, and is easy to deal with. The larger, primarily herbivorous species, however, have three parts to their excrement: a brown stool, a white blob, and quite a bit of liquid, mostly water, which has a consistency much like raw egg. This can be quite messy, especially with adult specimens.

The iguanid owner must assume all waste management duties. As previously mentioned, you must choose a substrate for the bottom of the cage that is easy to keep clean. Minor cuts or scrapes can become infected when iguanids are living in dirty conditions. Also, the cleaner the cage is kept, the less chance that mites will decide to move in. (See Common Problems, later in this section.) If it is determined that the more exotic substrates such as wood chips cannot be kept clean, you must change the substrate to something easier to clean, such as carpet or paper.

REPRODUCTION

With few exceptions, all iguanians are oviparous. Fertilization is always internal, followed by a gestation period which can last from 2-10 weeks, and then an incubation period which can last from 4-12 weeks. The chapter on Egg Physiology and Biology has detailed information about eggs and incubation. This reproduction section describes only general requirements for egg-laying and incubation.

If iguanids are observed mating, there is a good chance that the female will become gravid. Some iguanids that have several clutches of eggs per year are able to store sperm; this indicates that mating may not be observed in between clutches because none takes place. When the female is getting ready to lay her eggs, it is usually evident because she has stopped eating and has gotten heavier. It is important to provide the female with an appropriate egg-laying site so that she does not become egg-bound. A nesting substrate that is commonly used is a mixture of vermiculite and water. A 1:1 ratio of moistened vermiculite and sand is also used. In either case, the medium should be wet, but formable. When the lizard digs in it, the medium should not slosh back into a flat surface.

You should also make sure the nesting area has several inches of egg-laying medium. For smaller species, only a couple inches is necessary, but for larger species, you should provide at least six inches of substrate. Also, the animal is usually most comfortable with a private area. For large species, a large plastic trash can with

TABLE III:

INCUBATION TIMES AND TEMPERATURES

Genus	Number of clutches	Number of eggs	Incubation temperature(C)	Incubation length (days)
Iguana	1	20-40	30	75-120
Dipsosaurus	1	3-8	30-32	73-87
Sauromalus	1	12-14	?	84
Cyclura	1	5-20	28-31	84
Ctenosaur	1	20-30	29.5	65-90
Amblyrhynchus	1	1-3	?	95
Anolis	several	1-2	28-30	60-90
Basiliscus	several	3-20	27.8	70-150
Laemanctus	?	3-5	?	?
Corytophanes	?	6-11	?	?
Crotaphytus	4	2-24	30	50-75
Gambelia	2	2-20	30	?
Sceloporous	1-3	4-12	30	30-90
Holbrookia	5	2-10	?	?

Eggs of the Bearded Dragon, *Pogona barbata*, incubating in moist sand. Photo by Isabelle Francais.

lid turned on its side works well. If you use a trash can and lid, cut a hole in the lid so the iguanid can enter the can when she is ready to lay. Smaller species are generally comfortable laying in their cages, as long as you have provided appropriate hiding places for the nests.

Table III gives an overview of incubation times and temperatures for the more commonly bred species. Generally speaking, the incubation temperature ranges from about 28°C - 32°C, and the incubation time shortens with higher temperatures. Iguanids have certainly hatched successfully at different temperatures than the ones given in Table III. For many species, captive breeding is still largely an experimental science.

As soon as the eggs have been lain, you should carefully move the eggs to an incubator. The eggs should be placed in a moist container of vermiculite (similar to the egg-laying medium). For best results, the eggs should be placed in the vermiculite in the exact orientation in which they were lain (Kaplan, 1995).

You can use either a commercial or home-made incubator. With commercial incubators, the temperature can easily be set and maintained throughout the entire incubation period. However, you will still need to manually maintain an appropriate humidity for the nest. You can make your own incubator by placing the container of eggs inside a receptacle such as a glass aquarium. Both temperature and humidity can be maintained by filling the aquarium with a couple inches of water and by employing a heater with thermostat, such as are used with fish tanks. The egg container can then be placed in the water, which should not be deep enough for water to get into the egg container. Both types of incubators should be lightly sealed, allowing some air flow. In addition, every couple of days the incubator should be completely opened for a moment to allow a complete air exchange. For more specific information on eggs and how they are best managed, read the chapter on egg physiology and biology.

Once lizards begin to hatch, they will be hungry. You can start feeding insectivores on pinhead crickets or wingless fruit flies. Herbivores simply need finely chopped vegetables. Add vitamin and mineral supplmentation every other day or so to the food items. Young specimens should not endure a drastic temperature drop at night. Rather, a couple of degrees is sufficient.

PREVENTIVE HEALTH CARE

The first step in keeping captive iguanids healthy is daily observation. Although reptiles are exceptional at appearing healthy even when they are not healthy, it is usually possible to detect subtle behavioral or physical changes when acute observation is employed. Perform a complete body check every day, beginning with the head and ending with the tip of the tail. Check for parasites, lumps, color changes, swelling, wounds, and any other abnormalities. Overall, check to see if the animal appears thin, overweight, listless, bloated, or otherwise not itself. Spotted early, most conditions can be easily treated.

It is a good idea to find and develop a good relationship with a reptile veterinarian. Hopefully, in most cases, the veterinarian's role will be purely a precautionary one, but he or she can be of assistance for routine checkups. For example, many people opt to have their iguanids checked for internal parasites once or twice a year through fecal analysis. Still others opt to treat their lizards for parasites once or twice a year, regardless of the results of fecal test. Veterinarians are able to perform the tests and prescribe proper worming medication.

In addition, the enclosure should always be clean. Bacterial infections and parasite infestations can be avoided by simply cleaning out all feces and uneaten food. Employing a weekly cleaning schedule is also a good idea. Each week the entire cage and cage toys can be cleaned with a dilute bleach solution (one part bleach to ten parts water) followed by a thorough rinsing and drying.

COMMON PROBLEMS

Reptiles in general experience a myriad of problems in captivity, most of which stem from mismanagement. Very few reptiles succumb to completely uncontrollable ailments such as cancer, or catch airborne bacteria or viruses. Instead, they develop internal parasitical infestations from eating feces or soiled food, respiratory infections from being kept in an environment which is too cold, and diseases stemming from malnutrition. The best things to do to avoid the common problems seen in reptiles are to take proper care of the reptile and to employ the preventive health measures mentioned earlier. Listed below are some common ailments, their general causes, and possible cures.

EXTERNAL PARASITES

Mites can accumulate under scales, in folds of skin around the head and neck, and in between spines. There they live, eat, breed, and cause their host general discomfort. Not only are they annoying, but they can also spread infection. The common invaders are *Hirstiella trombidiiformis*, the lizard mite, and Trombiculidae species, the chigger mites. They are either black or red, and a little larger than the period at the end of this sentence. They are not restricted to animals kept outdoors.

It is prudent to eradicate mites as soon as they are discovered. Squashing works well on the mites that are out in the open, but that is a very slow process as there may be hundreds of mites present, all laying hundreds of eggs. A better first step would be to draw a lukewarm bath for the lizard and let it swim around for a while. A good portion of the mites will drown, and this will also help cleanse the lizard. While it is bathing, the enclosure can be cleaned and disinfected. Not only will this kill any mites present, but it will kill their eggs, which are lain off the lizard host. (Mader and Palazzolo, 1993.) A bleach solution (one part bleach to ten parts water) works well, followed by a thorough rinsing. In addition, as long as there are still mites present on the animal, this whole process should be repeated every day or two until the mites are gone.

Cape Spinytail Iguana, *Ctenosaura hemilopha*, with mite in ear. Photo by W. P. Mara.

If desired, a pest repellent can be used to help eradicate the mites. They are available as either sprays or solid strips. The effective ingredient to eradicate these mites is pyrethroid. If using a spray, the lizard should be completely covered with it (don't get it in the eyes or mouth) and then the spray should be thoroughly rinsed off. If using a strip, it should be placed in the same room as the affected iguanid, or a very small portion of the strip can be placed in the cage with the animal. If this is done, it is essential that the iguanid is not able to come into direct contact with the strip. In addition, the portion of the strip should only be placed in the cage for a few hours a day until the mites are gone. This method should be used very carefully.

Another messy, but effective way to eradicate mites on iguanids is to douse them with olive oil or another similar cooking oil. A kitchen brush type baster can be used to coat their bodies with the oil. It is like a prolonged bath because it drowns the mites. If this method is employed, be very careful not to get any oil into the nostrils. This method kills almost 100% of the mites present on the lizard's body. Lizards can be coated with oil in the evening and then bathed in the morning. This is a messy, primitive method, but it is relatively safe (as long as the oil stays away from the nostrils) and effective.

Mites on iguanids can also be treated with ivermectin, a medication that can be obtained from a veterinarian. (Mader and Palazzolo, 1993.)

Unfortunately, mites lay lots of eggs. Even when all of the mites seem to be gone, it is a good idea to keep cleaning and disinfecting for 2-3 weeks. This helps to ensure that the eggs will be washed away and will not hatch.

INTERNAL PARASITES

Reptile veterinarians can diagnose internal parasites with a fecal sample. If an iguanid is acting peculiar, typically not eating, growing, or acting lethargic, it could be due to internal parasites. They can take control inside an iguanid's alimentary canal and generally wreak havoc. If the fecal exam identifies parasite eggs in the stool of an iguanid, there are effective, easy-to-use worming medications available that should easily take care of the problem.

If multiple animals are kept in the same enclosure and only one of them is diagnosed as having internal parasites, the affected animal should be quarantined from the others until a fecal test reveals that the parasites are gone. Usually, if one iguanid is diagnosed with internal parasites and it has been living in the same quarters as another iguanid, both will be given the medicine. This is one good reason for yearly check-ups: sometimes

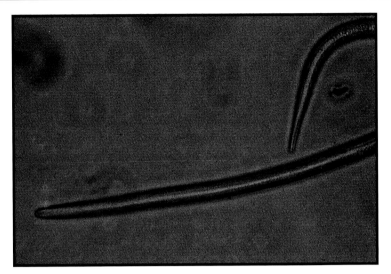
Ascarid (hookworm) larvae. Photo by Eric Rundquist.

it is not evident without fecal analysis that an iguanid has contracted an internal parasite.

ANOREXIA

There are three basic reasons why an iguanid would refuse to eat: a psychological problem, a physiological problem, or both. One common solution to the problem is raising the temperature of the iguana's enclosure. Many people tend to keep their lizards at temperatures that are too low for the animals, and consequently, abnormal behavior ensues. Many times, correcting the temperature will motivate an iguanid to start feeding. In addition, many iguanids will eat voraciously in the summer months, then slow down considerably during the winter months.

If the problem is not temperature or season, it could be stress. Sometimes reptiles do not respond well to human activity around their cages. Iguanids that are particularly skittish could be moved to a quiet corner of a room where there are not as many external stressors.

An improper photoperiod can also bother iguanids. As discussed in the housing, heating, and lighting section, iguanids like a consistent light/ dark cycle. If lights are on all night in the lizard's room, the animal can become stressed, which can lead to anorexia.

Finally, the iguanid might be ill. Internal parasites, external parasites, any kind of bacterial or fungal infection, as well as most other illnesses will cause a reptile to go off feed. Commonly, the only symptom a sick iguana will present to its owner is anorexia. Once a reptile stops eating, there is definitely a problem at hand. It is important to remember that food refusal is not a disease, but a symptom of some other problem. First, you should determine that there are no stressors at work on the lizard. If the lizard is living in an appropriate environment, consult a veterinarian. Sometimes, a quick fecal analysis can pinpoint the problem; in some cases, just two doses of medicine can get an iguanid back to normal eating habits.

LETHARGY

Similar to anorexia, lethargy in iguanids is a symptom of a larger problem. It usually accompanies disease. If an iguanid seems listless, review the temperature, photoperiod, and diet you are providing to the animal. If those environmental factors seem to be correct, you should take the animal to the vet. A quick blood test can tell much about an iguanid's health. All reptiles and amphibians are good at masking their illnesses. When a symptom becomes visible, it is important to act quickly so that the problem can be reversed.

GENERAL WOUNDS AND ABSCESSES

Iguanids sometimes injure themselves with their acrobatic antics. These lizards frequently break their toes and pull out claws when they leap through the air, and those injuries are not considered to be very serious. However, iguanids can also break legs. If your lizard begins to limp or begins to move strangely in some other way, it needs medical attention.

Iguanids are also prone to abrasions and lacerations. Usually, scratches are the result of contact with other lizards, but they can also happen accidentally in other ways. When an iguana gets a scratch, the first and foremost thing to do is keep the wound clean. You can use povidone-iodine scrub, hydrogen peroxide, or alcohol to clean a minor cut. Because these do not need to be used at their full strengths, they may be diluted with water. After cleaning out the wound, use a triple antibiotic ointment daily to keep the wound clean and protected against infection. If a wound is deep, consider a trip to the vet to see if stitches are in order. Generally, for minor wounds and burns, there is little chance of infection when the wound area is kept clean and medicated.

Sometimes, what starts out as a minor cut or puncture can turn into an abscess. Basically, this is just a pus-filled, infected lump. It is necessary to seek veterinary attention to eliminate abscesses. The lump should be lanced and drained, and antibiotics should be administered. The sooner attention is given to abscesses, the better.

BURNS

Thermal burns are relatively frequent for iguanids in captivity, mainly due to the use of hot rocks, which can overheat. Iguanids can also burn themselves on lights that are used for heating. Lights should not be placed inside the cage; rather, they should be positioned outside the cage so they can shine into the cage. Many burns are relatively minor and can be treated with a triple antibiotic ointment. If the burn seems to be very bad, a veterinarian should be consulted. In general, if a burned iguanid is acting normally (eating, pooping, etc.) then all it probably needs is triple antibiotic ointment. Never hesitate to contact a veterinarian, however, if there is any doubt.

NOSE ABRASIONS

Nose abrasions, or rostral rub, is a common problem in many lizards that are housed in cages that have wire or screen on the sides. If an iguanid is unhappy with its cage, it may spend much of its time rubbing its nose against the sides, trying to escape. Some lizards rub their noses against the cage so often that their flesh is rubbed away.

METABOLIC BONE DISEASE (FIBROUS OSTEODYSTROPHY)

One of the most common nutritional ailments among iguanines in captivity is metabolic bone disease (MBD). MBD is also called fibrous osteodystrophy. This condition is generally caused by calcium deficiency. You can easily avoid MBD by following the diet and husbandry guidelines in this chapter. The following symptoms are almost always indicative of MBD. If you observe any of these symptoms in iguanian lizards in captivity, immediately correct your diet and husbandry techniques. For more specific information on metabolic bone disease, the reader is referred to the chapters on rehabilitation, internal medicine and nutrition.

When an iguanid has MBD, it does not have enough calcium in the blood. This is due to a calcium-poor diet. When the iguanid's blood cannot get enough calcium from the food it eats, it starts to take calcium from the bones. This results in the bones becoming soft. If an iguanid starts breaking its bones easily, it could be indicative of MBD.

There are other signs that usually develop before broken bones. One sign is a crooked back. If an iguanids spine seems to be bent—no matter what position it is in—it might be curving due to MBD. Another symptom is lack of toe use. If an iguanids toes twitch frequently (this is called tetany) or don't seem to be very strong, it could also be indicative of MBD. Perhaps the two most common symptoms are the swelling of the limbs and the jaw. If an iguanid appears muscle-bound in its limbs, but it hasn't changed its exercise routine, it could be due to the body's attempt to strengthen the weak bones by surrounding them

with fibrous connective tissue. The lower jaws can also become swollen or appear to be caved in when they get very weak. If an animal's mouth does not close all the way, it could be indicative of MBD. Also, sometimes the jaw will appear to be normal, but be soft. You can give the jaw a very gentle squeezing to tell if the jaw does not seem to be well calcified.

MBD is a reversible disease, especially when caught early. A good reptile veterinarian will easily be able to tell if an iguanid is suffering from MBD, and can help nurse the animal back to health. The most common cure is simply a change to a better diet and more exposure to unfiltered sunlight. When veterinary help is employed, calcium as well as a hormone called calcitonin-salmon (which helps return calcium to the bones) can be injected into the iguanid (Wissman and Parsons, 1994).

MBD is most frequently observed in I. iguana, but it is also seen in insectivorous lizards that are fed nothing but unsupplemented crickets. MBD can occur in any iguanid that is fed a poor diet.

SALMONELLOSIS

Salmonella is a bacteria that is usually contracted by eating undercooked or spoiled poultry, usually chicken. It can, however, be present in other foods. When only a small amount is present in the body of either a human or an iguanid, it may never be noticed. Like its close cousin, *E. coli*, it is present in humans who suffer no ill effects. Healthy adults (human or iguanian) whose immune systems are not compromised are usually able to fight off the bacteria if it is not present in large numbers. The young, the old, and those whose immune systems are already compromised are the ones at risk.

Reptiles have recently become notorious for transmitting salmonella to humans. The animals might contract the bacteria from their food or from the feces of other infected animals. It can be passed along to humans through contact with infected feces or when we are scratched by an reptile's dirty claws. Humans are at the greatest risk of *Salmonella* infection after cleaning the cage and after handling reptiles. Always wash your hands, preferably with antibacterial soap, after being in contact with a reptile. If a reptile has *Salmonella* and the bacterium is transferred to your hands, chances are that the bacterium will make it to your mouth as well. In addition, always thoroughly wash cuts or bites (inflicted by a reptile) with an antibacterial soap to avoid infection. Salmonellosis can be very serious in humans and medical attention is required. For more specific information, see chapter on zoonotic conditions.

A good reptile veterinarian can check a reptile's feces for salmonella to determine if the animal is infected. You can also treat an animal for *Salmonella* as a safety precaution. Although a reptile infected with salmonella may appear to be healthy, if it contracts another illness or its system is otherwise comprimised, *Salmonella* can again prove itself harmful. Having a reptile checked and cleared of salmonella is beneficial for both the reptile and the human. Also remember that a clean bill of health today does not ensure that *Salmonella* will not have invaded again by tomorrow, so it is important to keep both hands and wounds clean.

RECOMMENDED READING

—Ball, JC:
A Comparison of the UV-B Irradiance of Low-Intensity, Full-Spectrum Lamps with Natural Sunlight. *Bulletin of the Chicago Herpetological Society*, 1995; 30(4): 69-72.

—Bartlett, D:
The Anoles of the United States. *Reptiles*, 1995; 2(5): 48-65.

—Bernard, JS; Oftedal, OT; Barboza, PS; Allen, ME; Citino, SB; Ullrey, DE; Montali, RJ:
The Response of Vitamin D-Deficient Green Iguanas (Iguana iguana) to Artificial Ultraviolet Light. *Proc. Am. Assoc. Zoo Vet.* 1991: 147-150.

—Blair, DW:
Chuckwallas. *Reptiles*, 1994; 1(3): 16-22.

—Blair, DW:
Rock Iguanas. *Reptiles*, 1994; 1(4): 40-63.

—Bricker, K:
Follow-up: Third-generation Green Anoles, *Anolis carolinensis. Bulletin of the Chicago Herpetological Society*, 1995; 30(5): 89.

—DeVosjoli, P:
The General Care and Maintenance of Green Water Dragons, Sailfin Lizards and Basilisks. Advanced Vivarium Systems, Lakeside, CA, 1992; 31 pp.

—_____:
The Green Iguana Manual. Advanced Vivarium Systems, Lakeside, CA, 1992; 71 pp.

—Elfstrom, B:
The Paleate Spiny-Tailed Iguana, *Ctenosaura palearis* Stejneger: Distribution and Life History. *Iguana Times*, 1994; 3(4): 2-9.

—Fitch, HS:
Variation and Clutch Size in New World Reptiles. University of Kansas Museum of Natural History, Miscellaneous Publications, 1985; 76: 1-76.

—Frost, DR; Etheridge R:
A Phylogenetic Analysis and taxonomy of Iguanian lizards (Reptilia: Squamata). Misc. Publ. Univ. Kansas Nat. Hist. Mus. 1989; 81: 1-65.

—Frye, FL; Townsend W:
Iguanas: A Guide to Their Biology and Captive Care. Krieger Publishing Company, Malabar FL, 1993, 145 pp.

—Gehrmann, WH:
No UV-B From Tungsten Filament Incandescent Lamps. *Bulletin of the Association of Reptile and Amphibian Veterinarians*, 1992; 2(2): 5.

—Iverson, JB:
Adaptions to Herbivory in Iguanine Lizards, in Iguanas of the World: Their Behavior, Ecology and Conservation. G. M. Burghardt and A. S. Rand, eds. Noyes Publishing, Park Ridge, NJ, 1982; 60-76.

—Kaplan, M:
Iguana: A Guide to Care, Feeding and Socialization. Melissa Kaplan: Rohnert Park, CA, 1995; 44 pp.

—Mader, D. R. and C. Palazzolo.
Mite & Tick Infestations. *Reptiles* 1(1): 64-72. 1993.

—Meyer, J. R. and L. D. Wilson. 1985.
The Snakes of Honduras, 2nd edition. Milwaukee Public Museum, Milwaukee.

—Obst, F. J., K. Richter and U. Jacob.
The Completely Illustrated Atlas of Reptiles and Amphibians for the Terrarium. TFH Publications, Neptune City, NJ, 1988, 830 pp.

—Pennington, JAT:
Food values of portions commonly used. HarperCollins, New York, 1989, 328pp.

—Rundquist, E.M. 1995.
Lizards in the Mists: Basilisks. *Captive Breeding* 3(1): 26-28.

—Sharp, C. R. The Galapagos Marine Iguana:
A Natural History. *Reptile & Amphibian Magazine*, May-June 1994: 76-83.

—Thirkhill, L. 1995.
Breeding Western Collared Lizards. *Reptile & Amphibian Magazine* May-June 1995: 74-77.

—Villers, L.M. 1995.
Captive Propagation of the Desert Iguana. *Captive Breeding* 3(1): 5-7.

—Wissman, M. and B. Parsons, 1994.
Hypocalcemia in a Green Iguana. *Reptiles* 1(2): 89-93.

—_____, 1994.
Metabolic Bone Disease in Green Iguanas. *Reptiles* 1(3): 68-72.

—_____, 1995.
Dermatophytosis of Green Iguanas. *Reptiles* 3(3): 78-80.

—Zug, G. R. 1993.
Herpetology: An Introductory Biology of Amphibians and Reptiles. San Diego CA: Academic Press, Inc.

MONITOR LIZARDS (VARANIDAE) AND TEGUS (TEIIDAE)

By: Michael J. Balsai
4223 Pine Street
Philadelphia, PA 19104

Michael J. Balsai received his B.A. (with honors) in biology from Lehigh University in 1975. Presently he is a Ph.D. dissertation student at the University of Pennsylvania, pursuing studies in "lower" vertebrate paleontology. He has been working on the husbandry of various species of tegus and monitor lizards for about 13 years and has published widely in herpetological subjects over the past seven years. iIn addition, his other "vivarium" interests include Solomon Island prehensile-tailed skinks, European glass lizards, and royal pythons. He is a member of: American Zoo and Aquarium Association, Association of Reptilian & Amphibian Veterinarians, American Federation of Herpetoculturists, American Society of Ichthyologists and Herpetologists, The Herpetologist's League, Society for the Study of Amphibians and Reptiles, Chicago Herpetological Society, Australasian Affiliation of Herpetological Societies, the Victorian Herpetological Society, Society of Vertebrate Paleontology, Society of Systematic Biologists, and Society for the Study of Evolution.

BASIC TAXONOMY, LIFESPAN AND HABITAT PREFERENCES

Monitors and tegus may share a superficial resemblance, but are not closely related to each other. Monitors belong to the family Varanidae while tegus belong to the great lizard family Teiidae. One consequence of these relationships is that monitors are much more closely linked to helodermids (e.g., gila monsters and beaded lizards - *Heloderma* sp.) and anguids (lizards such as the "glass lizards" - *Ophisaurus* sp.) and alligator lizards (e.g., *Gerrhonotus* sp.) than they are to tegus, and these, in turn, are more closely aligned to lacertids and skinks than they are to monitors (Zug 1993; Estes et al 1988). One other interesting aspect of monitor systematics is that many experts believe these lizards are probably more closely related to snakes than are any other lizards, and certainly more so than tegus (Estes et al 1988). Biogeographically, monitors are all Old World lizards with a wide distribution through Africa, southern and south-

White-throated Monitor, *Varanus albigularis*. Photo by Mark Bayless.

east Asia, Australasia, and various archipelagos in the Pacific and Indian Oceans. Tegus, on the other hand are only New World and are found broadly distributed in South America.

All monitors are currently classed as members of a single genus *Varanus* and there are at least about 40 or so species of these lizards (Card 1995c; Green and King 1993; King et al 1991). Among the more commonly kept species are: the savannah monitor (*Varanus exanthematicus*), The white-throated or Cape monitor (*V. albigularis*), the Nile monitor (*V. niloticus*), the Asian water monitor (*V. salvator*), the Dumeril's or brown rough-necked monitor (*V. dumerilii*), the black rough-necked monitor (*V. rudicollis*), the mangrove monitor (*V. indicus*), and the argus monitor (*V. gouldii horni*), a subspecies of Gould's monitor. There are currently four species of monitors that are recognized by CITES as Appendix I which means they are considered endangered. These are the Komodo dragon (*V. komodoensis*), the bengal monitor (*V. bengalensis*), the desert monitor (*V. griseus*) and the yellow monitor (*V. flavescens*). All other species of monitors are listed on the Appendix II and thus, they are considered to be threatened and could be vulnerable to exploitation if trade their numbers are not regulated. The tegus are all in the single genus *Tupinambis* containing two or three species depending upon which author is consulted

(Peters and Donoso-Barros 1970; Presch 1973; Hoogmoed and Lescure 1975; Luxmoore et al 1988). These species are: the so-called "black and white" or "white" tegu (*Tupinambis teguixin*), the red tegu (*T. rufescens*), and the contested (considered by some to be synonymous with *T. teguixin*) third species, commonly called the golden tegu (*T. nigropunctatus*). Presently, no tegus are listed as CITES Appendix I, but they are all listed on the Appendix II.

No studies on longevity seem to have been conducted for either monitors or tegus in the wild. However lists (see Slavens 1989; Slavens and Slavens 1993; Bowler 1977) do indicate that both genera are reasonably long lived as captives. Captive records for at least some species of monitors indicate ages of about 14 + years at the time of death (Slavens 1989), while those of some tegus may be as much as 16 + years (Slavens and Slavens 1993). It does not seem improbable that as husbandry techniques continue to improve, longevity for captive monitors may increase even more.

A few species of monitors can be very cosmopolitan in habitat preference by virtue of their extended ranges (e.g., Gould's monitors) while the surroundings of others need to be rather well defined (e.g., desert monitors, or tree monitors). Certainly some monitor species show particular adaptations to their preferred habitats. For example, tree monitors (e.g., *V. beccari*, *V. prasinus*, *V. teriae*, and *V. bogerti*) have prehensile tails and somewhat sticky soft black colored tissue on the soles of their feet (Wilson and Knowles 1988) to enhance their abilities as tree dwellers and climbers. Many aquatic and semi-aquatic species show keeled tails that may enhance their proficiency as swimmers. Monitors seem to occupy four broad habitat types: (1) the arboreal/aquatic, (2) the rocky outcrop, (3) the arboreal, and (4) the ground or purely terrestrial (Cogger 1959, Greer 1989, Sprackland 1992). Most of the aquatic species and some of the arboreal, inhabit the first habitat type and include mangrove monitors and Dumeril's monitors as well as many more aquatic species such as Nile monitors and Asian water monitors. Those that prefer the rocky outcrop habitat would include such species as the spiny-tailed monitor (*V. acanthurus*), and the perentie (*V. giganteus*) (Greer 1989). The purely arboreal species include all the tree monitors, probably the crocodile monitor (*V. salvadorii*) and black rough-necked monitor (*V. rudicollis*), and possibly the Timor monitor (*V. timorensis)* and Gray's monitor *(V. olivaceus)* (Greer 1989, Auffenberg 1988, Sprackland 1992, Card 1995b,c). The last category (purely terrestrial) would include a vast array of species, many which excavate burrows. Examples would include savannah monitors, white-throated monitors, desert monitors,

Gould's (and argus) monitors, Bengal monitors and Komodo dragons (Auffenberg 1981, 1994, Sprackland 1992, Green and King 1993). Readers must always bear in mind that these categories are not necessarily "strict" and certain species will not necessarily be restricted to any of these general habitats (Greer 1989) and the preferences can change over the life of the animal. Successful rearing of monitors, particularly with the intent of breeding should definitely include research by the herpetoculturist to discern as much about the natural history, habitat preferences, temperature needs, etc. Monitors living under specialized conditions may show interesting adaptations to such habitats. For example, many arid adapted species may have adaptations of the kidneys to conserve water and some have glands for ridding their bodies of excess salts (Greer 1989).

Tegus are generally associated with a wide variety of habitats and the fact that only two or three species are known, can make the herpetoculturist's job somewhat easier than with monitors. Habitats for *Tupinambis* include dense jungle, marshes, arid scrubland, prairies, and savannahs (Luxmoore et al 1988), vegetative islands during floods (Dixon and Soini 1986) and they are apparently partial to cleared areas (Norman 1987; Milstead 1961; Ditmars 1933). These lizards are well known to be somewhat opportunistic and are very hardy, both as captives and as free-ranging animals. Red tegus are more associated with arid regimes than either the white or golden tegus, though, they too, prefer the edges of rivers and ponds (Donadio and Gallardo 1984; Luxmoore et al. 1988). Tegus tend to be fossorial, and captives will usually tunnel below the substrate. They can be arboreal (Mercolli and Yanosky 1994: Yanosky 1991; Luxmoore et al. 1988), though probably not often (Sprackland 1992) and may sleep submerged even in cool water (Olmos 1995)! Quite possibly, tegus may fill an ecological niche (presumably that of a large carnivorous lizard) in South America, similar to the one monitors occupy in the areas where they are found (Laurent 1979; Tyler 1979). Both tegus and monitors are diurnal and depending upon where they are native, some will undergo seasonal periods of inactivity resembling hibernation (Auffenberg 1994; Langerwerf 1992/93; Stanner and Mendelssohn 1991; Branch 1988; Luxmoore et al 1988).

PHYSICAL CHARACTERISTICS

Some obvious general physical characteristics of monitors are their long, slender, deeply forked tongues, sharp (usually) fang-like, compressed

Emerald Tree Monitor, *Varanus prasinus*. Photo by Mark Bayless.

Common Water Monitor, *Varanus salvator*. Photo by Mark Bayless.

teeth, their (usually) long necks with fairly short bodies, large eyes with round pupils, the moderately large, deeply inset openings of their ears, long heads with (usually) pointed snouts, five-toed feet with large, sharp, recurved claws, long, muscular, non-breakable tails, and the absence, for most species, of femoral pores and anal glands (Halliday and Adler 1986). Monitors are alert and often curious about what is occurring in their immediate surroundings. They can also react to stimuli surprisingly fast and are capable of moving very quickly. Monitors vary greatly in size, though all are considered large for lizards, and include members that are the largest living lizards (komodo dragon and crocodile monitor). Varanids usually bear relatively uniform sized scales which ensure that their skins are both tough as well as supple (Greer 1989). To be sure, monitors look pretty similar, differences being in specific details, such as lengths and shapes of snouts, tails (as well as tail shape, lack or presence of keels, and whether the tail is spiny), position of the nostrils, neck length and nuchal scale sizes, and teeth shapes (whether serrated, recurved, molariform, etc) (Greer 1989; Balsai Pers. Obs.).

Tegus are also large lizards, and as mentioned previously, superficially resemble monitors causing confusion for some inexperienced herpetoculturists. Specific similarities are, their tapering snouts, forked tongues (though these tongues are nowhere near as gracile as those seen on monitors) and long powerful tails (though the tails do not bear any sort of keel on any species of tegu). Mature male tegus, as with many monitor species tend to be larger and more robust than females and old males may have what could be called jowls (unlike any varanid species). In contrast to monitors, these lizards can loose their tails and regrow them. Evidence of such tail loss may be common, particularly but certainly not exclusively among wild-caught golden tegus (Balsai pers. observ.). Tegu tails range from about the same length to somewhat longer than the SVL while in some monitor species, the tail can be about the same as the body length to as much as twice the body length. The scales along the dorsal side of the head and also along the lateral aspects of the muzzle in front of the eyes, are quite large, much more so, in fact, than on any species of monitor. The rest of the tegu's body, however, is entirely covered with somewhat small, lustrous, shiny, almost glassy bead-like scales. Tegus are strongly built heavy-bodied lizards. Comparatively speaking, tegus show much more noticeably shorter necks when compared to their body lengths than any monitor lizard. Their limbs are strong with sharp claws (though the claws are not nearly as talon-like as those of many monitors). Their limbs do appear somewhat shorter when compared to their bodies than is the leg to body ratio of varanids.

SELECTION AND ACQUISITION

It is important to prepare for the acquisition of any monitor or tegu species by doing some research before purchase. Familiarity with the temperature, space, lighting, water, humidity, and food requirements of the species being considered is paramount. Do not acquire a species that requires a large amount of space with the intent of forcing it to confinement in a small area. Provide arboreal species with adequate three dimensional space. Desert species will require year round dry climatic regimes which must be considered when living in areas with continuous high humidity. Certain species do not tame very well (e.g., Nile monitors, golden tegus) and these differences in temperament are important considerations for long term handling. Some monitor species spend much time in water and will require large vessels of water for swimming and soaking. The American Federation of Herpetoculturists' *Guidelines for Keeping Monitor Lizards* (Anon. 1993) are very useful when considering the maintenance of these lizards and they are pretty much applicable to tegus as well. Consider that most of these reptiles can inflict significant injury via their claws, sharp teeth and powerful jaws. Monitors are known to whip their tails at adversaries and a few species can rear up on their hind legs for attacking (e.g., Gould's and Bengal monitors).

It is unwise to purposely purchase animals in obvious poor health with the intent of salvaging them. It is also good practice to avoid the acquisition of aggressive or otherwise ferocious individuals. While they may be seemingly in good health at the time of purchase, these animals are actually quite stressed. They may eventually refuse to eat and their psychological and physiological stress will eventually depress their immunological system (making them candidates for disease). In addition, these individuals will be difficult to care for properly, both from sanitary considerations as well as when treatment becomes required for any illness.

Captive born or raised animals in good health are normally good choices for selection and acquisition, particularly individual animals that are alert and somewhat extroverted (but not aggressive). Such animals exhibit hardy appetites and are at least reasonably handleable. In addition, very young wild-caught animals will usually adapt to captive conditions. In general, select animals that

Bengal Monitor, *Varanus bengalensis*. Photo by Mark Bayless.

are alert, active, and in good flesh (i.e., perhaps even slightly "chubby" but not fat or obese). The vent or cloacal areas should be clean and free of any wet or dry caked stool. The eyes should be clear, with no injuries or disease. Both tegus and monitors will flick the tongue when picked up or in any way disturbed (as well as when they walk about). Monitors may defecate when picked up though this habit usually declines after long term captivity (tegus seem to lack this unpleasant trait).

BEHAVIOR

Monitors and tegus have recognizable suites of behavior that arise from the appropriate motivations, and these behaviors are often somewhat different for these two groups of lizards. The categories most commonly observed would probably be: feeding/hunting, mating (described under breeding), and threat/fear. Some other behaviors are performed as normal daily routines, such as burrowing and digging about the cage. In general, it is my experience that adult monitors are normally much more active, at least as captives, than tegus, though the juveniles of both tend to be more active than adults.

Red Tegu, *Tupinambis rufescens*. Photo by R. D. Bartlett.

Acclimation is when an organism becomes habituated to a different, usually abnormal, climate or environment. This term is often applied to descriptions of animals adjusting to captive conditions. Whether a captive acclimates successfully, will depend upon housing, maintenance, temperature, general state of health, temperament, and nutrition. Generally, new captives require some time to adjust to the new environment, and captive bred or long-term captive raised animals adjust faster and better to changes in captive conditions than wild-caught lizards. My experience has shown that adult wild-caught animals are usually highly stressed by captivity and rarely adjust well to handling, many being quite difficult and even aggressive toward the keeper, for long periods or for their entire life. Some captives become so "stressed" by captivity they can fail to thrive (see: DeNardo 1990; Patton 1991).

It is interesting that monitors and tegus can exhibit a wide range of "personalities", from very extroverted and tame, to nervous and fierce. This is true across, as well as within, species. It is also true that certain species have "reputations" concerning their general demeanor as captives. For example: golden tegus and Nile monitors tend to make ferocious captives, while dumerils monitors and red tegus are reputed to be relatively easily tamed. Additionally, some individuals can undergo developmental changes in "personality" where they may change from a nervous, flighty even aggressive animal to a mature and calmer lizard. However, a few may become even worse in temper.

It is useful to be able to recognize some so-called "stereotypical" behaviors exhibited under different conditions. Probably the most critical behaviors from the perspective of a herpetoculturist are threat behaviors. Sometimes an angry monitor lizard will turn toward a keeper with its mouth wide open. This is normally followed by a sudden lunge if approached too closely. At other times these lizards will often turn to show their broad sides, raise their bodies very high on all four legs, arch their backs hiss loudly (this can be incredibly loud at times), inflate their throats, and by producing pronounced curvature in their necks by bowing their heads (this is called a raised "roach" [Auffenberg 1978, 1981]). These behaviors may be accompanied by somewhat violent twitching, curling and possibly lashing of the tail as a threat and a "smack" by any species can be rather unpleasant.. Sometimes they may actually sway their bodies. When monitor lizards are angry or afraid, they can be amazingly aggressive, and handling the animal at that time may result in a serious bite. Injuries by large specimens may require serious medical attention.

Some species of monitors, such as the argus (Gould's) and Bengal monitors will also occasionally assume a bipedal posture. This can be quite amazing and often intimidating to witness. These monitors will sporadically do this to take stock of their surroundings, and not necessarily out of anger. Ditmars (1933) remarked that placing monitor lizards in natural sunlight can sometimes cause even the most docile specimens to become unexpectedly aggressive. I have had this observation verified for me by many keepers of monitor lizards.

On some occasions, other behaviors may be observed, particularly when monitors interact with conspecifics. These are usually observed when the lizards are mating or while several individuals are establishing social hierarchies and/or territories. Most of these behaviors involve posturing and assuming various stances with respect to one another. Males of several species (e.g.., Asian water monitors, Nile monitors, Timor monitors, Savannah monitors, White-throated monitors, and argus/Gould's monitors) will engage in ritualistic combat for the purpose of establishing dominance and securing territories. Sometimes they may inflict damage upon each other with the teeth and claws, but usually it is only after dominance is established that the victor bites the defeated animal. Some species do not normally bite each other (e.g., Asian water monitors) while others usually do (e.g., Nile monitors) (See Horn et al. 1994).

When foraging, monitor lizards will exhibit a somewhat swaying or swinging walk, accompanied by side to side head motions. These head movements are always accompanied by frequent tongue flicks. Food placed in the cage at this time, will be quickly located and seized. Detailed descriptions about monitor behavior can be found in Auffenberg (1978, 1981, 1983, 1988, 1994), Daltry (1991), and Green and King (1993). Further information about mating behaviors will be given under reproduction.

Tegus tend not to be quite as impressive in their threat displays. They will produce a peculiar puffing sort of hiss which repeats in a series of short rapid bursts. They will lunge if approached too closely and often signal threat by facing their adversaries with the mouth open. They do not inflate their throats in anywhere near as dramatic a fashion as monitors and also do not exhibit anything like the "raised roach". Like monitors, they can give serious bites. Male tegus can show aggression towards each other though females seem to cohabit with little or no fighting (Beltz 1989). Both tegus and monitors can be aggressive feeders, so this must be considered whenever several individuals are housed together (a situation I do not recommend for several reasons).

HANDLING

Both monitors and tegus require some care when grasped and during handling. If the animal is angry or in some way annoyed or normally has a fierce temper (particularly if the lizard is an adult) it may be quite difficult to grab hold. In many zoos, large fierce monitors are lassoed when necessary. If approach becomes difficult, individual handlers could drop a cloth over the head of the lizard to obscure its vision and ease the capture). It is necessary to secure the head of such animals and I find this is best achieved by firmly gripping the lizard behind the head, much like one would do with a snake. Holding the animal about the neck may be required, but care must obviously be taken to avoid strangling the animal. Note that tegus have much shorter necks and often wider heads than monitors of similar size. Keep the claws blunt so that they cannot also be used to inflict damage during handling. A method for trimming claws is described in Balsai (1992, In Press). Tame animals can be held with one hand controlling the head and front end while the body is supported with one arm (hand about the pelvic area) and the lizard's body braced against the body of the restrainer (tail might be held under the arm). Ferocious animals may even require several handlers for restraint. Occasionally the mouth may be taped if the lizard must be handled for a fairly long period. Large fierce tegus and monitors could be handled similarly to crocodilians (see Wise 1994). Be aware that many monitors, particularly when angry or frightened, will expel copious amounts of fecal matter upon the handler, so care must be made to ensure the cloacal area is held away from the body. This feces may even come out with such force as to be almost like a projectile (Card 1995c). This unpleasant trait is not normally part of the tegu's repertoire.

HOUSING, HEATING, AND LIGHTING

Monitor lizards are large diurnal foragers and require as capacious an enclosure as is humanly possible. I cannot stress enough that the larger the enclosure, the better. This is particularly true for certain very active species, such as argus (Gould's) monitors (Card 1995a c). Some other species, such as black rough-necks or crocodile monitors require an arboreal set-up with plenty of vertical space as well. Certainly, "minimal enclosures" are not recommended and any monitor lizard housed under such conditions may exhibit stress, become aggressive, and will certainly not breed. That said, minimal sized enclosures should be at least one and one half to two times the snout-vent length of the

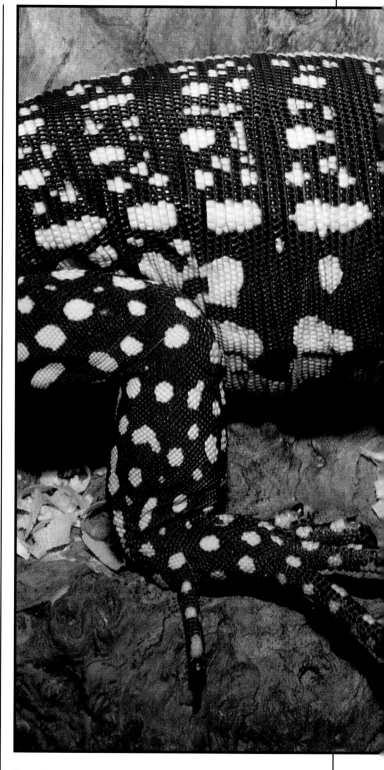

lizard, at least two-thirds to one times the total length of the animal in width and at least one and one-half times the total length of the lizard in height (ensure the lizard cannot not peer over the top). Cages need to be of extremely strong construction and any materials used for the "windows" (ie., glass, plexiglass, or screening) must be strong enough to withstand the assaults the lizard will inflict upon them. Wood, metal, fiberglass, etc has been used successfully, but with wood, remember that these lizards have strong claws and may dig away at corners, potentially causing significant damage in the process. Hinges must be very strong.

Black Tegu, *Tupinambis teguixin.*
Photo by R. G. Sprackland.

Avoid the use of screening in places the animal can frequently contact, because rostral abrasions can be a problem. All cages must be secure against escape. Consideration must be given to ease of cleaning and disinfection. Probably, room sized enclosures are best with some kind of drainage for easy cleaning (Card 1994a,b; Sprackland 1992; Balsai 1993, In Press). Tegus tend to be less active than monitors and tolerate somewhat smaller enclosures than monitors of similar sizes, but should none-the-less, be given as much space as is possible. General suggestions for captive conditions for reptiles can be found in Perry-Richardson and Ivanyi (1995) and McKeown (1996). Attempts to simulate naturalistic habitats should, however, be guided by ease of sanitation, potential for injury for the animal, and ease for maintenance of proper humidity, light, and temperature conditions.

What substrate to use is a commonly debated issue among herpetoculturists. I have found that newspaper works well for privately held captives, though it lacks aesthetics for public displays which usually entail some sort of stone, cement, etc. surface that can be easily cleaned. Other substrates used by private collectors are wood chips and/or bark, pebbles, pine shavings, rabbit or alfalfa pellets, outdoor car-

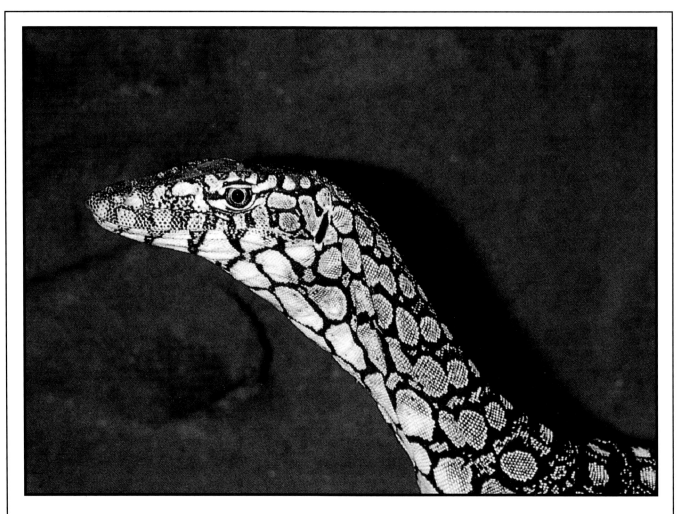

Perentie, *Varanus giganteus*. Photo by K. H. Switak.

peting, and Astroturf® or some similar type mat. Cedar shavings must not be used because they are quite toxic. I have found that loose substrates often get piled to one side of the enclosure and may be accidently ingested (possibly causing intestinal blockage) [see also McKeown 1996], outdoor carpeting fibers may become snared about a digit causing circulation problems for the toe, and both Astroturf® and outdoor carpeting can require near continuous cleaning, due to the frequent and copious defecations monitors (and to a lesser extent, tegus) may deposit in the cage. Newsprint is cheap and easily replaced. Alternatively, Sprackland (1992) recommends a bare floor, composed of an easily cleaned, waterproof, nonslippery and claw resistent material.

Most tegus and monitors prefer some sort of shelter, particularly, though not exclusively when they are young. Shelters of some sort aid greatly toward the lizard acclimating to captive conditions and helps to reduce stress. For young and medium sized lizards, cardboard boxes, inverted, with a hole cut in front are cheap and easily replaced, when damaged or soiled. For larger specimens, wooden, metal, or plastic shelters can be purchased or made (the enclosed cat litter boxes are good for this purpose). If the enclosure has a floor, the animal can often be induced to enter it during cleaning and

can possibly be maintained within it for the entire process (reducing the need to handle fierce individuals). Branches for some of the occasional climbers may also be a useful piece of cage "furniture" to include, as well as hollow logs or rocks. I do not recommend adding any sorts of plants because they will almost certainly be wrecked during attempts to tunnel in the soil or even during normal daily activities in the cage.

Both monitors and tegus, as reptiles require areas in their enclosure where they may obtain sufficient heat from the environment to enable their daily activities. They live in places that would be considered tropical to subtropical and thus require warm environments (but see Langerwerf 1995 for black andwhite tegus). This is best ensured by providing for a temperature gradient through their enclosure, as well as a basking area. The basking area is best heated via incandescent heat lamps or the newer ceramic heaters (eg., those marketed by Ram Network or Zoo Med, both in California). These must be properly shielded to prevent the lizard from gaining physical contact with them. In addition, if the surrounding ambient temperature is too cold additional heat may be provided by space or room heaters. When using these devices keep in mind that temperature gradients may stratify in a horizontal plane (ceiling fans can help disperse these gradients) and be alert to the danger of the ambient temperature becoming too warm (use only those connected to thermostats). Day time ambient temperatures should range somewhere into the low 30's °C while nighttime ranges should be roughly in the mid 20's °C. Many authors advise against heating pads, "hot rocks", and other such devices that rely on warming the animal through the ventral area (Card 1995c; McKeown 1996). It is true that improper use can expose the lizard to the danger of burns and sometimes they can overheat. Certainly, the use of basking sources and adequate ambient temperatures normally dispenses with the need to use "hot rocks" and other such devices.

Most animals require circadian (24 hour) light/dark cycles. Monitors and tegus, coming from the warmer ares of the globe should be provided with about 12-14 hours of daylight, using, when possible, combinations of artificial and natural light. Many advocate the use of full spectrum lights, such as VitaLites®, however, I have had no problems with the use of regular fluorescent lights. It is possible, though, that some subtle benefits, particularly when attempting to breed animals, may be derived by the use of full spectrum lights that would merit the extra expense. Be aware that the UV radiation of these full spectrum lights drops to about 85% after 2000 hours and they should be replaced about every six months (Perry-Richardson and Ivanyi 1995; Behler 1987). In addition, there is some controversy about the pros and cons of UV light ("black" light) use. Interested readers are referred to Perry Richardson and Ivanyi (1995) and Gehrmann (1994, 1996).

FEEDING AND WATER REQUIREMENTS

All species of monitors with the exception of Gray's monitor are completely predatory and carnivorous. The Gray's monitor regularly feeds upon fruits, as well as invertebrates, with the total being about 50:50 plant to animal derived food for adults within a year. Juveniles favor animal derived food (Auffenberg 1988; Green and King 1993; Card 1995b). Free ranging tegus have been shown to consume much larger amounts of plant derived foods than previously suspected (Mercolli and Yanosky 1994; Beebe 1945). The ratio was shown to be as high as 66:33 plant to animal derived food (Mercolli and Yanosky 1994) for *T. teguixin*. However, captive specimens were observed regurgitating plant foods (Hall 1978) and my experience has been that captives tend to prefer animal derived foods to plant.

Dumeril's Monitor, *Varanus dumerili*. Photo by R. G. Sprackland.

A young *Varanus spenceri* from the Northern Territory, Australia. Photo by Karl. H. Switak

Card (1995c) notes that there may be some controversy about what constitutes a proper captive diet for varanids. He attributes this to lack of natural history information for most species. However there was a study (Losos and Greene 1988) that noted the stomach contents from some free-ranging individuals for most species. The results indicated that invertebrates and carrion constituted the diet for most monitor lizards. One study for Cape monitors (Alberts 1994b) showed that they seemed to eat only vertebrate eggs and invertebrates. Alberts argued that monitors are diurnal and thus do not encounter rodents which are nocturnal in their habitat, and that it is improper to feed rodents to this species. Gaulke (1991) also noted the enormous numbers of arthropods eaten by Asian water monitors but cautioned that this might actually be a result of habitat destruction limiting what was available as prey. Lemm (1994) claimed that he has seen many savannah monitors dying from "hair impactions" and that rodent diets induce kidney and liver failure due to obesity and, presumably, too much protein. I have never observed any of my specimens of savannah monitor to show stress or impaction from the hair of rodents. I suspect that what Lemm observed was actually a product of the obesity of the animals he saw, and not necessar-

ily the rodent diets. It should be clear, however, that more work needs to be done on this aspect of varanid husbandry.

Card (1995c) recommends a varied diet of whole fish, rodents (and other mammals, such as rabbits) chickens, insects and other invertebrates. He also notes that occasional use of commercial canned dog and cat foods should be OK if not overdone. The exceptions to this diet are tree monitors and, of course, the Gray's monitor (which presently does poorly as a captive). Tree monitors feed largely on terrestrial arthropods and occasionally eat small lizards, small birds, and their eggs. As captives they can occasionally be induced to accept canned dog food and strips of beef. Tegus can be maintained on a diet similar to the regimen Card (1995c) recommended for most monitor species. They should also be offered fruits and other plant parts, as well, but it has been my experience, as well as others (Fagan 1994; Beltz 1989; Hall 1978) that they prefer the predatory diet. I have found that golden tegus are very fond of canned cat food, especially poultry flavors. I have maintained tegus for many years on a purely carnivorous diet which includes canned cat food, rodents, insects, and embryonated eggs. For a good general discussion of nutrition for carnivorous reptiles, I recommend consulting the article by Allen and Oftedal (1994).

WASTE MANAGEMENT

The living quarters of monitors and tegus will need regular hygienic maintenance. Feces and other waste products as well as any soiled substrate must be removed, usually at frequent intervals. Cages should be cleaned with some sort of mild disinfectant, at least once a week. I prefer either a dilute solution of Nolvasan-S® (chlorihexidine), or dilute (to between 5% and 15%) sodium hypochlorite bleach (common household bleach solution such as Clorox®). Another possibility is Roccal-D at between 1:200 (small cages) to 1:400 (Large cages) [McKeown 1996]. *Never use phenolic compounds such as Lysol® because their residues are toxic! All traces of disinfectant must be removed.* Water containers should also be washed, disinfected, rinsed, and refilled with fresh water when ever necessary. If the water vessels are large enough, monitors and tegus may climb into them and soak. In the process, these lizards may defecate, so removal of such soiled water should occur as soon as possible. If housed in large quarters (especially room sized), it would probably be very convenient to install a drain to allow for frequent hosing down and washing away of the waste.

REPRODUCTION.

MONITORS

Before attempting the captive breeding of any reptile species, consideration must given to a multitude of factors including: the sexual behavior of the females and males, "energy budgets", territoriality, possible effects of hibernation, neuroendocrine physiology, the influence of the environment on both mating behavior and, egg incubation, etc. Lack of space precludes discussion, but interested readers are referred to the following references: the entire reproductive biology section of *Captive Management and Conservation of Amphibians and Reptiles* (1994) edited by James B. Murphy, Kraig Adler, and Joseph T. Collins; as well as: Murphy and Collins 1980; Duvall et al. 1982; Gregory 1982; Hubert 1985; Saint Girons 1985; Frye 1991; Gans and Crews 1992; Vitt and Pianka 1994; Licht 1995, DeNardo 1996.

Captive breeding of monitors as of this writing, is still a developing study. Repeated and consistent breeding remains somewhat elusive for most species. Certainly, captive breeding for any species of varanid do not usually seem to be well publicized, particularly by private individuals.

No "recipe" for the breeding of monitor lizards exists, as there is for the breeding of many other reptiles and there are several impediments. Certainly one could claim that the space, costs and labor of developing a captive breeding program for monitor lizards does not appear to be a profitable venture, particularly with the less expensive species now imported in large numbers (such as the savannah monitor). Better management of wild populations and possibly the development of field culture in the countries of origin are a better course of action with the larger species. Nonetheless, continued efforts should be made in this area by herpetoculturists, particularly with the rarer species, to develop a methodology for sustained multigeneration propagation. The knowledge derived from developing this methodology may prove invaluable in the future conservation of varanid species.

One major problem, sexing monitors has always been a difficult procedure and any attempts to differentiate male from female based upon external criteria have been inconclusive. Probing and various methods to evert the hemipenes (eg., the method of Stewart 1989) have only varying degrees of reliability and success (Card 1994). Endoscopic methods have been used, but they are invasive and incur some risk to the animal (Schildger 1987; Schildger and Wicker 1992). Fiber-optic laparoscopy was successfully utilized with Dumeril's monitors (Davis and Phillips 1991). A method involving measurements of the pelvic bones derived from radiographs can be used but require very accurate measurements of the ischium (Card and Mehaffey 1994). Additionally, certain monitor species have ossifications in their hemipenes which can be seen on radiographs (Shea and Reddcliff 1986; Greer 1989) though it is not known at exactly what age these can be detected in most species (Card 1994).

Sexual maturity can be difficult to discern. Size can offer a reasonably valid criterion. Readiness to breed, at least for females, can actually be related to body length (Andrews 1995; Alberts 1994b). De Buffrénil et al. (1994) showed that for male Nile monitors, growth is faster and steadier than females and that males slowed down in growth later than females. It seems reasonable to assume that monitors two and one half feet or greater in total length are likely to be sexually mature animals. They should also preferably be three years or more years old. The growth rate of adult monitors is drastically reduced compared to that of immature monitors and reduced growth rate could be another indicator of sexual maturity.

Captive breeding success may be higher with captive-raised animals. In addition, the animals should be given as much three dimensional space as is possible. Height may be as important as length and width. Ensure that the available animals are the same species and even subspecies. Chances of

Above: White-throated Monitor, *Varanus albigularis*. **Photo by Mark Bayless. Below: Rough-neck Monitor,** *Varanus rudicollis*. **Photo by Paul Freed.**

success will be greatly increased with the availability of several potentially breeding pairs. Switching partners may also be helpful. It is important to keep all individuals housed separately until breeding is to be attempted, and after the animals show no further interest in breeding separate them again (Card 1994a). According to Card (1994a) animals are introduced for mating when the photoperiods begin to lengthen.

The lizards must have a good weight but should not be grossly obese. Of course, a good diet is essential. This is particularly true of course, for female animals, which need to produce and yolk eggs. In the wild, many species of monitors are influenced by a seasonal availability of their food, where egg-laying and hatching is coordinated to periods of higher food availability for the neonates. So a fairly sudden increase in the frequency and amount of food offered, just prior to a breeding attempt, might stimulate mating.

As a rule, many reptiles do not breed when environmental conditions remain constant. A period of rest/cooling/fasting may be tried that may also include a period of reduced day length. Upon concluding the rest period, temperatures are re-established, preferably in the high range. The photoperiod should also be raised to 14 or more hours of daylight per day (even up to 24 hours for short periods, has been recommended by some herpeticulturists to induce breeding). Feed more heavily than is usual, and supplement the diet with vitamins and minerals. During the following weeks, introduce the female into the male's enclosure for regular and increasingly longer intervals. Maintain surveillance, because some animals may fight, but avoid confusing combat with mating behavior (See Bayless 1992a, 1994).

Once copulations cease, the animals should be separated, again. If successful breeding has occurred, egg-laying will usually follow four to six weeks after the observation of copulation. What effect the type of substrate has upon egg retention by female monitor lizards is poorly understood at present. Generally, monitors will place the eggs down on the substrate when necessary (Bayless and Huffaker 1992).

The eggs can be incubated in moistened vermiculite (Terralite, grade 3) at the proportions of 50% vermiculite and 50% water (by weight) at 85-86°F (29-30°C) [see Card 1994a; Douglas 1994 (1993); Packard and Phillips 1994]. Card (1994a) recommends opening the containers on occasion to allow fresh air to enter. They should hatch in 165-195 days, though incubation temperature is an important factor when figuring hatching times. Eggs should never be turned. The effect incubation temperatures upon the development of the sex of monitor lizards is not known. Current indications seem to suggest that it

does not (Wright 1993b; but see Phillips and Packard 1994 for a discussion about the importance of temperature and humidity for hatchling physical characteristics).

TEGUS

"Rumors" indicate that breeding tegus is relatively easy, compared to monitor lizards. However, actual reported instances are rather slim. Hall (1978) used several attributes to distinguish male and female tegus (*T. teguixin*) and due to high interspecific physical similarity, these characteristics can presumably be applied to all the species. Males have enlarged jaw muscles whereby their necks appear as wide as the body (Hall 1978; Fitzgerald et al. 1991). They also tend to be larger, and the circumference of the tail, just posterior to the cloaca, tends to be wider. Males also weigh more than females and their femoral and pre-anal pores are more numerous. Fitzgerald et al. (1991) reported that male tegus have, two "buttons" of enlarged scales on the postanal region. However, Hall notes that all the above criteria vary widely by age and condition of the individual animals and only manual probing has proven totally reliable for her.

Hall (1978) provided a description of the mating behavior of tegus in significant detail and reported that intense feeding activity is often observed during courtship. Langerwerf (1992/93) reported that his tegus (*T. teguixin*) reach sexual maturity at about three years of age. Fitzgerald et al (1991) noted that among one captive population they observed, female *T. teguixin* would prefer "large" males as mates and reject small ones. Fitzgerald et al (1993) recorded that red tegus also show a sexual dimorphism in size, and again the males are larger. Finally, they believe that red tegus are probably about 3 years old when they reach maturity and that males seem to compete for mates and are more active during breeding season. From what is known about the reproduction of free-ranging tegus, they seem to be seasonal breeders (Luxmoore et al. 1988; Fitzgerald et al. 1991 claim mating occurs from September through early January for *T. teguixin* and begins "a few weeks later depending on the start of the rainy season" for *T. rufescens*).

Eggs are deposited within burrows about 0.5 m deep and 1.5 m long. The egg chamber is furnished with a layer of dry vegetation into which the eggs are laid. Some reports (Luxmoore et al. 1988; Fitzgerald et al. 1991) have claimed that the females guard the eggs until they hatch (which usually occurs in late December to early January). There is also some possibility that a second brood may be laid towards the end of the summer. This may not be unreasonable, since I had a report (Andre Ngo pers. comm.) that between one to two clutches per year could be expected from captive golden tegus. Eggs can be handled as described above for monitors

Further detailed information concerning the reproduction of tegus, consult the following sources (again, no claim is made for exhaustiveness): Beebe 1945; Hall 1978; Luxmoore, Groombridge and Broad 1988; Fitzgerald, Chani and Donadío 1991; Langerwerf 1992/93, 1995; Hurt 1995; Balsai In Press.

PREVENTIVE HEALTH CARE

Appropriate husbandry, with a maintenance schedule to assure good hygienic conditions, is essential for the health of any species of captive monitor or tegu. In addition, it is a good practice to follow proper quarantine procedures whenever a new specimen is introduced into the collection (see Stahl 1992; Wright 1993a). Most disease results from initial selection of an unhealthy animal, improper or inadequate husbandry, poor diet, bad hygiene, or maladaptation. In addition, if there is any way your lizard can injure itself, it frequently will do so after an escape.

The selection, stocking, and use of a "monitor medicine cabinet", as described by Olson (1992) is both very useful and recommended and these same items are equally useful for tegus. At the very least, such a kit should contain: Tweezers, Betadine®, Polysporin® (or "Triple Antibiotic"), nail scissors or clippers, Monoject 412 or some similar item (a curved tube-syringe for mild force feeding, rehydrating, and flushing the mouth), cotton swabs, eye droppers and plastic-tipped syringes.

Ailments must be discovered early. Early disease discovery will be aided a "quick-check" method that should become automatic and allow for the recognition of any disease or other disorder as quickly as possible. It may even be a good idea to have "routine lab tests" run on the collection (Cauble 1992a,b) Check for:

General responsiveness/alertness; abnormal behavior of any kind; sluggishness; inappetence; vomiting; abnormal breathing; frequent gaping; wheezing; gasping; abnormal breathing rhythms; mucous discharges; swelling or clinging debris or lumps about the mouth; eyes that show unusual wetness, dryness, swelling, discharge or cloudiness; Any sort of injuries to the body; evidence of skin disease; lumps or necrosis on the body; head tilts; paralysis; peculiar gaits; swollen feet toes or limbs; loose skin clinging to the body; something entangled about a digit; watery and/or bloody stools; swollen vent or fecal matter smeared about the vent; constipation.

Finding veterinarians with experience in the treatment of reptiles and other exotic animals can be difficult. Check with local herpetological societies for information about veterinarians with knowledge of treating reptiles. With the willing cooperation of a local veterinarian, it is reasonable to presume that diagnosis and appropriate treatment of many reptile diseases can be accomplished.

COMMON PROBLEMS

THERMAL BURNS

This usually results from improper shielding of the lizard from spotlights or some other very

hot heating device. Superficial burns will eventually heal, but scarring may result. Serious burns will require veterinary care. Always ensure the protection of the animal from any direct contact with a heat lamp or spotlight. Frequently check the temperatures of all hot rocks and similar such devices, modifying or removing those that are overheated. Burns may also easily become infected worsening an already bad situation.

NOSE RUB (ROSTRAL ABRASION).

This occurs when captive lizards endlessly rub their snouts against screen mesh or hard (such as glass) surfaces. This usually happens because the animal is improperly housed (screening should be avoided for the sides of monitor and tegu cages) or if the cage is too small or poorly designed. When a monitor or tegu rubs its snout, it indicates that conditions in the cage are somehow uncomfortable (such as: the cage is too warm or cold, too bright, etc.), or the reason may not be immediately obvious, for example, the animal may be trying to reach a location, for whatever reason, that it has spotted, through the cage in some inaccessible part of the room. If the lizard does not stop rubbing its snout, the trauma will become progressively worse. Early treatment with an antibiotic salve can help the wound heal and often with little scarring. In extreme cases, your lizard can cause such damage to its snout that bone and teeth may actually be exposed! Additionally, reptiles have no conception of glass or other transparent

Red Tegu, *Tupinambis rufescens*. **Photo by R. D. Bartlett.**

barriers and thus may ceaselessly try to penetrate them. Frye (1991) noted that the U.S. National Zoo's reptile facility places a visual barrier of dark paint or tape on the glass front (and where ever else the animal can see through), along the lower-most few cm. This inhibits pacing and rubbing. The animals apparently perceive a barrier and do not attempt to cross.

SKIN AND FOOT INFECTIONS

If monitors or tegus are kept in conditions that are too humid or wet (especially if hygiene is not the best), they can develop skin and toe infections. These infections appear as whitish or more commonly, brownish to blackish raised areas. The toes will usually swell as well and be stained as above. Put the animal on a dry surface (such as clean newspaper). Keep its enclosure scrupulously clean and dry and periodically disinfect it. Apply topical antibiotics to the lightly infected surfaces. Swollen toes or feet will require veterinary treatment.

EXTERNAL PARASITES

TICKS

Animals obtained from a reliable source,

should never be infested with ticks. The treatment for ticks is fairly easy, however. Application of some rubbing alcohol to the tick's surface (often several applications may be needed), will soon cause the parasite to withdraw its mouth parts. Simultaneously, grasp the arachnid with forceps and gently, but steadily, pull it off the lizard. Save the tick for later identification by preserving it in alcohol. Apply some topical antibiotic to the area where the tick was extracted. An infested animal can safely be treated with a spray or powder form of some pesticide containing pyrethrins or carbaryl (Sevin®). Just be sure to avoid the eyes, ears, mouth, and vent area. See Klingenberg (1993) and Mader (1993, 1996) for more information about tick treatments.

MITES

Monitors and tegus are normally not good candidates for harboring mites, the bane of snake keepers, but they may sometimes be seen on recently imported animals or they may spread from an infested reptile introduced to a collection without implementing proper quarantine procedures. Infested animals will show signs of irritation and may be seen to be rubbing up

Asian Water Monitor, *Varanus salvator*. Photo by Robert Pearcy.

against the sides of the enclosure or soaking themselves more often than usual. Sometimes these parasites specifically attack the eyes and if not treated, can cause severe eye infections (from excessive rubbing against objects). While pyrethrins or Sevin® can be used to treat most infestations (except those of the eye), Vapona® *No Pest Strips®* (2.2 dichlorovinyl dimethyl phosphate) usually will take care of the problem very well. Use a small section of strip (about 1 or 2 in.) wrapped in a small piece of nylon screen and suspend it in the cage by attaching this to a length of thin wire (such as a "twist-tie" used for closing plastic bags). Remove all water, food, cage furniture, and substrate, and leave the strip for 2 to 4 days. It may help to place a small piece of this strip in a plastic trash bag together with any cage furniture or empty water bowls. Clean and disinfect the cage. Repeat the procedure for the same length of time about 3 weeks later. Disinfect all cage furnishings before putting them back.

There is one major disadvantage to Vapona® treatment. Lizards seem to be particularly prone to idiosyncratic responses to this chemical. In other words, it could prove toxic to your pet. Symptoms of a toxic reaction will often include a chronic, progressive, total paralysis of the lizard that seems to always be fatal (see Mader 1996, who strongly discourages the use of this substance)! Prolonged or high dose exposure to these pest strips can also cause liver damage. This author once lost a beautiful Dumeril's monitor to use of Vapona®. However, this remedy can be one of the most effective at eliminating mites, and most monitors so treated by the author have had no ill effects. See Klingenberg (1993) and Mader (1993, 1996) for more information about mite treatments.

INTERNAL PARASITES

Cestodes, some digestive tract inhabiting nematodes, and a few protozoans, (e.g., *Entamoeba invadens* or some coccidia) are the commonest internal parasites found to inhabit monitors and tegus. Quarantine all new additions to the collection and have fecal samples checked by a qualified veterinarian to identify internal parasites and prescribe the best course of treatment (see: Cauble 1992b; Frost 1992; Klingenberg 1993; Mader 1994; Lane and Mader 1996).

NUTRITIONAL DISORDERS

If the captive monitors and tegus are getting the proper diet, these problems should not appear. However, here a few potential sources of trouble.

METABOLIC BONE DISEASE/CALCIUM DEFICIENCY

This will normally not be a problem with adult monitors or tegus (unless they are feed almost exclusively upon muscle and organ meats [Boyer 1996; Donoghue and Langenberg 1996]), but it could become one when improperly feeding juveniles. Calcium deficiencies are not merely the result of a lack of available calcium, because merely feeding supplemental calcium will not solve the problem. The proper absorption of calcium, via the intestinal lining is accomplished with an adequate amount of vitamin D3 and a proper calcium/ phosphorus ratio. Lizards seem to require 1 to 2 parts calcium to 1 part phosphorus (Frye 1991b). A common reason why juveniles can be a source of trouble is because neophyte herpetoculturists may feed them crickets and/or "pinkie" mice, exclusively. These are not totally balanced diets and should be supplemented with a mineral/vitamin mix. For those who use insects to feed very young monitors, I recommend consulting de Vosjoli (1990 or 1994). Canned cat or dog food may be also be a reasonable way to help ensure adequate nutrition for young tegus or monitors fed a largely insect or pinkie diet.. Feed two or three times a month and use poultry flavors which are more "natural" and somewhat less fatty. One of the major brands (such as Purina® or Alpo®) will be sufficient. By doing this, I have never encountered metabolic bone disease in monitors or tegus.

The usual symptoms of calcium deficiencies in lizards are "soft" jaws which may be further complicated by back and limb deformities (in juveniles), and, in adults, swollen "smooth" hind limbs, and/or swollen deformed lower jaws. The latter symptoms are indicative of a condition whereby the animal compensates for thin and weak bones by depositing spongy tissue (see Frye 1991a; Boyer

Mangrove Monitor, *Varanus indicus*. Photo by R. D. Bartlett.

1996; Donoghue and Langenberg 1996). In monitors and tegus, this should NEVER be allowed to become a problem!

INDUCED THIAMIN (VITAMIN B1) DEFICIENCY

This can be a problem for some species of monitor lizards (unlikely for tegus), particularly Nile monitors, mangrove monitors, or water monitors fed almost exclusively on diets of thawed, frozen fish. If oily fish or obese rodents are used, steatitis (inflammation of fat, which will require vitamin E treatment) can also be a problem (Frye 1991a; Done 1996). The most common symptom of B1 deficiency is twitching of limbs or fine muscular tremors (Frye 1991a) and other symptoms can include: ataxia, blindness, bradycardia, etc. (Donoghue and Langenberg 1996). Muscular atrophy can result if this condition is left untreated too long (Frye 1991a). Change the diet, and if symptoms are severe, consulting a veterinarian will be required.

INDUCED BIOTIN DEFICIENCY

A problem seen in monitors and tegus that are fed largely on raw non-embryonated whole eggs. This is because raw egg white contains avidin which binds the biotin and induces this deficiency (Frye 1991a; Donoghue and Langenberg 1996).

Change to a more varied and balanced diet and avoid raw non-embryonated eggs because of the additional hazard of salmonellosis.

OBESITY

Commonly, when captive tegus and monitors are overfed and inactive, they will become very fat. If this continues, the fat can deposit in and upon the internal organs, especially the liver, with eventually fatal results. Eliminate overfeeding and restrict the lizard's intake when it is becoming fat. Encourage exercise by providing adequate space for moving about and exploration. Monitor lizards, in particular, are very active in the wild and appear to patrol fairly large territories in search of food.

RESPIRATORY INFECTIONS

Respiratory infections usually result from keeping monitors and tegus at inadequately warm temperatures (although there can be other causes, Murray 1996). This results in lowering the lizards resistance to infections and creates a situation where the immune system cannot function properly. Elevated mucous content is usually noted in the mouth and nostrils, and the mucus may appear somewhat foamy. In young animals, gently pressing the thumb against the throat will cause mucus to exude from the nostrils. Other early symptoms are: sluggishness, decreased or lack of appetite and slightly labored breathing. Slight gaping and puffing of air in and out of the throat and lungs are sure indications of pneumonia. The sick lizard will spend much of its time with its eyes closed. As the disease progresses, all these symptoms will worsen and the animal will begin to spend time with its head elevated and bubbly mucus will begin to exude from the mouth and nose (Ross and Marzec 1984; Frye 1991a; Murray 1996). If the disease is discovered early, elevated temperatures (30-32°C) will help the monitor fight off the infection. If it does not improve after a few days of elevated temperature, then treatment with injectable antibiotics will be required. A veterinarian must be consulted as early as possible to determine and administer the most effective treatments and antibiotics. Drinking water must be available at all times during the course of treatment.

GASTROINTESTINAL DISEASES

Sometimes monitors and tegus may develop diarrhea, which may be discolored, foul smelling, and/or bloody. This condition can occur in imported animals and in captive-raised or born animals that are fed raw chicken parts or carrion or kept with foul water on a regular basis. Inadequate maintenance temperatures also contribute to the susceptibility to pathogens. If the symptoms persist for more than a few days, your monitor may have a serious gastrointestinal disease. A veterinarian should be contacted for diagnosis and treatment (see Funk 1996). With early diagnosis and treatment, the prognosis for recovery is usually good.

EYE DISEASES

Frye (1991a) reported that juvenile monitor lizards may be prone to cataracts. Why this should occur is unclear, but one suggestion was dietary. Frye suspects it could possibly be genetic because this syndrome does not occur in other lizards, including helodermids, fed the suspected diet. The cataracts can vary in their severity, with some monitors appearing to suffer little from this condition, while others can exhibit virtual blindness, especially in low light. Cataract surgery could be done but it is prohibitively expensive (Wright pers. comm.). I have, so far, not observed this syndrome in any monitors, but Bayless (pers. comm.) noted that it has been observed in the desert monitor, *V. griseus*. For information concerning other possible opthalmic conditions see Williams (1996) for a thorough review.

QUARANTINE FOR NEW ACQUISITIONS.

It is always a good practice to quarantine new monitors and tegus brought into a collection. Wright (1993a) advises that all transport materials should be considered potentially infested with parasites and treated accordingly. This may include freezing the materials, disinfecting them, etc. The new animal should be examined as above for any potential problems and it is probably a good idea to see a veterinarian for tests for internal parasites and treatment for any found. Wright recommends a quarantine period of at least 60 days and that new lizards should have their quarters cleaned last and the owner should always wash after handling the new animal so as not to contaminate others. A new animal should also have its own "set of husbandry tools" (Wright 1993a). A quarantine enclosure should be large, well ventilated, and easily disinfected. Wright recommends choosing newspaper as a substrate during quarantine.

REFERENCES AND RECOMMENDED READING

Acharijyo, LN and S Mobapatra:
Eggs of the water monitor (*Varanus salvator*) laid in captivity. *Indian Forester* 1989, 106(3): 230.

—**Alberts, A: Off to see the lizard:**
Lessons from the wild. *The Vivarium* 1994b, 5(5): 26-28.

—**Allen, M E and O T Oftedal:**
The nutrition of carnivorous reptiles. In: Murphy, J. B., K. Adler and J. T. Collins (eds.) *Captive Management and Conservation of Amphibians and Reptiles*. Society for the Study of Reptiles and Amphibians, Ithaca, NY. *Contributions to Herpetology, V. 11*, 1994. pp. 71-82.

—**Andrews, H:**
Varanus salvator. *VaraNews* 1991, 1(6): 4.

—**Andrews, H V:**
Sexual maturation in *Varanus salvator* (Laurenti, 1768) with notes on growth and reproductive effort. *Herpetological Journal*. 1995, 5: 189-194.

—**Anon:**
Varanus salvator breeding at Madras Snake Park. *Hamadryad*. 1978, 3(2): 4.

—**Anon:**
American Federation of Herpeticulturists Leg-

Author wishes to acknowledge Mark Bayless and Peter Strimple for ceaselessly supplying difficult references.

islative Packet. AFH, Escondido, CA. 1993. 8 sections (pages numbered accordingly).

—Anon:
1994 Proceedings of the Association of Reptilian & Amphibian Veterinarians. Association of Reptilian & Amphibian Veterinarians (A.R.A.V.), Chester Heights, PA. 1994. 121 p.

—Anon:
1994-1995 Directory: A Guide to North American Herpetology. Reptile & Amphibian Magazine, Pottsville, PA. 1994-1995. 310 p.

—Auffenberg, W:
Social and feeding behavior in *Varanus komodoensis.* In: Greenberg, N and P D MacLean (eds.). *Behavior and Neurology of Lizards An Interdisciplinary Colloquium.* National Institute of Mental Health, Rockville, MD. 1978. pp. 301-331.

—Auffenberg, W:
The Behavioral Ecology of the Komodo Monitor. University of Florida Press, Gainesville, FL. 1981. 406 p.

—Auffenberg, W:
Courtship behavior in Varanus bengalensis (Sauria: Varanidae). In: Rhodini, A. G J and K Miyata (eds.). *Advances in Herpetology and Evolutionary Biology: Essays in Honor of Ernest E. Williams.* Museum of Comparative Zoology, Harvard University, Cambridge, MA. 1983. pp. 535-561.

—Auffenberg, W:
Gray's Monitor Lizard. University of Florida Press, Gainesville, FL. 1988. 419 p.

—Auffenberg, W:
The Bengal Monitor. University of Florida Press, Gainesville, FL. 1994. 560 p.

—Balsai, M J:
Two wide ranging "Asian" Monitors. *VaraNews* 1991, 1(6): pp. 57.

—Balsai, M J:
The General Care and Maintenance of Savannah Monitors and Other Popular Monitor Species. Advanced Vivarium Systems, Lakeside, CA. 1992. 55 p.

—Balsai, M J:
Popular monitor species. *Reptiles* 1993, 1 (2): 36-57.

—Balsai, M J:
(In Press) *The Savannah Monitor Mauual.* Advanced Vivarium Systems, Lakeside, CA.

—Barker, D G:
Maintenance and reproduction of green tree monitors at the Dallas Zoo. In: Hahn, R. A. (ed.) *8th. Annual Reptile Symposium on Captive Propagation & Husbandry.* 1984, Zoological Consortium Inc. Thurmont, MD. 91-92.

—Bayless, M K:
Notes on the reproductive behavior of the Nile monitor lizard, *Varanus niloticus* Linnaeus (1766). *VaraNews* 1992a, 2(4): 5-6.

—Bayless, M K:
African varanids: Diets in captivity and in the wild. *VaraNews* 1992b, 2(5): 2-3.

—Bayless, M K
Zur Vortflanzungsbiologie des Steppenwarans (*Varanus exanthematicus*). *Salamandra.* 1994a, 30(2): 109-118.

—Bayless, M K and R Huffaker:
Observations of egg deposition and hatching of the savannah monitor (*Varanus exanthematicus* Bosc, 1792) in captivity. *VaraNews* 1992, 3(1): 5-6.

—Bayless, M K and T Reynolds:
Breeding of the savannah monitor lizard in captivity (*Varanus exanthematicus* Bosc, 1792). *Herpetology* 1992, 22(1): 12-14.

—Bayless, M K, R Huffaker, and O Maercks:
Notes on the egg deposition and incubation of the Argus monitor (*Varanus gouldii horni*) Gray 1838) in captivity. *VaraNews* 1994, 4(1): 5.

—Beebe, W:
Field notes on the lizards of Kartabo, British Guiana, and Carpito, Venezuela. Part 3. Teiidae, Amphisbaenidae and Scincdae. *Zoologica*, 1945, 30 (Part 1, No. 2): 7-32.

—Behler, JL:
Ultraviolet light and reptile propagation. *Proceedings of the American Association of Zoological Parks and Aquariums.* 1987: 162-169.

—Behrmann, H:
Haltung und nachzucht von *Varanus timorensis* [Care and reproduction of the Timor monitor, *Varanus timorensis*]. *Salamandra* 17 1981, (3/4): 198-201 [translation by Paul Gritis for *VaraNews* 1992], 2(6): 6].

—Beltz, E (ed.):
Care in Captivity: Husbandry Techniques for Amphibians and Reptiles. Chicago Herpetological Society, Chicago, IL. 1989. 87 p.

—Bowler, JK:
Longevity of Reptiles and Amphibians in North American Collections. Society for the Study of Amphibians and Reptiles and the Philadelphia Herpetological Society, Athens OH, 1977. 32 p.

—**Boyer, D and W E Lamoreaux:**
Captive reproduction in the pygmy mulga monitor *Varanus gilleni* at the Dallas Zoo. In: Tolson, P. J. (ed.) *7th. Annual Reptile Symposium on Captive Propagation & Husbandry.* 1983. Zoological Consortium Inc. Thurmont, MD. 59-63.

—**Boyer, T H:**
Metabolic bone disease. In: *Reptile Medicine and Surgery.* Mader, D (ed.) WB Saunders, Philadelphia, PA, 1996. pp.385-392.

—**Branch, W R:**
Field Guide to the Snakes and other Reptiles of Southern Africa. Ralph Curtis, Sanibel Island, FL. 1988, p. 326.

—**Bredl, J and T D Schwaner:**
First record of captive breeding of the lace monitor, *Varanus varius* (Sauria:Varanidae). *Herpetofauna* 1983, 15(1): 20-21.

—**Card, W:**
A reproductive history of monitors at the Dallas Zoo. *The Vivarium* 1994a, 6(1): 26-29, 44-47.

—**Card, W:**
Double clutching Gould's monitors (*Varanus gouldii*) and Gray's monitors (*Varanus olivaceus*) at the Dallas Zoo. *Herp. Review* 1994b, 25(3): 111-114.

—**Card, W:**
Emerald monitors. *Reptiles* 1994c, 1(6): 4.

—**Card, W:**
Captive maintenance & reproduction of Gould's monitor lizard (*Varanus gouldii*). *Reptiles* 1995a, 3(3): 84-91.

—**Card, W:**
Gray's monitor lizard (*Varanus olivaceus*) at the Dallas Zoo. *Reptiles* 1995b. 3(5): 78-85.

—**Card, W:**
Monitor lizard husbandry. *Bulletin of the Association of Reptilian and Amphibian Veterinarians,* 1995 c; 5(3): 9-17.

—**Card, W and D Mehaffey:**
A radiographic sexing technique for *Heloderma suspectum. Herp. Review* 1994, 25(1): 17-19.

—**Carlzen, G:**
Breeding green tree monitors. *Herpetology Journal* 1982, 12(2): 4-6.

—**Carter, D B:**
Courtship and mating in wild *Varanus varius* (Varanidae: Australia). *Mem. Queensland Mus.* 1990, 29 (2): 333-338.

—**Cauble, C:**
Routine laboratory tests for monitors. *VaraNews* 1992a, 2(1): 7.

—**Cauble, C: 1992b.**
Internal Parasite Detection. *VaraNews* 1992b, 2(2): 7.

—**Chippindale, P:**
Captive breeding of the Timor monitor (*Varanus timorensis similis*) *Herp Review* 1991, 22(2): 52-53.

—**Cogger, HG:**
Australian Goannas. *Aust. Mus. Mag.* 1959 13(3): 71-75.

—**Cooper, J E and O F Jackson (editors):**
Diseases of the Reptilia, 2 volumes. Academic Press, London, England. 1981. 584 p

—**Cowles, R B:**
The life history of *Varanus niloticus* (Linnaeus) as observed in Natal South Africa. *J. Ent. Zool.* 1930, 22: 1-31.

—**Davis, R B and L G Phillips, Jr:**
A method of sexing the Dumeril's monitor. *Herp. Review* 1991, 22(1): 18-19.

—**de Buffrénil, V, C Chabanet, and J Castanet:**
Données préliminaires sur la taille, la croissance et la longévité du varan du Nil (*Varanus niloticus*) dans la région du lac Tchad. *Can. J. Zool.* 1994, 72(2): 262-273.

—**DeNardo, D:**
Stress: A real but not well understood phenomenon. *The Vivarium* 1990, 2(5): 25-27, 29.

—**DeNardo, D:**
Reproductive Biology. In: *Reptile Medicine and Surgery.* Mader, D. (ed.) WB Saunders, Philadelphia, PA, 1996. pp. 212-224.

—**de Vosjoli, P: 1990.**
The Right Way to Feed Insect-Eating Lizards. Advanced Vivarium Systems, Lakeside, CA. 1990. 32 p.

—**de Vosjoli, P:**
The Lizard Keeper's Handbook. Advanced Vivarium Systems, Lakeside, CA. 1994. 175 p.

—**Ditmars, R L:**
Reptiles of the World. Macmillian, NY. 1933. 321 p.

—**Dixon, JR and P Soini:**
The Reptiles of the Upper Amazon Basin, Iquitos Region, Peru. Part 1: Lizards and Amphisbaenians. Part 2: Crocodilians, Turtles and Snakes. Milwaukee Public Museum, Milwaukee, WI. 1986. 154 p.

—**Donadio, OE and J M Gallardo:**
Biologia y conservacion de las especies del genero *Tupinambis* (Squatamata, Sauria, Teiidae) en el Republica Argentina. *Revista del Museo Argentino de Cie*

—Done, L B:
Neoplasia. In: *Reptile Medicine and Surgery.* Mader, D (ed.) WB Saunders, Philadelphia, PA, 1996. pp.125-141.

—Done, L B:
Postural abnormalities. In: *Reptile Medicine and Surgery.* Mader, D (ed.) WB Saunders, Philadelphia, PA, 1996. pp. 406-411.

—Donoghue, S and J Langenberg:
Nutrition. In: *Reptile Medicine and Surgery.* Mader, D (ed.) WB Saunders, Philadelphia, PA, 1996. pp.148-174.

—Douglas, R M:
High water potential Vermiculite as an incubation medium for reptile eggs. *Australian Herp News* 1994 [1993], May (#13): 4-8 [reprinted from: *British Herpetological Society Bulletin* #45, 1993]

—Duvall D L J Guillette, Jr., and R E Jones:
Environmental Control of Reptilian Reproductive Cycles. In: Gans, C. and F. H. Pough (eds.) *Biology of the Reptilia: Physiological Ecology*, V. 13, Physiology D. Academic Press, London. 1982. pp. 201-271.

—Eidenmüller, B:
Zwillingsanlage bei *Varanus (Varanus) mertensi* Glauert, 1951. *Salamandra* 1991, 27(4): 282-283.

—Eidenmüller, B:
Einige Bermerkungen über die Zeitgungsparameter von Warangelegen. *Monitor.* 1992, 1(1): 14-20.

—Eidenmüller, B:
Successful breeding of Mertens' monitor lizard, *Varanus mertensi. The Vivarium* 1995, 7(2): 18-20.

—Enright, B:
Notes on breeding the Nile monitor, *Varanus niloticus*, in captivity. *VaraNews* 1992 2(6): 5 [reprinted from *Ontario Herp Society News,* 1989].

—Estes, R, K De Queiroz, and J Gauthier:
Phylogenetic relationships within Squamata. In: *Phylogenetic Relationships of the Lizard Families*, R. Estes, and G. Pregill (eds.) Stanford University Press, Stanford, CA, 1988, pp. 119-281.

—Fitzgerald, L A, J M Chani, and O C Donadío:
Tupinambis lizards in Argentina: Implementing management of a traditionally exploited resource. In: Robinson, J. G. and K. H. Redford (eds.) *Neotropical Wildlife Use and Conservation.* 1991. University of Chicago Press, Chicago, IL. pp 303-316.

—Fitzgerald, L A, F B Cruz, and G Perotti:
The reproductive cycle and the size at maturity of *Tupinambis rufescens* (Sauria: Teiidae) in the dry chaco of Argintina. *J. Herpetology* 1993, 27(1): 70-78.

—Frost, M:
Acquiring a new monitor: Purchase & parasite prevention. *VaraNews* 1992, 3(6): 1-2.

—Frye, F L:
Biomedical and Surgical Aspects of Captive Reptile Husbandry. VM Publishing, Edwardsville, KS. 1981. 456 p.

—Frye, F L:
Biomedical and Surgical Aspects of Captive Reptile Husbandry, 2nd. Ed., V. 1 & 2. Krieger, Malabar, FL. 1991a. 637 p.

—Frye, F L:
A Practical Guide for Feeding Captive Reptiles. Krieger, Malabar, FL, 1991b. 171 p.

—Funk, R S:
Vomiting and regurgitation. In: *Reptile Medicine and Surgery.* Mader, D (ed.) WB Saunders, Philadelphia, PA, 1996. pp.425-426.

—Gaulke, M:
On the diet of the water monitor, *Varanus salvator,* in the Philippines. *Mertensiella* #2 1991, Bonn, Germany: 143-153.

—Gans, C and D Crews (eds.):
Hormones, Brain, and Behavior: Biology of the Reptilia, V. 18, Physiology E. University of Chicago Press, Chicago Il. 1992. 564 p.

—Garrett, C M and M C Peterson:
Varanus prasinus beccarii behavior. *Herp. Review* 1991, 22(3): 99-100.

—Gehrmann, WH:
Light requirements of captive amphibians and reptiles. In: *Captive Management and Conservation of Amphibians and Reptiles,* JB Murphy, K Adler, and JT Collins (eds.) Society for the Study of Amphibians and Reptiles, Ithaca, NY. 1994, pp. 53-59.

—Gorman, D:
Breeding the Bengal Monitor in captivity. *VaraNews* 1993, 3(4): 2.

—Gowen, R L (ed.)
Captive Propagation and Husbandry of Captive Reptiles and Amphibians. Northern California Herpetological Society, Special Publication #5. 1989. pp. 57-63

—Gregory, P T:
Reptilian hibernation. In: Gans, C and F H Pough (eds.) *Biology of the Reptilia :Physiological Ecology, V. 13*, Physiology D. Academic Press, London. 1982. pp. 53-154.

—Green, B and D King:
Goanna: The Biology of Varanid Lizards.

New South Wales University Press, Kensington, NSW, Australia, 1993, 102 pp.

—Greer, A E:
The Biology & Evolution of Australian Lizards. Surrey Beatty & Sons Pty Limited, NSW, Australia. 1989. p. 264.

—Hairston, C S and P M Burchfield:
The reproduction and husbandry of the water monitor (*Varanus salvator*) at the Gladys Porter Zoo, Brownsville. *Int. Zoo Yb.* 1992, 31: 124-130.

—Hall, B J:
Notes on the husbandry, behavior and breeding of captive tegu lizards. I*nt. Zoo Yb.* 1978, 18: 91-95.

—Halliday, T R, and K Adler:
All the World's Animals: Reptiles and Amphibians. Torstar Books, NY. 1986. 160 p.

—Hoogmoed, MS and J Lescure:
An annotated checklist of the lizards of French Guiana, mainly based on two recent collections. *Zoologische Mededlingen* 1975 49 (13): 141-172.

—Horn, H:
Breeding of the lace monitor (*Varanus varius*) for the 1st time outside of Australia(Reptilia: Sauria: Varanidae) *Mertensiella* #2 1991. Bonn, Germany: 168-175.

—Horn, H & G J Visser:
Review of reproduction of monitor lizards *Varanus spp.* in captivity. *Int. Zoo Yb.* 1989, 28: pp. 140-150.

—Horn H and G J Visser:
Basic data on the biology of monitors. *Mertensiella* #2 1991. Bonn, Germany: 176-187.

—Horn, H, M Gaulke, and W Böhme.
New data on ritualized combats in monitor lizards (Sauria: Varanidae), with remarks on their function and phylogenetic implications. *Zool. Garten N. F.* 1994, 64 (5): 265-280.

—Hubert, J:
Embryology of the squamata. In: Gans, C and F Billett (eds.) *Biology of the Reptilia :V. 15, Development* B. John Wiley, NY. 1985. pp. 1-34.

—Hurt, C 1995.
The red tegu: Notes on captive breeding. *Reptiles* 1995, 3(1): 80-89.

—Irwin, B:
Captive breeding success: *Varanus mertensi, Varanus gouldii. Thylacinus* 1986 11(2) [*VaraNews* 1991, 1(7): 6-7].

—Jacobson, E R and G V Kolias (eds.):
Exotic Animals. Churchill Livingstone, NY. 1988.

—James, C D, J B Losos, and D R.King:
Reproductive Biology and diets of goannas (Reptilia:Varanidae) *Australian J. Herpetol.* 1992, 26(2): 128-136.

—King, D, M king, and P Baverstock:
A new phylogeny of the Varanidae. *Mertensiella* #2 1991; 2:211-219.

—Klingenberg, R J:
Understanding Reptile Parasites: A Basic Manual for Herpetoculturists and Veterinarians. Advanced Vivarium Systems, Lakeside, CA. 1993. 81 p.

—Lane, T J and D R Mader:
Parasitology. In: *Reptile Medicine and Surgery.* Mader, D (ed.) WB Saunders, Philadelphia, PA, 1996. pp.185-203.

—Lange, J: 1989.
Observations on the Komodo monitors in the Zoo-Aquarium Berlin. *Int. Zoo Yb.* 1989, 28: 151-153.

—Langerwerf, B:
The reproduction of the Argentine black and white tegu, *Tupinambis teguixin*, in captivity. *British Herpetological Society Bulletin* 1992/93, 42: 18-23.

—Langerwerf, B:
Keeping and breeding the Argentine black and white tegu, *Tupinambis teguixin. The Vivarium* 1995, 7(3): 24-29.

—Laurent, R F:
Herpetofaunal relationships between Africa and South America. In: Duellman, W. E. (ed.) *The South American Herpetofauna: Its Origin, Evolution, and Dispersal.* Museum of Natural History, The University of Kansas Monograph 1979, No. 7: 55-71.

—Lemm, J:
Captive husbandry of white-throated monitors (*Varanus albigularis*) at the San Diego Zoo's Center for Reproduction of endangered species (C.R.E.S.). *VaraNews* 1994, 4(2/3): 4-5.

—Licht, P:
Reproductive Physiology of Reptiles and Amphibians. In: *Conservation of Endangered Species in Captivity: An Interdisciplinary Approach.* Gibbons, EF Jr., BS Durrant, and J Demarest (eds.) State University of New York Press, Albany, NY. 1995. pp.169-186.

—Linville, P:
Komodo dragons and the National Zoo. *Reptiles* 1995, 3(8): 56-67.

—Losos, J B and H W Greene:
Ecological and evolutionary implications of diet in monitor lizards. *Biological Journal of the Linnean Society* 1988, 35: 379-407.

—Luxmoore, R, B. Groombridge, and S Broad (eds.):
Significant Trade in Wildlife: A Review of Selected Species in CITES Appendix II. Volume 2: Reptiles and Invertebrates. International Union for Conservation of Nature and Natural Resources, Cambridge, UK, 1988, 306 pp.

—Mader, D R:
Mite and tick infestions. *Reptiles* 1993, 1(1): 64-72.

—Mader, D R:
Reptile endoparasites. *Reptiles* 1994, 1(4): 64-71.

—Mader, D R (ed.):
Reptile Medicine and Surgery. WB Saunders, Philadelphia, PA, 1996. 512 p.

—Marcus, L C:
Veterinary Biology and Medicine of Captive Amphibians and Reptiles. Lea & Febiger, Philadelphia, PA. 1981. 239 p.

—Markwell, K:
The artificial incubation of lace monitor (*Varanus varius*) eggs. *Herpetofauna* 1983, 15(1): 16-17.

—McCoid, M J:
Reproductive output of captive and wild mangrove monitors (*Varanus indicus*). *VaraNews* 1993, 3(3): 4-5.

—McCoid, M J and R A Hensley:
1991. Mating and combat in *Varanus indicus. Herp. Review.* 1991, 22(1): 16-17.

—McKeown, S:
General husbandry and management. In: *Reptile Medicine and Surgery.* Mader, D (ed.) WB Saunders, Philadelphia, PA, 1996. pp. 9-19.

—Mercolli, C and A A Yanosky:
The diet of adult *Tupinambis teguixen* (Sauria: Teiidae) in the eastern Chaco of Argentina. *Herpetological Journal* 1994, 4 (1): 15-19.

—Milstead, WW:
Notes on the teiid lizards in Southern Brazil. *Copea* 1961 (4): 493-495.

—Murphy, J B:
Notes on the care of the ridge-tailed monitor (*Varanus acanthurus brachyurus*) at the Dallas Zoo. *Int. Zoo Yb.* 1971, 11: 230-231.

—Murphy, J:
Notes on Indo-Australian varanids in captivity. *Int. Zoo Yb.* 1972, 12: 199-202.

—Murphy, J B K Adler and J T Collins (eds.):
Captive Management and Conservation of Amphibians and Reptiles. Society for the Study of Reptiles and Amphibians, Ithaca, NY. Contributions to Herpetology, V. 11. 1994 408 p.

—Murphy, J B and J T Collins (eds.):
Reproductive Biology and Diseases of Captive Reptiles. Society for the Study of Amphibians and Reptiles, Ithica, NY. Contributions to Herpetology V. 1. 1980. 277 p.

—Murray, M J:
Pneumonia and normal respiratory function. In: *Reptile Medicine and Surgery.* Mader, D (ed.) WB Saunders, Philadelphia, PA, 1996. pp. 396-405

—Norman, DR:
Man and tegu lizards in Eastern Paraguay. *Biological Conservation* 1987, 41: 39-56.

—O'Dell, J:
Successful captive propagation of the freckled monitor (*Varanus tristis orientalis*). *VaraNews* 1992, 3(2): 4-6.

—Olmos, F:
Tupinambis teguixen (tegu lizard) aquatic behavior. *Herpetological Review* 1995. 26(1): 37.

—Olson, W:
Monitor Medicine Cabinet. *VaraNews* 1992, 2(2): 4.

—Packard, G C and J A Phillips:
The importance of the physical environment for the incubation of reptilian eggs. In: Murphy, James B., Kraig Adler and Joseph T. Collins (eds.) 1994 *Captive Management and Conservation of Amphibians and Reptiles.* Society for the Study of Reptiles and Amphibians, Ithaca, NY. Contributions to Herpetology, 1994, V. 11. pp. 195-208.

—Patton, KT:
Understanding stress in captive reptiles. *The Vivarium* 1991, 2(6): 18, 36-7, 39.

—Perry, G, R Habani, and H Mendelssohn:
The first captive reproduction of the desert monitor (*Varanus griseus griseus*) at the Research Zoo of Tel Aviv University. *Int. Zoo Yb.* 1993, 32: 188-190.

—Perry-Richardson, J J, and CS Ivanyi:
Captive Design for Reptiles and Amphibians. In: *Conservation of Endangered Species in Captivity: An Interdisciplinary Approach.* Gibbons, EF Jr., BS Durrant, and J Demarest (eds.) State University of New York Press, lbany, NY. 1995. pp. 205-221.

—Peters, J A and R Donoso-Barros:
Catalogue of the Neotropical Squamata: Part II Lizards and Amphisbaenians. *Bulletin of the US National Museum* 1970, 297: 1-293

—**Phillips, J A and G C Packard:**
Influence of temperature and moisture on eggs and embryos of the white-throated savanna monitor *Varanus albigularis*: Implications for conservation. *Biological Conservation* 1994, 69 (2): 131-136.

—**Presch, W:**
A review of the tegus, lizard genus *Tupinambis* (Sauria: Teiidae: Lacertilia). *Copea* 1973 (4): 740-746.

—**Radford, L and F L Paine:**
The reproduction and management of the Dumeril's monitor. *Int. Zoo Yb.* 1989, 28: pp. 153-155.

—**Roder, A and H Horn:**
Über zwei Nachzuchten des Steppenwarans (*Varanus exanthematicus*). *Salamandra* 1994, 30(2): 97-108.

—**Ross, RA and G Marzec:**
The Bacterial Diseases of Reptiles. Institute for Herpetological Research, Stanford, CA, 1984. 114 p.

—**Saint Girons. H:**
Comparative data on lepidosaurian reproduction and some time tables. In: *Biology of the Reptilia : V. 15*, Development B. John Wiley, NY. 1985. pp. 35-58.

—**Schildger, B:**
Endoscopic sex determination in reptiles. *Proc. 1st. Int. Conf. on Zoo and Avian Med.* 1987. pp. 369-375.

—**Schildger, B and R Wicker:**
Endoscopie bei Reptilien und Amphibien Indikationen, Methoden, Befunde. *Der praktische Tierarzt* 1992, 6: 517-526.

—**Shea, G M and G L Reddacliff:**
Ossifications in the hemipenes of varanids. *J. Herpetology* 1986, 20(4): pp. 566-568.

—**Slavens, F.L:**
Reptiles and Amphibians in Captivity: Breeding Longevity and Inventory. F.L. Slavens, Seattle, WA. 1989. 474 p.

—**Slavens, FL and K. Slavens:**
Reptiles and Amphibians in Captivity: Breeding Longevity and Inventory. Slaveware, Seattle, WA. 1993. Xxp.

—**Sprackland, R G:**
Mating and waiting: A status report on reproduction in captive monitor lizards (Sauria: Varanidae). In: Gowen, R. L. (ed.) *Captive Propagation and Husbandry of Reptiles and Amphibians 1989.* Northern California Herpetological Society, Special Publication #5. pp. 57-63

—**Sprackland, R G:**
Giant Lizards. TFH Publications, Neptune City, NJ. 1992. 288 p.

—**Sprackland, R G:**
Dumeril's monitor lizard. *Reptiles* 1995, 3(7): 56-69.

—**Stahl, S:**
Monitoring medicine. *VaraNews* 1992, 2(3): 5-6.

—**Stanner, M and H Mendelssohn:**
Activity patterns of the desert monitot (*Varanus griseus*) in the Southern Coastal Plain of Isreal. *Mertensiella* 1991; 2: 253-262.

—**Stewart, J S:**
Techniques for sex identification in large reptiles. In: Gowen. pp 201

—**Strimple, P:**
The savannah monitor, *Varanus exanthematicus* (Bosc, 1792). Part 1. *The Forked Tongue* 1988, 13(12): 8-13.

—**Strimple, P D and J L Strimple:**
Australia's largest goanna: The perentie. *Reptiles* 1996, 4(2): 76-87.

—**Thissen, R:**
A double clutch and successful hatching of Australian spiney-tailed monitors, *Varanus acanthurus* Boulenger. *VaraNews* 1991, 1(7): 5-6.

—**Thissen, R:**
Breeding the spiny-tail monitor (*Varanus acanthurus* Boulenger). *The Vivarium* 1992, 3(5): 32-34.

—**Tyler, M J:**
Herpetofaunal relationships of South America with Australia. In: Duellman, W. E. (ed.) *The South American Herpetofauna: Its Origin, Evolution, and Dispersal.* Museum of Natural History, The University of Kansas Monograph 1979, No. 7: 73-106.

—**van Kalken, C:**
Captive breeding success with the mangrove monitor. *VaraNews* 1993, 3(6): 2.

—**Visser, G:**
Notizen zur Brutbiologie des Gelbwarans *Varanus (Empagusia) flavescens* (Hardwicke & Gray, 1827) im Zoo Rotterdam (Sauria Varanidae). [Notes on the breeding biology of the yellow monitor *Varanus (Empagusia) flavescens* (Hardwicke & Gray, 1827) in the Rotterdam Zoo. (Sauria Varanidae)]. *Salamandra* 1985, 21 (2/3): 161-168. [Translated by Margaret Berker, edited by Ennis Berker, *VaraNews* 1992, 2(3): 2-5].

—**Vitt, L J and E R Pianka (eds.):**
Lizard Ecology: Historical and Experimental Perspectives. Princeton University Press, Princeton, NJ. 1994. 403 p.

—**Walsh, T, R Rosscoe, and G F Birchard:**
Dragon tales: The history, husbandry, and breeding of the Komodo monitors at the National Zoological Park. *The Vivarium* 1993, 4(6): 23-26.

—**Williams, D L:**
Opthalmology. In: *Reptile Medicine and Surgery*. Mader, D (ed.) WB Saunders, Philadelphia, PA, 1996. pp.175-185.

—**Wilson, S K and D G Knowles:**
Australia's Reptiles: A photographic Reference to the Terrestrial Reptiles of Australia. Collins, Sydney, NSW, Australia. 1988. pp. 447.

—**Wise, MA:**
Techniques for the capture and restraint of captive crocodilians. In: *Captive Management and Conservation of Amphibians and Reptiles*, JB Murphy, K Adler, and JT Collins (eds.) Society for the Study of Amphibians and Reptiles, Ithaca, NY. 1994, pp.401-405

—**Wright, K:**
Suggested quarantine procedures for monitors and tegus. *The Vivarium* 1993a, 5(3): 22-23.

—**Wright, K:**
Nile monitors. *Reptile & Amphibian Magazine* September-October 1993b: 36-44.

—**Yanosky, A A:**
Arboreality in the teiid lizard *Tupinambis teguixen* (Reptilia, Lacertilia, Teiidae). *Sphenidiscus* 1991, 9: 11-13.

—**Zug, GR:**
Herpetology. Academic Press, San Diego, CA, 1993, 527 pp.

INDEX

Please Note: This Index includes page references for all three volumes of
The Biology, Husbandry and Health Care of Reptiles.

Capillaria, **697**
Captive breeding,
  of lizards, 503-506,
      of tegus, 545-546,
      of varanids, 543-545,
  of snakes, 398-400,
  of turtles, 430, 433-436,
      TSD, 433,
Cardiac shunting, 153,
Caretta caretta, **89, 248, 411**
Carettochelys insculpta, **95**
Carpet Python, **340**
Cataract, **741, 743**
Catheter, 853, 879
Cayman Island Rhinoceros Iguana, **522**
Cayman Islands Ground Iguana, **242, 243, 244**
Celiotomy, **756,** 757, 761, 764-766
Cerastes cerastes, **774**
Chamaeleo calyptratus, **568**
Chamaeleo hoehneli, **308**
Chamaeleo jacksoni, **299**
Chamaeleo lateralis, **95**
Chamaeleo melleri, **736**
Chamaeleo montium, **201**
Chamaeleo parsoni, **607**
Chamaeleo petteri, **255**
Chamaeleonidae, 470
Chameasaura anguina, **187**
Charina bottae, defensive behavior, 383
Chelonia mydas, **161,** 670
Chelonia, 3
Chelonians,
  auditory sensitivity, 190-191,
  bacterial diseases, 667-668,
  captive breeding, 430, 433-436,
  conservation, 247-250,
  ear anatomy, 189,
  eggs, 110,
  external parasites, 670,
  feeding behavior, 417-418,
  feeding, 426-430,
  fungal disease, 668-669,
  growth, 412-413,
  heating, 423-424,
  hibernation, 419,
  housing, 421-423, 424-425,
  incubation, 435,
  lifespan, 404,
  lighting, 424,
  locomotion, 417,
  morphology of nasal passage, 199-200,
  radiography, 685,
  reproductive behavior, 430,
  reproductive cycles, 72, 73,
  selection, 416,
  senses, 405,
  sexing, 43, 413-414,
  skin diseases, 667-670,
  stress, 436,

  surgery, 728-733,
  TSD, 45-46,
  ultrasonography, 619-623,
  viral disease, 597-598,
  vocal communication, 192,
Cheloniidae, reproductive cycles, 72,
Chelus fimbriatus, **423,**
  feeding behavior, 418
Chelydra serpentina, **130, 431,**
  feeding behavior, 418
Chelydra serpentina osceola, **409**
Chinemys reevesi, **425**
Chinese Alligator, **251**
Chinese Crocodile Lizard, **242**
Chlamydosaurus kingi, **470, 482**
Chondropython viridis, **309, 791, 908**
Chromatophores, 656
Chrysemys picta, **668,**
  stress, 74
Chrysemys picta belli, **731**
Chrysemys picta dorsalis, **417, 421**
Chrysemys picta picta, **174**
Chuckwalla, **490**
Citrobacter fruendi, 667
Claudius angutatus, 448, 450
Clemmys guttata, **192**
Clemmys insculpta, **410**
Clemmys muhlenbergi, **416**
Cnemidophorus deppei, **505,** 134
Cnemidophorus sexlineatus, **297**
Cnemidophorus tigris, **131**
Cnemidophorus uniparens, **158**
Coachwhip Snake, **807, 829, 873, 899**
Collared Lizard, **139, 514, 835**
Coluber constrictor, **370**
Coluber constrictor constrictor, **101**
Common Agama, **97**
Common Flat-tailed Gecko, **502**
Common Garter Snake, **25, 126**
Common Mud Turtle, 450-452, 455
Common Musk Turtle, **335,** 448, 450, **452, 454,**
457
Common Spiny-tailed Lizard, **187**
Common Viper, **226**
Common Water Monitor, **535, 549**
Conjunctivitis, **562,** 566, 634, **743,** 743, 745, **921,**
922
Conolophus pallidus, **163**
Conolophus subcristatus, **112**
Conservation, 235-260,
  chelonians, 247-250,
  crocodilians, 250-252,
  legislation, 256,
  lizards, 241-244,
  private sector management, 259-260
  reintroductions, 256,
  snakes, 244-247,
  species management plans, 258-259,
  wild populations, 253-254,